T0291545

Financing the Future

Financing the Future

*Multilateral Development Banks in the
Changing World Order of the 21st Century*

CHRIS HUMPHREY

OXFORD
UNIVERSITY PRESS

OXFORD
UNIVERSITY PRESS

Great Clarendon Street, Oxford, OX2 6DP,
United Kingdom

Oxford University Press is a department of the University of Oxford.
It furthers the University's objective of excellence in research, scholarship,
and education by publishing worldwide. Oxford is a registered trade mark of
Oxford University Press in the UK and in certain other countries

© Christopher Humphrey 2022

The moral rights of the author have been asserted

All rights reserved. No part of this publication may be reproduced, stored in
a retrieval system, or transmitted, in any form or by any means, without the
prior permission in writing of Oxford University Press, or as expressly permitted
by law, by licence or under terms agreed with the appropriate reprographics
rights organization. Enquiries concerning reproduction outside the scope of the
above should be sent to the Rights Department, Oxford University Press, at the
address above

You must not circulate this work in any other form
and you must impose this same condition on any acquirer

Published in the United States of America by Oxford University Press
198 Madison Avenue, New York, NY 10016, United States of America

British Library Cataloguing in Publication Data
Data available

Library of Congress Control Number: 2022943633

ISBN 978–0–19–287150–3

DOI: 10.1093/oso/9780192871503.001.0001

Printed and bound by
CPI Group (UK) Ltd, Croydon, CR0 4YY

Links to third party websites are provided by Oxford in good faith and
for information only. Oxford disclaims any responsibility for the materials
contained in any third party website referenced in this work.

To Lena, Nicolas, and Rebecca

Acknowledgments

Whatever insights this book might contain are built on the experience and knowledge of very many people in development cooperation, governments, academia, and think tanks—far too numerous to mention here. I am extremely grateful to all who have generously offered their time to patiently answer my questions over the past twenty years.

I would like to offer special thanks to those who have offered me professional opportunities that took me down the path leading to this book: Maria Correia, Wendy Cunningham, Vicente Fretes, Marcelo Giugale, Pia Peeters, and the rest of my colleagues from the Latin America vice-presidency (World Bank); Raghavan Narayanan (International Finance Corporation); Kapil Kapoor, Carlos Mollinedo, and Tim Turner (African Development Bank); Koldo Echebarría and Verónica Zavala (Inter-American Development Bank); Paulo Nogueira Batista (New Development Bank); Daniel Birchmeier, Joël Farronato, and Ivan Pavletic (Swiss State Secretariat for Economic Affairs); Admassu Tadesse (Trade and Development Bank); Amar Bhattacharya and Marilou Uy (Inter-Governmental Group of 24); Mattia Romani (Global Green Growth Institute); Neil Saravanamuttoo (Global Infrastructure Hub); Rashad Kaldany (World Economic Forum); Federica Diamante (Italian Ministry of Finance); Hugo Jones (UK Treasury); and Ed Hedger, Philipp Krause, Mark Miller, and Annalisa Prizzon (Overseas Development Institute). In academia, I am grateful for the support of and engagement with: Ken Shadlen, Robert Wade, and my amazing PhD colleagues (London School of Economics); Katharina Michaelowa (University of Zurich); Isabel Günther and Fritz Brugger (ETH Center for Development and Cooperation); Stephany Griffith-Jones (Colombia University); and Kevin Gallagher (Boston University Global Development Policy Center). I owe a particular thanks to Eric Helleiner (University of Waterloo) who inspired me through his own excellent scholarship and offered valuable critiques and suggestions on earlier drafts of this book.

Contents

List of Figures, Tables, and Boxes

Figures

Tables

Boxes

Multilateral Development Banks in a Fast-Changing World

From Bretton Woods to the BRICS

For twenty-three days in July of 1944, delegates from forty-four countries and colonial territories gathered in a palatial hotel secluded in the forested mountains outside of Bretton Woods, New Hampshire. Led by the U.S.'s Harry Dexter White and British economist John Maynard Keynes, the main topic of the Bretton Woods conference was the creation of the International Monetary Fund (IMF), while a secondary goal was to found a new kind of public bank to help rebuild Europe after the war and support economic development elsewhere.

Christened with the unwieldy name of the International Bank for Reconstruction and Development, what quickly became known as the World Bank first opened its Washington D.C. office in 1946. The first president quit after just six months, the first two loans used up all the World Bank's available resources, and the New York investor community showed little interest in buying its bonds. The largest shareholder, the U.S., lost patience with this slow start and launched the Marshall Plan to rebuild Europe, thus eliminating the bank's original main purpose.

Nearly eight decades after this inauspicious beginning, the World Bank is the leading international development organization, with 189 member countries, 12,400 full-time staff and 5,500 consultants across the globe, and a loan book of over $400 billion across its four operational divisions. Beyond its own spectacular growth, the World Bank has served as the template for a unique type of international organization: the multilateral development bank (MDB). Depending on the precise definition, thirty MDBs currently operate around the world, ranging from the massive European Investment Bank to the tiny East African Development Bank. And new ones are still being created: 2016 saw the launch of the China-led Asian Infrastructure Investment Bank and the New Development Bank founded by Brazil, Russia, India, China, and South Africa (the "BRICS").

Not only has the number of MDBs risen steadily, but many formerly small MDBs are growing in size and relevance. The Development Bank of Latin America, created in 1970 by a group of Andean nations and best known by its Spanish acronym, CAF, now lends as much each year as either the World Bank or Inter-American Development Bank in the same group of countries. The loan book of

Financing the Future. Chris Humphrey, Oxford University Press. © Christopher Humphrey (2022).
DOI: 10.1093/oso/9780192871503.003.0001

Africa's Trade and Development Bank grew by nearly 1000 percent in the past decade, after twenty-five years of minimal growth. Asian Infrastructure Investment Bank has attracted nearly one hundred member countries in just five years of operations, including five of the G7 nations. The MDB model remains useful for governments the world over, despite the tremendous geopolitical and economic changes that have taken place since Bretton Woods, and is central to global efforts to achieve the Sustainable Development Goals, face the challenges posed by climate change, and recover from economic and social shocks like the Covid-19 pandemic.

At the same time, MDBs face a constant barrage of criticism and calls for reform. For some, MDBs are bloated, inefficient public bureaucracies wasting taxpayer money to support corrupt dictators and high staff salaries. For others, they are tools of a few imperialist rich countries rewarding their allies and punishing their enemies, and making the world safe for rapacious capitalism. And for still others, they are purveyors of misguided development ideologies cooked up by economists with little understanding of how the world really works, crowding out the private sector, clumsily causing all sorts of unintended consequences, and saddling poor countries with too much debt.

What's going on here? Why have MDBs come to be one the most useful and replicated types of international organization ever invented, while at the same time one of the most criticized? The answer to these questions lies in the mechanics of how MDBs function—in particular, how they manage financial resources and how they are governed. The core operational model is exactly the same for all MDBs, from the World Bank to the East African Development Bank to the Asian Infrastructure Investment Bank, and is highly successful at channeling mostly private investor resources toward public policy goals at minimal budgetary cost. But this core model is poorly understood by outside observers—and even by some MDB staff and member country government officials—hidden by political rhetoric, organizational complexity, and financial technicality, confusing external observers about key factors driving MDB policies and actions.

MDBs are also in the process of major change, driven by the tectonic shifts underway in the global economy and geopolitical relations. The international context in which most MDBs were created is disappearing. The Cold War is over, the U.S. is facing myriad new challenges, the role of the G7 powers is uncertain, and new nations—most notably China, but also others like Turkey, Brazil, Indonesia, India, and South Africa—are asserting themselves on the global stage. These new political and economic realities are fueling pressure for change at the World Bank and major regional MDBs, the rapid growth of smaller MDBs, and the creation of new ones like Asian Infrastructure Investment Bank and New Development Bank. At the same time, the growing international consensus on the urgent need for action to address climate change, rising global inequality, and stagnating living standards in many countries has led to increasing calls for MDBs to do more, without a clear idea of how and where the MDBs will find the resources to do so.

Despite their central and fast-evolving role in global governance and international development, no book exists examining the core aspects of the MDB model and showing how that model plays out in different MDBs around the world. Dozens of books and hundreds of articles have been written about the World Bank, a modest but growing number of studies on the major regional MDBs, and a handful on smaller MDBs. While many of these studies are valuable in their own right, they do not situate the individual cases into the broader set, comparing and contrasting how different MDBs have resolved the tensions built into their organizational model. As well, much research has only a partial understanding of the mechanics of how MDBs actually operate, in particular the underpinnings of MDB finances.

Too much of the discussion around MDBs is detached from how this specialized set of international organizations function, the trade-offs they face in pursuing development goals, and how they might be improved to better address the development challenges of the twenty-first century. This book is an effort to shift the debate in both policy and academic communities by offering a new perspective to explain MDB policies and actions grounded in the practical realities of how they are governed and operate.

Why Do MDBs Matter?

MDBs are of far more than academic interest. These organizations are key public policy tools allowing different countries to cooperate with one another to face some of the most pressing problems affecting all of us. No other kind of organization combines a public policy mandate, a multilateral cooperative framework, global expertise, and the financial firepower to make investments at scale. No single MDB perfectly exemplifies these attributes, and all have weaknesses that need to be remedied to become more effective. But they play a role that national governments, the private sector, and other types of international organizations like the United Nations are not able to fulfill. As one recent policy study put it, "if the MDBs no longer existed today, the international community would have to reinvent them" (Birdsall and Morris 2016, x).

Essentially, the role of MDBs is to invest in projects that no one else can or will support, but which are critical for the social, economic, and environmental sustainability of our planet. MDB investments generate public goods that benefit all members of the cooperative. For a smaller MDB, these might be to stimulate greater economic activity in a particular region like Central America, West Africa, or the Black Sea region. For larger MDBs, investments have global implications, which is why so many wealthy non-borrower nations join MDBs. It is not simply out of largess or a feeling of moral obligation (although that might also play a role), but a clear-eyed awareness that inadequate infrastructure, social services, and institutions perpetuate poverty, inequality, lack of opportunity, and an unsustainable use of natural resources. These, in turn, lead to social and political instability, low economic growth, migration, environmental destruction, pandemics, and accelerating climate change. Tackling those challenges is in the interest of the entire global community.

Take, for example, physical infrastructure. Anyone who has lived in or traveled to a lower-income country is immediately aware of the lack of basic infrastructure that citizens of wealthy countries take for granted. Tap water and sanitation are often unavailable in rural areas and peripheral neighborhoods of major cities. Transportation is time-consuming on poor-quality road and rail networks. Electric power comes and goes in cities and isn't available at all in more remote regions. And the population is growing rapidly many parts of the world, which means even more infrastructure will be needed in the coming years. Africa is adding 22 million people to its cities each year, and its total urban population is projected to triple to 1.3 billion by 2050 (Hajjar 2020). According to one study, $63 trillion in infrastructure investment is needed in emerging market and developing countries (EMDCs) between 2016 and 2030—an increase of $1.8 trillion per year beyond current levels (New Climate Economy 2016).

It's not just the amount of infrastructure investment, but also the quality. As EMDCs urbanize and industrialize, they are building infrastructure networks that will operate for decades into the future. The quality of these networks will go a long way to defining the potential for economic growth, patterns of urban development, and the trajectory of our planet's climate. If EMDCs install electric generation capacity to keep up with their population and economic growth powered by cheap coal, or neglect public mass transportation, global carbon emissions will continue to climb unsustainably. We are at a critical juncture in our planet's climate trajectory, and the quality of infrastructure put in place in the coming few years will have tremendous implications for decades to come.

MDBs cannot do all this on their own, but they are uniquely well-placed to lead the way. They have the financial capacity to make their own direct investments in sustainable infrastructure facilities, to demonstrate proof of concept and open the path for private investors and governments to follow. They have the technical expertise and relationships with EMDC governments to help design multi-year strategies and regulatory frameworks for sustainable infrastructure, and the international standing to help coordinate with bilateral donors and private investors. No other set of institutions can play all of these roles. United

Nations agencies lack a sustainable and powerful financing model, and do not have the same depth of project expertise. Bilateral donors have their own fiscal constraints and are oriented in part by their own national interest. Most private sector actors are too risk-averse and focused on short-term profit motives rather than the public good.

MDBs are far from perfect, and face numerous political, financial, and bureaucratic constraints. They require close oversight and leadership from shareholders, and must be adapted to changing times and circumstances. But the core MDB model remains powerful and extremely useful if it is deployed well by member country shareholders. It combines a degree of market discipline that makes MDBs more responsive and adaptive compared to budget-funded public aid institutions with the public policy aims and international cooperative nature absent from private sector firms. At a time when the interconnectedness of the globe makes environmental, financial, and social challenges a collective threat to us all, MDBs are more relevant than ever.

What Is an MDB?

In the simplest terms, an MDB is a cooperative financial institution created and owned by the governments of a group of countries for the purpose of financing long-term development projects. This definition results in a set of thirty

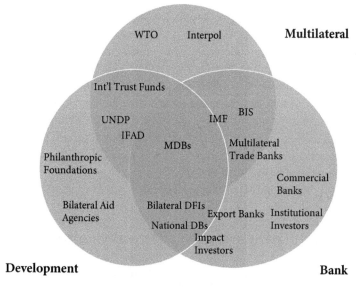

Figure 0.1 Multilateral Development Banks and Other Organizations.

organizations, according to available information as of 2020 (see Annex for a complete list).

To better understand what does and does not qualify as an MDB, and what the definition implies for how MDBs operate, it is useful to explore the three words "multilateral development bank" (Figure 0.1).

Multilateral

MDBs are created and owned by a group of national governments and are legally based on an international treaty signed and ratified by each member. While a few MDBs have some non-sovereign shareholder members (as discussed in Chapter 2), they are always subordinate to government shareholders. Historically MDBs have mainly lent directly to governments, and although they now engage in substantial (and growing) lending to the private sector and subnational governments, it is always done with the permission of the host national government. This character as an intergovernmental organization has a number of implications. From an analytical standpoint, it means that the nation state is a fundamental factor that cannot be ignored in understanding MDB actions. They are the creators, owners, and ultimate authority for all MDBs.

On an operational level, the multilateral nature of MDBs gives their activities a degree of international legitimacy. All countries that receive MDB resources are also members and part-owners of the cooperative.[1] As such, they have a stake in the survival of the organization, and also a say in its decision-making. The degree of this legitimacy is of course open for debate. Certainly the World Bank and major regional MDBs have long been perceived, with considerable justification, as controlled by the U.S. and G7 nations. But even in these cases, recipient nations can make their voices heard, and they know that many operational staff are committed development professionals rather than political appointees. The relationship between MDB and recipient is fundamentally different from with a bilateral aid agency of a wealthy donor country or a commercial bank. While power politics and national interests of major shareholders clearly play a role, MDBs can address issues of international concern with a degree of credibility and acceptance by wealthy countries and EMDCs alike.

Examples of other **multilateral** organizations that are not MDBs:

- *International Monetary Fund*: The IMF is a fund that pools resources committed by member countries (not a bank). Its main purpose is to

---

[1] The Arab Bank for Economic Development in Africa (BADEA) is the only MDB that is owned by one set of countries (a group of Arab nations) but lends entirely to another set of countries that are not members (African nations).

provide short-term liquidity assistance to any member country, including high-income countries, to help overcome financial crises (not development). In recent years, IMF owners have included a stronger poverty reduction orientation in its mandate, but that has never been its main purpose.[2]

- *World Trade Organization.* Created to support the growth of international trade and resolve trade disputes among nations of all income levels (not development), the WTO has no powers to borrow money or extend loans (not a bank).
- *United Nations Development Programme:* UNDP is a specialized UN agency oriented toward long-term development promotion in middle- and low-income countries, just like MDBs. It is funded directly by member contributions and does not make loans or borrow from capital markets (not a bank).
- *International Fund for Agricultural Development:* IFAD has traditionally followed the same basic model as UNDP in receiving contribution from member countries. However, in October 2020 it became the first UN agency to receive a bond rating, indicating it may be in the process of converting into an MDB and accessing capital markets to support its project funding (IFAD 2020).

Development

The mandate of MDBs is not to generate profit, but to promote development. As a result, they can lend to projects that do not necessarily generate direct financial returns, but rather long-term social returns. Along with their multilateral character, this nonprofit development mandate gives MDBs a degree of legitimacy in their operations. Some MDBs (particularly the larger ones) are at times accused of hidden agendas like the supporting the political and/or economic interests of major shareholders. But they do not seek short-term profit with their operations, as commercial banks do, and recipient countries know they can count on MDBs to remain engaged with them year after year, including (and perhaps especially) during times of crisis. This makes the relationship between borrowers and MDBs more than merely transactional and financial.

But what is "development"? The short answer is that there is no single definition. Reducing poverty and inequality, improving living standards, equalizing opportunity, promoting economic growth, creating job, industrializing—all of these and

---

[2] In 2022, the IMF created the Resilience and Sustainability Trust (RST) to make long-term development loans, although details were still being finalized at the time of writing. The RST was to be funded by Special Drawing Rights (SDRs)—the IMF's synthetic currency—from the $650 billion allocated to members in the summer of 2021 in response to the Covid-19 crisis. This moves the IMF toward work normally done by MDBs, and was done as a means to channel "surplus" SDRs from wealthy countries to EMDCs. See IMF 2022.

more can be considered development, depending on one's point of view. The World Bank's slogan, "Working for a world free of poverty" may sound self-evident, but the bank prioritized economic growth and industrialization in its early years, rather than poverty reduction.[3] MDB foundational documents all have some language about their developmental goals, but it is invariably vague and broad. Without a clear definition it is impossible to define success, much less attempt to measure it. On the one hand, this vague mandate allows adaption and operational flexibility according to circumstances, but on the other, it leads to endless debates and disagreements about what MDBs should be doing.

Examples of other **development** organizations that are not MDBs:

- *Bilateral aid agencies:* The donor agencies of high-income governments, like the German Corporation for International Cooperation, USAID, or the Swedish International Development Cooperation Agency, fund development projects mainly in lower-income countries. These agencies are backed by a single government (not multilateral) and are funded almost entirely by direct budget allocations (not banks). Most of their project resources are donated rather than lent.
- *Bilateral development finance institutions:* A number of higher-income countries have created specialized agencies to provide funding through loans, guarantees, and equity investments to private sector projects in lower-income countries. Some, like the U.K.'s Commonwealth Development Corporation and French Development Agency, are entirely owned by a single government, while others like the Entrepreneurial Development Bank of the Netherlands are partly owned by investors (not multilateral). Some raise money from borrowing like MDBs, while others rely on budget allocations like bilateral agencies.
- *National development banks:* Numerous developed and developing countries have public banks to promote economic and social development. Examples include Germany's KfW, the Brazilian Development Bank, China Development Bank, and the Development Bank of Ethiopia (see Box 0.1). Their primary purpose is to fund domestic rather than international development (not multilateral), although some like KfW and China Development Bank do fund projects in other countries.
- *Trust funds:* Governments have created a variety of trust funds for developmental purposes, including freestanding ones like the Green Climate Fund and others that are managed by other agencies, including many housed at MDBs (see Reinsberg et al. 2015). Trust funds resources come

---

[3] Poverty reduction was at least partly in the minds of the World Bank founders at Bretton Woods, as examined in Helleiner (2014).

directly from donations from the founders (not banks). Some are created by several governments (multilateral), whereas others are supported by a single government.

- *Philanthropic foundations:* Wealthy individuals have set up foundations to promote development, including the Gates Foundation, Tata Trusts, and Aga Khan Foundation. These are nongovernmental organizations funded by an endowment, and they almost always donate rather than lend out their resources (not multilateral and not banks).

Box 0.1: National Development Banks

MDBs are only one of a variety of different types of organizations supplying development finance, and they are not the largest. According to one recent estimate (Ocampo and Ortega 2020), over 400 national development banks operate across the globe today, with about $10 trillion in assets and making about $2 trillion in annual financing commitments. China Development Bank alone had assets of $2.5 trillion in 2020, more than all the MDBs reviewed in this book combined. Other major national development banks with decades of experience and substantial financial firepower include Germany's KfW ($485 billion in assets), Italy's Casa de Depositi e Prestiti ($425 billion), Brazil's BNDES ($220 million), and Korea Development Bank ($225 billion).

The interface between national and multilateral development institutions has evolved substantially (Griffith-Jones and Ocampo 2018). In the Great Depression and post–World War II era, national development banks were perceived as an essential policy tool in wealthy countries and EMDCs alike. The World Bank worked hand in hand with many national development banks, providing considerable funding and technical assistance. This support dwindled and at times turned into opposition the era of neoliberal reforms in the 1980s and 1990s, but sentiment has swung back with renewed appreciation for their potential in recent years (World Bank 2018a).

National development banks are by definition owned by a single country, and as a result decision-making is deeply enmeshed in domestic political and economic interests and with none of the multi-country attributes of MDBs. Financing models are often very different from one another and from MDBs. While some national development banks rely on market borrowing and have a strong financial performance, others receive subsidized funding of some type and have a realistic prospect of being bailed out by their parent government in the event of financial difficulties (Xu et al. 2020, Griffith-Jones and Ocampo 2018, Humphrey 2015a).

> Although some larger national development banks—notably China Development Bank and KfW—are active in other countries, the vast majority of lending is in domestic markets. MDBs, by contrast, are by definition involved in multiple countries. Hence, despite their huge scale, national development banks are fundamentally different kinds of organizations than MDBs. Their importance as sources of development finance is undisputable, and their engagement with MDBs appears to be growing after years of decline. The two types of organizations occupy different though equally important roles in the international development finance landscape.

Bank

MDBs are specialized financial institutions that share many but not all attributes of what are commonly considered "banks." They have a normal balance sheet with assets, liabilities, and equity, and they can borrow resources and extend loans. Many MDBs also can purchase equity stakes and offer guarantees and insurance products, but lending remains their main business. They must manage financial risks, and if they collapse, their member governments would lose their shareholding stake. Unlike most retail commercial banks (but similar to many investment banks), MDBs do not fund themselves mainly by taking deposits, but rather borrow from bond markets, commercial banks, or official financing sources like global funds, export–import banks, or bilateral aid agencies. Unlike commercial banks, they are not licensed and have no formal regulators.

Whether MDBs are exactly banks or not, the essential point is that they must concern themselves with financial as well as developmental considerations due to their funding model. Member governments do not want to lose their shareholding stake and have no interest in bailing out an MDB in danger of going bust because its borrowers don't pay back their loans. Nor will bond markets or commercial banks want to lend an MDB the money it needs to operate if they don't think the MDB will be able to repay them. Hence, an MDB must balance its development goals with financial concerns like loan portfolio quality, an adequate level of shareholder capital, and funding costs.

Examples of **banks** that are not MDBs:

- *Commercial banks*: Retail and investment banks all lend money to a huge array of customers, including governments and private enterprises in low- and middle-income countries for projects that could be construed as developmental. But their over-riding purpose is to generate profit for their shareholders (not development). While commercial banks may have a government shareholder, they are mainly owned by private investors and are created by a legal business contract rather than an international treaty (not multilateral).

- *Impact investors:* A rising segment of the financial sector is comprised of investors, including banks, seeking to combine profit with a positive social impact. Profit remains the priority, even if investors may be willing to accept a lower return than they otherwise obtain. These are overwhelmingly private investors and they are bound by legal contracts rather than a treaty (not multilateral).

- *Export–import banks:* Many individual governments (not multilateral) have specialized agencies that make loans for projects in EMDCs, often to support infrastructure. The most well-known currently is the China Export-Import Bank, but most wealthy nations and an increasing number of upper-middle-income countries have similar agencies. The proceeds of their loans are usually "tied" by requiring that they be spent on companies based in the bank's country—hence while projects may have positive developmental impacts, their priority is to promote the national industry of the lender country (not development).

- *Bank for International Settlements:* The BIS is a specialized financial agency created by international treaty among member nations (multilateral). Like MDBs, it can issue bonds and provide loans, but it does so only to central banks and other international institutions, not to country governments or private borrowers. Its main goal is to provide services to central banks and support international financial stability (not development).

Power of the MDB Model

What is it about this combination of characteristics that make MDBs attractive enough that thirty have been created since 1944 and just about every country in the world belongs to at least one? The main reason for the enduring popularity of this model of international organization is simple but often overlooked: MDBs allow governments to pursue collective public policy goals at very little fiscal cost. Most of the money for their operations comes not from the budgets of member governments, but rather from MDB borrowing, mainly from international capital markets. At their core, MDBs are government-owned mechanisms to channel private investor financing toward public policy goals.

The MDB financial model is explored in more detail in Chapter 1, but the essence is as follows. Member countries capitalize an MDB by buying capital shares, and then the MDB borrows most of the resources needed to fund projects from elsewhere. Since MDBs are international institutions with the backing of member governments and (in most cases) a strong financial track record, they borrow at very good terms. These resources are then on-lent by the MDB for development projects, and borrowers are charged slightly higher rates than the MDB's own low funding costs. The difference between the terms at which MDBs lend to borrowers and the terms at which it funds itself, along with any investment income, covers MDB administrative costs. Apart from a relatively small amount of shareholder capital, MDBs do not require regular budgetary contributions from member governments. They mostly pay for themselves.

The MDB model has proved to be a highly effective mechanism for channeling mainly private resources into projects that serve the public interest. Most of projects supported by MDBs do not generate short-term financial returns, and hence would never attract private investors. Buying a highly-rated MDB bond, on the other hand, is a very safe investment in high demand by the biggest pension funds, insurance agencies, and central banks across the globe. Hence, MDBs borrow resources from some of the most conservative, risk-averse investors in the world, and on-lend for things like rural roads in sub-Saharan Africa, maternal health care in south Asia, and primary education in Central America—projects that will never generate private returns but do have long-term social benefits.

The amount of money needed to capitalize MDBs is very small in relation to their financial output. For example, 189 member countries contributed a grand total of $18 billion share capital to the World Bank's main International Bank for Reconstruction and Development (IBRD) lending window from 1944 to 2020 (Table 0.1). With that capital, IBRD extended over $750 billion in loans, essentially all of which have been or are being repaid. The income of IBRD loan repayments generated nearly $30 billion in retained earnings, $23 billion in donated grants to the poorest countries, and covered the costs of creating the most comprehensive body of global development data and expertise in existence. And the original share capital has not been used up—it is still on the books of the World Bank and will support operations for years to come.

Table 0.1 Shareholder Capital, Reserves, and Lending (US$ Billions)

	Total Paid-In Share Capital	Retained Earnings	Cumulative Financing (to 2020)
World Bank IBRD (1944)	18.0	28.8	754.8
IDB (1959)	11.9	23.2	296.5
ADB (1966)	7.6	45.1	264.5
AfDB (1963)	7.3	3.9	151.0
EBRD (1991)	7.5	14.2	201.2
Total	**52.3**	**115.2**	**1,668.0**

Source: MDB 2020 financial statements.

Looked at in this light, the fact that nations delegate development finance at least in part to MDBs is not as surprising as some (for example Milner 2006 or Kellerman 2018) have suggested, especially when compared to the financial results of bilateral aid agencies. The total contribution of the U.S. to the IBRD share capital through 2020 was about US$3.1 billion, less than one-sixth of the *annual* 2020 budget of the U.S. government's main development agency (USAID 2020). Of course, the U.S. can align USAID spending directly with its policy priorities and geopolitical interests in a way that it cannot with IBRD operations, as Milner (2006) points out. Nonetheless, in terms of value for money in generating development impact, the contrast is almost laughable. On top of that, numerous studies have shown that MDBs are more efficient, have higher development impact, and are more trusted by recipients than bilateral aid agencies (see for example Gulrajani 2016, Brookings Institution and Center for Global Development 2018, and Prizzon et al. 2022).

This model comes with trade-offs, however. Joining a multilateral institution to undertake development work means that governments delegate a degree of authority to MDBs, which leads to agency problems and requires negotiations with other members of the collective. The MDB model also gives a role to two other sets of actors that are not relevant to bilateral development agencies. On the one hand, MDBs must concern themselves with the perceptions and interests of the external financiers from which they obtain their funding. And on the other, making loans that must be repaid gives an important demand-side aspect to MDB operations. Borrowers have to think MDB loans are worth it, unlike bilateral aid that is mostly free grant funding. In short, MDBs by design must be much more responsive to supply and demand forces compared to aid agencies or international bureaucracies that depend on budget allocations.

Why Do MDBs Act as They Do?

National governments are creators, owners, and main clients of MDBs, and scholars attempting to explain their actions appropriately take the interests of member countries as their starting point. Much of the academic focus on what drives MDBs and other international organizations (IOs) like the IMF or World Trade Organization has been on the G7 nations and, in particular, the U.S. To simplify, at one end of the spectrum are more "institutionalist" theories, which see the major powers creating IOs as cooperation mechanisms to address common goals (Keohane 1984; Koremenos et al. 2001). Others perceive IOs as more directly serving the interests of the hegemonic power (the U.S.), although sometimes balanced with give and take among other nations and supporting a more stable global system (Krasner 1981 and Ascher 1990 related to MDBs in particular; Gruber 2000 and Stone 2011 on IOs more generally). Still others in the "realist" tradition explicitly or implicitly see MDBs and other IOs as tools designed to further the direct interests of the most powerful member countries (Mearsheimer 1995, Thacker 1999, Vreeland and Dreher, 2014). Scholars interpreting MDBs and other IOs from a Marxist perspective (for example Payer 1982) are analytically similar to realist approaches in the sense that they are seen as controlled by the G7 nations, except here these governments are themselves tools for the interests of global capitalism.

There can be little dispute that the U.S. and other major shareholders have not been shy about furthering their own interests through the MDB to which they belong. Nevertheless, this is far from the whole story. The World Bank and four major regional MDBs are huge organizations undertaking thousands of lending, technical assistance, and research operations every year across the globe. Many of these operations have little direct bearing on the geopolitical interests of the U.S. and G7, and even if they did, these governments do not have the time, manpower, or energy to micro-manage all of them. Even a cursory review of their history shows that the management of these MDBs have often been at loggerheads with the U.S. and other major shareholders about aspects of their policies and strategy.

The power and interests of the U.S. and G7 at minimum define a "framing constraint" (Woods 2006, 12) that circumscribes the actions of the major MDBs. Within those limits, scholars see other forces at play. For Woods (2006), this includes the intellectual formation of MDB staff and the relations with borrower countries, while Nielson et al. (2006), Babb (2009), and Weaver (2008) examine issues such as ideological mandate, staff self-image, and expert knowledge. Vaubel (1986) and Frey (1997) take a public choice approach to focus on how the incentives and self-interest of MDB staff dovetail with those of domestic politicians of major shareholders. Gutner (2005), Hawkins et al. (2006), and Lyne et al. (2006), among others, employ principal–agent frameworks that look at information asymmetries and institutional rules to understand why MDBs do not always seem to obey the interests of their major shareholders.

The diversity of ways to understand MDBs makes sense, as they are situated at the intersection of geopolitics, global financial markets, and changing views of development economics, among others. The actors and interests shaping MDB operations are diverse and multilayered, meaning different theoretical lenses are needed to analyze different aspects of their activities. The research cited above, as well as a great variety of other academic and policy studies of individual or groups of MDBs,[4] have generated an impressive body of evidence supporting different theoretical approaches to explaining MDB behavior. However, the literature has

---

[4] The literature is vast, but a few citations are worth mentioning. World Bank: Kapur et al. (1997); Mason and Asher (1973), Mosley et al. (1995), Stiglitz (2002), Mallaby (2004), Woods (2006). IDB: Dell (1972), Tussie (1995). AfDB: Mingst (1990), English and Mule (1996). ADB: Kappagoda (1995). Regional MDBs: Culpeper (1997), Gutner (2002), Griffith-Jones (2008), Babb (2009), Park and Strand

two important gaps that, if filled, would greatly expand our understanding of this unique type of IO. On the one hand, the literature has not sufficiently engaged with the practical realities of how MDBs operate, and on the other, it is overly focused on a few specific cases.

Not digging into the details of how MDBs operate

The first gap in the literature is an incomplete or at times incorrect understanding of how MDBs actually operate, particularly their financial model. This is no surprise, considering that MDBs are enveloped in a cloud of acronym-filled jargon about poverty reduction, environmental protection, policy reform, and much else besides. The lack of precision on what exactly MDBs do can lead to mistaken assumptions, misguided questions, and faulty conclusions. To take a common example, much of the literature overlooks the fact that most of what MDBs offer is not donated aid, but rather loans that must be repaid with interest. An entire stream of international political economy literature has focused on asking why MDBs "allocate" their money to certain countries and not to others. This implicitly assumes that recipient countries will always want to take MDB loans, an assumption that is clearly false.[5] Many developing countries think very carefully about taking on debt, and often prefer other sources of external borrowing, or not borrowing at all, for a variety of reasons. Bilateral aid, on the other hand, is often (though not always) free grant money given to recipient countries, and in that case the supply-focused approach of the aid allocation literature makes more sense.

Another mistaken assumption is that wealthy member countries generously supply all the resources MDBs need to operate. In reality, member countries (including developing countries) pay in a small amount of share capital and MDBs raise almost all of their resources by borrowing, mainly on bond markets. This financial model is little understood in academia and has major implications. To give one example, Egypt was entirely cut off from lending by the African Development Bank between 2012 and 2014 in the wake of the Arab Spring

(2016) and Ben-Artzi (2016). Policy studies: Meltzer (2000), Institute for Development Studies (2000), Birdsall (2006), Zedillo (2009), Birdsall and Morris (2016) and G20 (2018).

[5] See Greenhill et al. (2013), Prizzon et al. (2016), Gulrajani (2016), and Humphrey and Michaelowa (2013 and 2019) for more on the issue of borrower demand. To give one personal example, the author worked for the World Bank in the mid-2000s in the Latin America region. At that time, Ecuador was governed by a leftist administration strongly opposed to U.S. foreign policy, and also refused to borrow from the World Bank despite intensive efforts by the Bank's country team to restart lending. Academic studies assuming that U.S. pressure on the World Bank to reduce lending to countries not allied with it would, in this case, incorrectly attribute causality to the supply side rather than the demand side as was actually the case.

revolutions. One might imagine all sorts of theoretical explanations for this, such as powerful shareholders wanting to shape the course of events in a strategically important country. The reality was more prosaic: because of political instability, credit rating agencies suddenly deemed Egypt to be extremely risky, and the African Development Bank had to cut back lending until the crises passed to protect its AAA credit rating (Humphrey 2017a).

Not seeing the forest from the trees

The second gap is that the vast majority of research on MDBs has focused on the World Bank and, to a lesser extent, the four major regional MDBs—the MDBs with the highest profile and greatest operational reach. Most studies utilize theoretical and empirical approaches appropriate to those specific MDBs and are careful not to generalize their conclusions. The problem is that the collective weight of the literature can tempt one to draw conclusions based on these cases about MDBs as a collective whole. Like the ancient Indian parable about the blind men touching different parts of an elephant, inductive reasoning based on partial evidence can lead to faulty conclusions. As well, not considering how some MDBs act in comparison to others misses an opportunity to gain greater insight into the factors driving MDBs as a unique type of institution.

To give an example of how a broader perspective can inform MDB research, consider the "principal–agent" frameworks used to explain the disjunction between what the major shareholders want and what MDB staff actually do. Principal–agent frameworks have been applied mainly the World Bank and help explain the myriad bureaucratic mechanisms shareholders put in place in an effort to ensure that staff implement shareholder mandates. But as Barnett and Finnemore (2004) note, these frameworks are less good at explaining why MDB staff need to be controlled in the first place. Comparing the World Bank to the experience of other MDBs sheds light on this problem.

MDBs dominated by borrower countries, like Latin America's CAF or the Black Sea Trade and Development Bank, have a streamlined administration, fast project approval procedure, and much more delegation to management than at the World Bank and the major regional MDBs. The principal–agent problem is simply less relevant here. The shareholders at these borrower-led MDBs are in broad agreement on their goals and transmit clear messages and mandates to MDB staff. At the World Bank and major regional MDBs, on the other hand, borrower and non-borrower shareholders often disagree vehemently, and staff are caught in the middle and pulled in different directions. Many of the mechanisms put in place to control MDB agents are at the behest of non-borrowers wanting to ensure that their policy priorities—and not those of borrower shareholders—are the ones guiding MDB staff. By comparing different MDBs, it becomes evident that what might seem like a principal–agent problem inherent to all MDBs is actually the symptom of a deeper "principal–principal" problem derived from the specific governance dynamics at a subset of MDBs.

Scholarship on MDBs has begun to diversify. Motivated in part by the winding down of the Cold War and the ebbing of U.S. global dominance, a number of researchers have begun turning their attention to the major regional MDBs (African, Asian, and Inter-American development banks and the European Bank for Reconstruction and Development) and an incipient but growing interest in smaller MDBs led by borrower countries.[6] This accelerated with the sudden burst in new scholarship around the creation of the Asian Infrastructure Investment Bank and New Development by China and other nations in 2016.[7] What has been lacking in the literature is to take a step back and consider these individual cases within the broader class of organization. The policy world has taken steps in this direction, including IDS (2000), Sagasti and Prada (2006), Griffith-Jones et al. (2008), and more recently Delakanli et al. (2018), among others, but academic work has lagged behind.

A notable exception, and driven by a similar motivation to this book, is the recent survey of MDBs by Bazbauers and Engel (2021). Despite the shared interest in MDBs as a class of international organization, their book takes a very different theoretical and methodological approach. Bazbauers and Engel position MDBs as a key component in the postwar evolution of a broad "system of debt" and trace the evolution of that system from a neo-Gramscian and constructivist perspective. The authors conceive of the thirty MDBs as themselves a single system and do not attempt to analyze variation among them. By contrast, this book suggests that while MDBs all have essentially the same organizational model, the differences among them driven by the different countries making up their membership are important and worth understanding in detail. Further, Bazbauers and Engel consider the basic approach of MDBs—providing debt to fund investments—as inherently problematic and driven by the logic of incorporating developing countries into the global capitalist system. This book, on the other hand, sees MDBs as useful tools for cooperation among nations to help improve living standards and economic opportunities, although with numerous flaws that limit their effectiveness. Despite these fundamental differences, the two studies complement each other well. Bazbauers and Engel's work is a useful source for readers seeking to understand the historical trajectory of MDBs as a group and individually, and to consider their activities from a viewpoint informed more by critical theory than this book adopts.

---

[6] Avalle (2005), Griffith-Jones et al. (2008), Humphrey (2014, 2016a, 2016b, and 2019), Humphrey and Michaelowa (2013 and 2019), Imre (2006), Zappile (2016).
[7] Serrano (2019), Wang (2019), He (2016), Yang (2016), Ren (2016), Ikenberry and Lim (2017), and Chin (2019).

A new approach

This book attempts to remedy the gaps in the existing literature outlined above by proposing a new theoretical approach that offers i) a more detailed examination how the financial imperatives and incentives of the MDB model shape their actions, and ii) a broader way of analyzing governance and national interests that can be applied to the universe of MDBs, rather than just a subset. The book develops a framework for analyzing MDBs as a distinct class of international organization that encompasses their individual complexity and allows for systematic comparisons to better identify the key factors that shape their activities. This framework is sketched out below and presented in more detail in Chapters 1 and 2.

Much of the scholarly literature on MDBs—and even a substantial portion of policy-oriented studies—has largely overlooked the mechanics of their **financial model**. Academic research on MDBs has mainly come from the fields of political science and economics, neither of which are inclined to delve into the complexities of balance sheets, financial instruments, or bond ratings. This is unfortunate, as their financial model is a key reason for the enduring relevance of MDBs, and their actions cannot be fully understood without it. "Following the money," as the journalist dictum goes, helps cut through much of the confusing rhetoric surrounding MDBs and gets to the core of their operational reality.

Organizational sociology focusing on resource constraints can help analyze the financial pressures arising out of the MDB model. Several authors—notably Pfeffer and Salancik (1978) and Barnett and Coleman (2005)—emphasize that the drive to ensure external resources can strongly shape the strategies and activities taken by an organization, even if these are not always in line with the organization's stated mission. Babb (2009) applies these insights to the legacy MDBs in a meticulous study of how the U.S. administration and U.S. Congress have leveraged approval of U.S. capital contributions to MDBs as a means of enforcing its national interests.

This book takes the resource dependence approach employed by Babb a step further, to encompass a broader range of financial pressures impacting MDBs. Obtaining shareholder capital is indeed critical for MDBs, but their financial exigencies go beyond that. MDBs face numerous choices on how to maximize their lending capacity within existing capital limitations. As well, MDBs raise almost all of their operating resources from external creditors, mainly international bond markets, and this brings a host of pressures along with it, many of which can conflict with an MDB's development objectives. Nor can the demand side of MDB activities be overlooked: MDBs can only function if they offer the kind of financial and advisory services attractive enough for borrowers to want to take out loans from them. All of these realities—capital, external funding, and borrower demand—deeply shape the actions and policies of MDBs.

This book's approach to **governance** builds on the institutionalist view that member countries work cooperatively through MDBs to achieve goals they cannot achieve on their own, combined with the realist notion that nation states act rationally in their own interests. Rather than focusing on one or a few powerful countries like the U.S. or G7, as with much existing MDB literature, this book's framework extends to include the entire set of member countries. As Lyne et al. (2009) point out in relation to the World Bank, the U.S. is far from the only shareholder able to influence an MDB. Gutner (2002) makes a similar point in her study of MDBs in Europe, as does Copelovitch's (2010) study of the IMF (which has similar voting and governance patterns as the World Bank, although it is not an MDB). Lyne et al. (2009) highlight the "complexity" of principals and attempt to understand World Bank social sector lending by considering views of different member countries balanced by their formal governance voting power. This is a valuable recognition of MDB governance complexity, although operationalizing such an approach is not analytically practical. A researcher cannot realistically aggregate the preferences of all 189 member countries on each of the hundreds of operational and policy decisions taken each year at the World Bank, much less repeat the process for two dozen other MDBs.

Instead, this study proposes a "reduced form" approach to evaluating complex principles by focusing on two key groups of shareholder countries: those that borrow from an MDB and those that do not. The dichotomy between borrowing and non-borrowing countries in the context of MDB governance defines two important groups of shareholders that tend to have aligned interests within each group, but divergent interests between the two groups. This is manifested in many aspects of how an MDB operates, including the types of projects supported, approval procedures and oversight, financial policies, efforts to influence recipient development strategy, approach to environmental and social issues, and more. The balance of governance power between borrowers and non-borrowers goes a long way to explaining why an MDB acts as it does.

Clearly this is somewhat of a simplification. Borrower countries might well agree with non-borrowers on a particular issue, or vice versa, for any number of reasons related to the issue itself or for strategic reasons and alliances. Some countries—notably China, but also Saudi Arabia, Korea, and others—occupy an intermediate position, technically still able to borrow from some MDBs but shifting to a non-borrower role on some issues (as explored in more detail in Chapter 5). This is not an iron-clad framework that explains everything about how national interests influence MDB actions. The governance framework sacrifices a degree of precision by abstracting away from the interests and power of each individual country, but makes up for that by providing a practical empirical approach to systematically analyze the broad interests of many countries in a way that captures a large degree of the variation in policies and operations across many MDBs of different sizes, geographies, and membership.

The financial and governance factors outlined above interact dynamically. All MDBs face essentially the same financial pressures—this is, in a sense, a constant built into the basic model defining an MDB. The multilateral nature of MDBs is also hardwired into their model, but the different constellations of shareholders across MDBs result in very different outcomes in terms of operational characteristics. This variation in governance in turn plays a major role in defining the financial pressures each MDB faces. To give a simple example, the World Bank has a AAA bond rating and superlative access to bond markets at very attractive financial terms, while Africa's Ecowas Development Bank has a junk bond rating that severely restricts its access to bond markets and makes it reliant on subsidized donor resources and expensive commercial bank loans. A major reason for this disparity in bond ratings is the country shareholders behind the two MDBs. The World Bank is supported by the wealthiest countries in the world, while Ecowas Development Bank has fifteen low-income African countries as shareholders. Further, a number of important MDB characteristics are shaped primarily by governance, even though they have rebound effects on the financial side. For example, whether an MDB has relatively strict environmental and social safeguards or not is driven almost entirely by political considerations among shareholders—MDBs controlled by non-borrowers tend to have strict safeguards, while those controlled mainly by borrowers tend to have looser policies. Strict safeguards, in turn, can reduce borrower demand for MDB lending. The dynamic relation between governance and finance can also be seen in MDB membership itself. The China-led Asian Infrastructure Investment Bank opted to accept European non-borrower shareholders in part to strengthen the MDB's financial position and obtain a AAA rating, even though it would complicate governance due to the policy stance of the non-borrowers. The BRICS-led National Development Bank, on the other hand, has not (as of end of 2021) taken on major non-borrowers despite the financial benefits, which has avoided the governance tensions that would have arisen.

The combination of a detailed understanding of the financial pressures MDBs face and a broader approach to evaluating national interest encompassing all shareholders can help analyze two aspects of MDBs:

- The main and most powerful use of the framework is to explain and compare the **operational characteristics** of different MDBs. This includes operational policies such as safeguards and procurement rules, the length and complexity of loan approval procedures, oversight and complaint mechanisms, financial issues such as capitalization, loan interest rate charges and net income usage, developmental priorities, and style of engagement with recipients, among others. These characteristics are key to defining the ways in which the MDBs operate not just on individual projects, but their broader engagement with a country or group of countries over several years, and how those countries perceive and want to work with the MDBs. Hence, the framework is not only relevant for an academic understanding of MDBs, but also to the policy community attempting to make MDBs more effective through reform.

- In some specific cases, this framework can help clarify **decisions on lending to specific countries**. For example, the need to protect a bond rating might play an important role in leading an MDB to reduce or halt lending to countries in a serious crisis (as with Inter-American Development Bank in Argentina in the early 2000s or Venezuela more recently, or African Development Bank with Egypt during the Arab Spring). However, the framework might be less appropriate for systematically analyzing large numbers of MDB lending decisions.

All MDBs face a specific set of governance and financial imperatives built into their "machine" that are fundamentally different from other international organizations or development agencies. The remainder of this book will examine how these imperatives shape all MDBs, and then consider how different groups of MDBs have gone about resolving them based on their particular set of country owners and operating context. The contention is that a close analysis of the main financial factors impacting MDB operations and the governance balance of power among shareholder governments will go a long way toward explaining why an MDB has specific policies and why it operates in certain ways.

Other factors beyond finance and governance also influence MDBs and can productively orient academic scholarship and policy studies. In particular, sociological concerns related to development ideology, internal norms, and the education background of MDB staff are clearly important in shaping MDB policies and actions, as described by Barnett and Finnemore (2004), Woods (2006), Chwieroth (2008), and Weaver (2008), among others. Bureaucratic self-interest, staff incentives, and domestic political concerns prioritized by public choice scholars like Vaubel (1986) and Frey (1997) also play a role. While numerous realist-oriented studies have examined how major shareholders like the U.S. might steer the loans of legacy MDBs, different work could be done in this direction. For example, researchers could seek more qualitative evidence to substantiate the predominantly statistical approaches of existing studies or branch out to see how major shareholders in lesser-known MDBs—like Saudi Arabia in the Islamic Development Bank or Russia in the Eurasian Development Bank—might try to direct lending. And lastly, it is worth stepping back to consider more critical theory perspectives on the role of MDBs in bringing developing countries into the globalized capitalist economy, as suggested by Bazbauers and Engel (2021) and Shields (2016). In short, this book does not purport to tell the entire story. It offers a detailed analysis of what drives MDBs and differentiates them from one another that will frame them in a new light and hopefully prompt new lines of research and be of use to policymakers considering MDB reform.

What the Book Will and Will Not Do

This book has two central parts. The first two chapters following this introduction examine the main financial and governance issues relevant to all MDBs. Chapter 1 delves into the MDB financial model, explaining the basic principles of the MDB capital structure, where MDBs obtain their resources, and the realities of borrower demand for MDB services. The chapter illustrates in concrete terms how these factors shape the ways MDBs act in attempting to fulfill their mandates. Chapter 2 considers governance, laying out the theoretical framework based around the interests and balance of power between borrowers and non-borrower member countries and looking at the different governance structures that define how countries make decisions at MDBs. Both chapters highlight the commonalities and diversity across the range of MDBs and show how these factors help define MDB operational characteristics.

Chapters 3–5 then turn to see how these factors play out at three different groups of MDBs, divided according to their governance balance of power between borrowers and non-borrowers. Chapter 3 examines the World Bank and four major regional MDBs that are under the control of wealthy non-borrower country members—the "legacy" MDBs, to borrow a term from Birdsall and Morris (2016). A group of twelve MDBs owned and controlled by borrowing countries are reviewed in Chapter 4. Chapter 5 considers the Asian Infrastructure Investment Bank and New Development Bank, the two most recently created MDBs that contrast with both the legacy and borrower-led MDBs, and also contrast with each other. The designation of MDBs into these three groupings highlights "family similarities" among the MDBs within each chapter, but is not intended to lump all the MDBs in each chapter together in a simplistic fashion, and indeed much effort is spent noting variations within each group.

The analysis in all chapters is guided by the aim of explaining the main factors shaping MDB operational characteristics and how they impact the ability of MDBs to pursue their development mandates. The book prioritizes considering MDB characteristics from the point of view of recipient governments—the "demand" side of development finance. Far too much of the academic and policy literature (with notable exceptions such as the pathbreaking study on the World Bank by Mosley et al. 1995 and more recently Greenhill et al. 2013 and Prizzon et al. 2016) has focused on the "supply" side, underpinned by a western-centric approach that misrepresents a much more complex reality on the ground. This leads to an incomplete understanding of how MDBs actually function and perpetuates neocolonialist approaches to development that are ineffective and not in keeping with current realities and international commitments such as the agreements on aid effectiveness from Paris (OECD 2005), Accra (UN 2008), and Busan (OECD 2011). As such, the book emphasizes issues of concern to borrowers, such as financial terms, project sectors, technical assistance quality, policy conditionality, bureaucratic hassles, and speed of delivery. It is precisely these issues that are leading many developing countries to turn away from the World Bank and four major regional MDBs to other financing sources, like Chinese export credit or expensive commercial loans. The views of borrowers are all too often overlooked in high-level discussions on international development but are essential to the effectiveness of MDBs.

The book brings to bear a wide range of qualitative and quantitative evidence gathered over the course of two decades working directly with MDBs and undertaking independent research on their activities. This includes 122 formal interviews with government officials managing external development finance in sixteen countries in Africa, Asia, and Latin America and scores of interviews and informal discussions between 2007 and 2021 with senior management, operational staff, and executive directors at twelve different MDBs (including all legacy MDBs) as well as ministry officials leading MDB policy in non-borrower countries including Canada, Denmark, France, Germany, Italy, Japan, Korea, Netherlands, Norway, Sweden, Switzerland, U.K., and the U.S. Primary source material includes MDB articles of agreement, annual reports, financial statements, policy papers, board proceedings, speeches, and strategy documents. Secondary inputs include external reports on MDBs by bond rating agencies (a particularly useful source), shareholder governments, and policy think tanks as well as academic studies and news media reports.

The goal of this book is analytical: understanding why MDBs operate in certain ways and why they are similar to or differ from one another. It is not a general primer of what individual MDBs like the World Bank do. Readers seeking such information should consider the excellent (though now slightly dated) overview by Marshall (2008). Nor is the focus historical, although in some cases the historical trajectory of individual MDBs is touched upon to explain specific points. Apart from the many excellent studies on individual MDBs already noted in this chapter—first and foremost the comprehensive history of the World Bank by Kapur et al. (1997)—those looking for background on a variety of different MDBs in one book should consult Bazbauers and Engel's (2021) recently-published volume, which contains a brief historical overview of thirty different MDBs.

Nor does this book attempt to evaluate the impact of MDB operations. As is often noted, MDBs are very good at showing their *outputs* (schools built, roads paved, etc.), but much less good at demonstrating lasting economic and social *impacts*. Evaluating impact in the aggregate or even at an individual project level is extraordinarily complex, especially in the absence of the rigorous conditions needed for randomized control trials. One could conceivably—though with difficulty—show that building a road resulted over several years in greater economic activity and job creation, as the legacy MDBs attempt to do in their annual development effectiveness reports. Causally linking aggregate MDB activity in a country to overall economic growth is far more challenging due to the almost end-less number of factors involved. In any case, evaluating the developmental impact of MDB activity is beyond the scope of this study. Instead, the intention is that by better understanding the basic parameters within which MDBs operate and the key factors driving them, policymakers can craft more effective reform proposals to improve MDB impact, however they might define and measure that.

While the book digs into the underpinnings of the financial and governance model common to all MDBs (especially in the next two chapters), the focus is on MDBs that operate in EMDCs rather than in upper-income countries. The reason for this focus is the author's belief in the urgent need to promote improved living standards, sustainable economic growth, and greater opportu-nities in EMDCs—both for moral reasons as well as to improve our planet's future—and the view that MDBs are critical tools in that endeavor. As such, the book does not examine the European Investment Bank, which is the world's largest MDB but is in some senses more akin to a national development bank for the European Union (see among others Griffith-Jones and Tyson 2018, Clifton et al. 2018, and Mertens and Thiemann 2019). It also does not take up the Council of Europe Development Bank, Nordic Investment Bank, or North American Development Bank.

MDBs operating within EMDCs offer financial services directly to public sec-tor borrowers, directly to private sector borrowers, or (most commonly) some combination of the two. This book is particularly interested in MDBs that ded-icate at least part of their activities to public sector borrowers, and as such does not include discussion of the World Bank's International Finance Corporation or IDB Invest, both of which engage exclusively with private sector borrowers. The reason for this focus is threefold. First, the majority of investments needed to reach the Sustainable Development Goals and climate finance targets will be done by the public sector, and this is where financial constraints are the most pressing. Second, the dividing line between private projects needing MDB financ-ing and those that can be financed directly by private investors—especially the rapidly growing impact investing segment—is blurry and constantly shifting. A meaningful analysis of this topic would require another book by itself. And third, governance dynamics are qualitatively different in MDBs in which a subset of shareholders are also borrowers than with an MDB that lends only to private sector borrowers.

MDBs are very far from perfect. They are riddled with all manner of bureau-cratic pathologies, they have funded many projects that proved misguided, and at times they lend to incompetent and corrupt governments. This is a direct result of their mission: grappling with the most complex, frustrating, and important challenges facing our world today. Trying to promote development is extremely difficult, and MDBs are at the front lines of this struggle. If we are to have any hope of achieving the Sustainable Development Goals, stabilizing our planet's climate, and coping with global crises like the Covid-19 pandemic or rebuilding in the aftermath of violent conflict, MDBs will be a critical part of the solution. They combine a mandate to serve the public good, unparalleled global reach, practical developmental expertise, and financial strength. They are unique platforms in which countries can work together to solve practical problems, even in a world where multilateral cooperation is under threat. MDBs can and should improve. The first step to reform is to understand what MDBs are and why they do what they do. This book argues that examining the core financial underpinnings of MDBs along with the governance arrangements and balance of power among member countries will go a long way toward accomplishing that.

1

Follow the Money

The Financial Machinery of MDBs

MDBs are, among many other things, banks. Their unique financial model is a key reason for their enduring importance in international development. Despite this obvious fact, the ways that financial factors shape MDB behavior are not well understood by the academic or policy communities. This knowledge gap can easily lead to misinterpreting MDB actions and—even worse—policy proposals that are divorced from the financial realities MDBs face and that can undermine their development effectiveness. The way MDBs obtain and manage their resources is central to what they are and why they remain such a useful type of international organization, nearly eight decades after they were first created.

Unlike most national and international governmental organizations, MDBs are not funded by regular allocations from the budgets of member countries. Rather, MDBs borrow most of the resources they use from external sources—mainly international capital markets. This is perhaps the single most important reason why MDBs have proliferated in the decades since Bretton Woods and remain a viable type of international organization to this day: they are able to pursue public policy goals at minimal fiscal cost to member governments. This oft-overlooked fact must always be kept in the forefront of any attempt to understand MDBs and shape their future policy role.

Consider, for example, the 2018 decision by the U.S. government to support a capital increase for the World Bank's main lending wing, the International Bank for Reconstruction and Development (IBRD). This came as a surprise to many, considering the notoriously anti-internationalist inclinations of then-President Trump. But the reality is that it simply didn't cost the U.S. much money—about $900 million paid in over five years. Between 1944 and 2020, the U.S. contributed only $3.1 billion to IBRD in total. That has been repaid many times over by IBRD procurement contracts won by U.S. companies and the economic impact of spending at IBRD's headquarters on the Washington D.C. area over nearly eight decades, to say nothing of the geopolitical and developmental benefits the U.S. has enjoyed from its influence on World Bank activities around the globe. Even the Trump administration could see the value in such a model.

Nothing comes for free, however. By designing MDBs to channel money borrowed from external sources to development projects rather than funding them directly, member governments have implicitly relinquished a degree of control

Financing the Future. Chris Humphrey, Oxford University Press. © Christopher Humphrey (2022).
DOI: 10.1093/oso/9780192871503.003.0002

over MDBs. Governments remain their undisputed owners, but the need to obtain external resources embeds a new set of pressures into MDB operations. These pressures are fundamentally the same across all MDBs, from the massive World Bank to the tiny East African Development Bank, but are fundamentally different from the budget-based model of bilateral aid agencies, trust funds, or international agencies like the United Nations. At the end of the day, MDBs must respond to financial imperatives in ways that limit their ability to act in certain ways and incentivize them to act in others—and these actions may not always align with the desires of member governments or development goals.

In short, financial imperatives act as a key driver shaping MDB behavior, but one that is "hidden" from most observers due to the lack of familiarity with the MDB financial model. This chapter explores this model to arrive at a fuller understanding of the incentives and trade-offs facing all MDBs—large and small alike—and how these shape policies, operations, and even membership. The chapter seeks to demystify key concepts and look underneath the financial jargon to reveal the inherently political nature of the trade-offs and decisions posed by the MDB financial model. These issues are described here in general terms across the spectrum of MDBs and then examined in more detail in Chapters 3–5 with reference to different groups of MDBs.

Section 1 begins with a brief overview of the MDB financial model and Section 2 discusses the implications of this model in explaining MDB behavior, building on literature considering the role of resource dependence in international organizations. Sections 3–5 explore how financial dynamics play out in practice in three areas matching up with the three components of a balance sheet: capital structure and net income (equity), how MDBs obtain funding MDBs obtain from external sources (liabilities), and how the demand for an MDB's loans by borrowers (assets) is influenced by its operational policies and processes.

Outline of the MDB Financial Model

Below is a simplified overview of the MDB financial model.

- **Step 1**. A group of countries decides to create and <u>capitalize</u> an MDB: each country allocates money from its own budget to buy shares in the MDB, just as private individuals buy stock shares in a company. This shareholder capital is an MDB's financial foundation.
- **Step 2**. Because shareholder capital is limited, MDBs obtain more resources to lend for development projects by <u>borrowing money from external sources.</u> Large MDBs mostly issue bonds on capital markets, while smaller MDBs raise funds from a mix of bond issues and loans or credit lines from commercial banks, other development finance institutions, or export credit agencies.

- **Step 3**. With their shareholder capital and borrowed resources, MDBs make loans for development projects. The interest rates MDBs charge for project loans are slightly above their own cost of funding from the external sources (Step 2). MDBs limit how much they lend by a multiple of their shareholder capital, similar to the "capital adequacy" of commercial banks.
- **Step 4**. Borrowers repay their loans to the MDB. The income MDBs receive from loan repayments (and from other investments they make) allows MDBs to repay their own external borrowings and covers MDB administrative costs such as staff salaries, project preparation, and research. MDBs can keep any leftover income as retained earnings (which acts like additional share capital) or spend it as shareholders decide.
- **Step 5**. Apart from the cost of share capital, member countries do not need to contribute further resources to an MDB—it is largely self-financing, apart from any MDB-operated trust funds or special lending windows offering interest-free loans or grants to low-income countries ("concessional" window) that shareholders might wish to create.[1] Should members decide that they would like an MDB to expand lending for whatever reason, they may decide to increase the share capital of an MDB, which requires additional resources from the budgets of member countries.

In purely financial terms, the MDB model has been extraordinarily successful in generating resources for development. With a total share capital of about US$50 billion paid in over their entire history, the five legacy MDBs have lent US$1.5 trillion dollars for development projects as of end-2020, without using up a penny of their original share capital (see Table 0.1 in the introductory chapter). MDBs generate substantial net income almost every year,[2] the majority of which is retained as reserves totaling US$110 billion across the legacy MDBs (i.e., more than double share capital). These reserves are functionally equivalent to shareholder capital, meaning MDB operations not only generate very large amounts of development finance (along with all the knowledge and other public goods paid for by administrative costs), but also are effectively increasing MDB share capital every year.[3]

---

[1] MDB members can donate to trust funds or concessional lending windows managed by an MDB to achieve particular goals, like climate change mitigation or providing grants or zero interest loans to poor countries. Trust funds are not on the balance sheet of the MDB itself. The legacy MDBs in particular have accumulated a plethora of smaller trust funds, especially in recent years (see Reinsberg et al. 2015).

[2] Net income is otherwise known as profit. Although technically permitted by the statutes of most MDBs, in practice MDBs essentially have never distributed profits to shareholders. The one exception is Trade and Development Bank, discussed in Chapter 4.

[3] Legally, shareholder capital and reserves would all be returned to member countries if an MDB ever closes, meaning reserves could be seen as a return on investment. However, MDB members cannot sell their share as can shareholders in a private company, and no MDB has ever ceased operations and returned resources to its members, so this remains only a theoretical possibility. Member countries join

Underpinning MDB finances is an extremely strong loan repayment performance from borrower countries, based on "preferred creditor treatment" (PCT). This means that borrower governments prioritize paying back loans from MDBs, even if they might have difficulties repaying other creditors. PCT is informal and not written into any loan contract, and is an implicit recognition on the part of borrowers that MDBs are official development agencies to which they are also members, and not profit-seeking commercial institutions. As a result of PCT, borrower governments almost always stay current on servicing their MDB loans. Even in the few instances where countries do stop paying MDBs, they have historically always eventually cleared their back debts, making "loan default" a misnomer for MDB government lending. The commitment to repaying MDB loans is a key contribution of borrower member countries to the financial strength of MDBs.

The legacy MDBs have advantages that help them achieve such strong financial results, in particular the backing of major industrialized country shareholders like the U.S., Germany, and Japan. But borrower-led MDBs have also found this financial model to be effective. By far the most impressive has been the Development Bank of Latin America (CAF), generating US$301 billion in loans and US$7.6 billion in retained income from 1970 to 2020, based on total share capital of only US$5.4 billion. Even a more modest example like the Central American Bank for Economic Integration, with US$35 billion in lending and US$2.5 billion in retained income since 1961 on US$1.1 billion in share capital, has proved a useful investment to its member countries.

An oft-overlooked aspect to the MDB model is that it channels mainly *private* financing into development projects that would otherwise have no chance of attracting private investors. Most investors avoid developing countries entirely, even for projects likely to generate a profit like a toll road or electric power station, due to perceptions of risk. And most investors have no interest at all in putting money toward training primary school teachers, building rural roads, or reforming subnational tax systems. These projects do not generate short-term financial returns but rather long-term benefits to a country's human capital and future growth potential, meaning investors cannot realize a financial profit. A low-risk, highly-rated MDB bond, on the other hand, is an extremely attractive option for many investors, including huge institutional investor like pension funds or insurance companies. The MDB financial model serves to channel substantial private investor resources to projects with social benefits on a financially sustainable basis.

As presented above, an MDB's financial model seems quite dry and technical. In reality, the choices different MDBs make on how they manage their finances and address the pressures inherent in their financing model are deeply political

an MDB for many reasons, but the aim of realizing a financial profit on their share capital investment is not among them.

and informed by the national interests and relative power of their shareholders. The financial imperatives built into the model have major implications for understanding MDB behavior, including explaining why they might act in ways that do not seem to align with their development mandates.

Resource Dependence and MDB Behavior

The unique merging of banking practices with development assistance in an international organization is a fundamental reason why thirty MDBs have been created since 1944, and why rising powers like China continue to find them so useful that it helped found two new ones in 2016. Nonetheless, research on how this financial model has impacted MDB actions and policies is remarkably thin.

In-depth academic analysis of MDB finances has thus far been limited mainly to case studies: Kapur et al.'s (1997) rich history of the World Bank, studies on the uses of World Bank net income (Kapur 2002, Mohammed 2004, and Chapter 7 of Woods 2006), and a series of books on the major regional MDBs that partly address financial issues (notably Tussie 1995, Kappagoda 1995, English and Mule 1996, Culpepper 1997, and Ben-Artzi 2016). A former World Bank senior financial official wrote a book on the financial mechanics of the legacy MDBs (Mistry 1995), which though excellent is not easily accessible to most readers and is now dated. More recently Delikanli et al. (2018) reviewed several aspects of MDB finances from a mainly practitioner lens, as the authors themselves work for an MDB (Black Sea Trade and Development Bank). Academic work attempting to understand how financial issues impact MDBs more generally does not exist. One major study examining financing needs and international organizations is Gould's (2006) analysis of IMF conditionality and the interests of supplementary financiers. Although the mechanics of what Gould describe for the IMF are very different from MDBs, her study highlights how nonstate external actors with no formal governance role can shape the policies of an international organization, due to their financial role.

The lessons of organizational sociology suggest that the need to secure operating resources is a key factor behind why an organization might act in certain ways. Barnett and Coleman (2005) extend earlier work in this direction by Pfeffer and Salancik (1978) and others to international organizations (IOs). They note that IOs, like other organizations, must adapt to ensure the resources needed to survive, even if they end up acting in ways that do not always perfectly match their stated organizational goals. "The more dependent they are on others, the more likely IOs will alter their activities in a way that conforms to these external demands and standards" (Barnett and Coleman 2005, 599). This suggests that MDBs will be highly responsive to the requirements of their financial model, to ensure a continued flow of resources.

But what are those requirements? Scholars have heretofore focused almost entirely on the shareholder capital that MDBs need to obtain from their member countries. Shareholder capital is interpreted as an analogue to an agency's budget, and member countries are seen to use this "power of the purse" to enforce their interests. Put in the terms of the principal–agent framework, principals (share-holders) use control over MDB capital as one of their main tools to ensure that agents (MDB staff and management) do their bidding. As Lake (2007, 207, italics added) put it: "A grant of authority from the principal to the agent must be conditional and revocable, and the principal retains all residual rights of control including the right to veto actions by the agent either directly or *indirectly by cutting funding or other means*."

Numerous researchers have explored the ways that powerful shareholders—especially the U.S.—have used their control over capital increases as well as donations to concessional lending windows for low-income countries to exert influence over the World Bank and four regional MDBs.[4] Babb (2009) is the most explicit in using resource dependence as a key factor to understand how the U.S. has been able to enforce its policy priorities. She describes in convincing detail how the domestic politics of approving MDB capital and concessional window donations in the U.S. Congress, combined with the U.S.'s effective veto power over capital increases at the legacy MDBs, have given it authority to shape the policies and actions of the legacy MDBs (see Chapter 3 for more on this).

Illuminating though these works are in explaining the mechanisms used by powerful shareholders to influence the MDBs, this is only part of the story. For a start, this principal–agent approach to resource dependence is most applicable to the World Bank and four regional MDBs. The majority of MDBs are controlled by borrower countries, and principal–agent dynamics are much less in evidence. With borrower shareholders in broad alignment on MDB goals, capital increases are not an opportunity for a subset of shareholders to enforce their policy priorities against the wishes of other shareholders. Instead, the issue is invariably the fact that many borrower countries don't have fiscal capacity to contribute more capital. Hence, the principal–agent approach to resource dependence makes sense mainly in the context of the legacy MDBs but is less useful for the rest.

More fundamentally, shareholder capital and concessional resources are far from the only resources MDBs depend upon to function. Most MDB operating resources do not come from government budget allocations, but rather from borrowing on capital markets or other sources. Shareholders are well aware that MDB staff must do what is necessary to obtain these external resources—that is the trade-off they implicitly made by not allocating budget resources to

---

[4] Among many others, see Ascher (1992), Kapur et al. (1997), Kapur (2002), and Woods (2006) for the World Bank; Tussie (1996) for IDB; English and Mule (1997) and Mingst (1990) for the AfDB; Kappagoda (1997) for ADB; Gutner (2002) for EBRD; and Morris (2016) for the major MDBs collectively.

them directly to fund their operations, as at the United Nations and many other international organizations. This gives MDB management an unusual degree of autonomy from shareholders,[5] although it also means that MDBs face other pressures.

Capital markets, and in particular the rating agencies that investors rely on to evaluate MDB bonds, have detailed criteria to assess an MDB's perceived creditworthiness. The criteria are primarily financial, but also include operational strategy, management quality, and more. Official lenders that many smaller MDBs depend on, such as bilateral aid agencies, international funds, and export–import banks, also have specific requirements that must be fulfilled for an MDB to access their resources. All of these requirements have profound impacts on MDB policies, lending patterns, and membership structure—impacts that are poorly understood by the academic and policy communities, and even by some MDB staff and shareholders themselves.

The third major resource MDBs need are borrowers who take out and repay MDB loans. No one can make countries borrow from MDBs if they do not want to. The fact that MDBs must respond to borrower demand to function effectively and achieve the goals of their members creates a very different dynamic to their operations compared to bilateral aid agencies and multilateral trust funds offering mostly free grant resources. Unlike MDBs, organizations offering free grants can be reasonably analyzed considering mainly supply-side factors. Not so MDBs. The interest rate charges and repayment period of loans, the speed and bureaucratic hurdles of project approval, policy requirements attached to loans, quality and usefulness of technical assistance, and more all have a substantial impact on the demand of borrowers to take an MDB loan.

If the World Bank offers a loan to a borrower at very low interest rates and with a long repayment period, but with onerous policy conditions and a two-year approval process, a borrower might prefer a loan from the Chinese Ex-Im Bank without the hassles and delays, even if the interest rate is slightly more expensive, the loan must be repaid more quickly, and the borrower must hire a Chinese firm. On the other hand, if the West African Development Bank can approve financing quickly and without any policy conditions, but at a high interest rate and without any useful technical assistance in project design, a borrower might prefer instead to approach the World Bank for a loan, even if it takes longer and is more complicated

---

[5] An interesting parallel is the career of Robert Moses, who oversaw the construction of much of the infrastructure in and around New York City from the mid-1920s to the late 1960s. As detailed in Caro (1974), Moses drew up laws that gave his Triborough Authority the power to issue bonds based on toll revenues, which he then used to fund many of his infrastructure projects. Moses developed a very strong relationship with New York investors, which gave him immense power and made it very difficult for political authorities to control him. The World Bank was created during the height of Moses' power, and much of the early Bank leadership came from the New York financial markets. The Bank's early obsession with establishing itself firmly with bond investors as a top priority may well have been inspired partly by Moses' example.

to approve. MDBs need to offer services that borrowers want, or they run the risk of sliding into irrelevance, unable to achieve the development mandate they were created to pursue. With a few exceptions (Greenhill et al. 2013, Prizzon et al. 2016, Swedlund 2017, Humphrey and Michaelowa 2013 and 2019, and Humphrey 2016b), the importance of borrower demand in shaping MDB behavior has not been systematically explored.

Taken together, the need to secure these three sets of external resources can help explain many aspects of MDB behavior and policies. In fact the latter two sets of resources—private investor funding and borrower demand—embed a degree of market-like discipline on MDBs that is largely absent from other types of publicly-funded aid organizations. This can complicate their ability to undertake their development mission, but also ensures that MDB management are highly attuned to changing circumstances, making them more responsive and inclined to adapt (within the policy limits permitted by shareholders).

Capital and Net Income

The basic financial building block of an MDB is its shareholder capital. This is the initial seed money that shareholders contribute to get the MDB up and running, and which is a key underpinning of its financial strength. Each member country must contribute capital to join, and the amount of capital they contribute defines their shareholding percentage (which in most cases also defines their voting power in MDB governance). There is no single rule to decide how much each country contributes—in most cases it is a political negotiation among members, often based partly on each country's ability to pay. The total amount of share capital is relatively small in relation to what MDBs intend to lend, and MDBs must supplement their capital by borrowing from external sources to be able to lend at scale for development.

MDB capital comes in two parts. The first is actual **paid-in capital** transferred by shareholders to the MDB, just as in any private company issuing stock shares. The second is **callable capital**, which is a guarantee from member countries that an MDB can call upon if facing financial difficulties. First created as part of the Bank for International Settlements (Lichtenstein 2018), the World Bank's designers included callable capital when it was founded in 1944, and it has been replicated by almost all other MDBs since. Although originally useful to convince financial markets that an MDB had government backing and hence its bonds were extremely safe, its current value is much less certain. This is partly because callable capital has never been called in the history of any MDB and the process for doing so is not entirely clear, and also because not all countries are equally likely to pay up in the case of a capital call. Nonetheless, callable capital remains the vast majority of total subscribed capital of almost all MDBs (Figure 1.1).

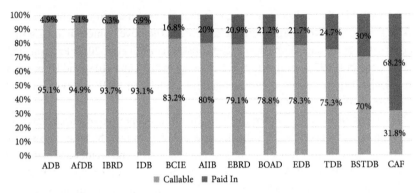

Figure 1.1 Structure of Shareholder Capital, Selected MDBs (2020).
Source: MDB 2020 financial statements.

Over time, an MDB may start to run up against the limits of how much it can lend based on its existing capital. An MDB's lending "headroom" is defined in three ways: the statutory limits written into its articles of agreement,[6] internal models that MDB staff use to calculate capital adequacy limits (similar to the Basel Committee guidelines on capital adequacy to protect the solvency of commercial banks), and the methodologies used by bond rating agencies to rate MDBs. At a certain point an MDB may find itself up against one or more of these limits and need more capital to keep lending. This can be for many reasons: growing financing needs as borrower countries urbanize and industrialize, the need for counter-cyclical lending to offset a crisis, or if an MDB takes on new tasks mandated by shareholders. The fastest way to expand lending headroom is through a capital increase paid by shareholders, or an MDB can build headroom more slowly by accumulating reserves each year out of net income.

MDB capital increases from shareholders are complicated and time-consuming affairs. At the legacy MDBs, competing budget priorities and dwindling political support for development in non-borrower countries make it difficult to convince legislatures to allocate new capital for MDBs. As well, non-borrowers use capital increase negotiations at the legacy MDBs as an opportunity to force through their priorities for MDB policy reforms (see among others Babb 2009, Woods 2003, Kapur et al. 1997 and Tussie 1995). For borrower-led MDBs, budget limitations on the part of many developing country shareholders restricts the amount of capital available.

Consequently, MDBs attempt to limit their need for capital increases by building lending headroom through the allocation of annual net income to an MDB's financial reserves (also sometimes called retained earnings). This avoids

[6] BADEA, CABEI, BOAD, CEDB, EDB, FONPLATA, and IIB are the only MDBs with no lending limits defined in their articles of agreement.

protracted negotiations among shareholders and the need to make political diffi-cult budgetary requests from member country legislatures. Once transferred from net income to an MDB's balance sheet, reserves are functionally equivalent to shareholder capital—together the two form shareholder equity. These reserves can be used just like shareholder capital to expand an MDB's lending headroom. The goal of generating net income to take the place of shareholder capital embeds a number of incentives into MDB behavior, some of which are not necessarily in line with development goals and might otherwise not make sense to an outside observer.

Raising the interest rate (and/or fees) on development loans is the easiest policy lever by which an MDB can raise additional net income. At the World Bank, for example, the interest rates on IBRD loans were increased three times between 2008 and 2014, and a new pricing scheme was introduced in 2018, specifically with the aim of generating additional net income (World Bank 2018b, 30). Similarly, the Asian Development Bank justified its loan interest rate changes in 2019 explicitly with the need to generate more allocable income (ADB 2019). The trade-off of raising loan costs is that it increases the budgetary burden to borrower countries—not the best outcome from a developmental point of view, and invariably opposed by borrower members. It can also weaken the demand for MDB loans, especially for smaller, non-AAA MDBs, thus reducing the MDB's relevance as a development financier.

Making more loans to larger middle-income countries (MICs) is a financially effective way to generate net income, compared to lending to lower-income coun-tries. MICs are better able to absorb much larger loans and, because they are usually considered less risky than lower-income countries, these loans use up less of an MDB's available lending headroom.[7] Hence, large loans to MICs generate more net income per dollar of MDB lending space. This is not the only reason why MDB staff have an incentive to promote lending to MICs—other reasons include greater implementation capacity, more complex and costly investment needs in an industrializing and urbanizing country, and more—but it is an important factor often overlooked in the discussion of lending to MICs. It is a contributing factor to why legacy MDB staff frequently resist pressure from non-borrower shareholders to reduce lending to MICs like China, Turkey, and Brazil.

Fast-disbursing budget support lending also generates more net income com-pared to slow-disbursing project lending. Budget support loans—also called struc-tural adjustment loans, development policy loans, or policy-based loans—are not tied to a specific project, and are often linked to policy reforms. They tend to be large and disburse immediately, unlike investment loans that disburse over many

---

[7] The amount of lending headroom used up by a loan is defined by the nominal face value of the loan combined with the perceived riskiness of the borrower. The riskier the borrower is thought to be, the more headroom is used up by the loan.

years. As a 2016 IDB evaluation put it, "From the Bank's perspective, PBLs [policy-based loans] are faster and cheaper to prepare and to implement than investment projects, and they generate more income per dollar approved" (IDB 2016a, 35). IDB calculated that the financial rate of return for PBLs was 2.2 percent, compared to 1.75 percent for investment loans (IDB 2016b, 39). As well, because large MICs tend to receive the most budget support, these loans tend to reduce the overall perceived riskiness of an MDB's loan portfolio (ibid., 40). Net income is far from the only incentive behind budget support lending, but it helps explain why fast-disbursing budget support loans lending still accounts for one-quarter to one-third of annual lending at the legacy MDBs. While borrower-led MDBs have generally avoided budget support lending—in part due to its association with policy condi-tionality at the legacy MDBs—CAF has begun offering it in recent years and the Central American Bank for Economic Integration has said it intends to. Despite their stated focus on infrastructure, the newly-created Asian Infrastructure Invest-ment Bank and New Development Bank both offered substantial budget support lending in 2020 in response to the Covid-19 crisis. While budget support lending has numerous developmental justifications, it helps the financial bottom line of the MDBs as well.

Reducing MDB administrative budgets also boosts net income. Net income con-siderations were a major factor behind the US$400 million cost-cutting drive at the World Bank under former President Kim (World Bank 2014, 8). They are also behind the much slimmer administrative arrangements, and hence lower expenses, of many of the borrower-led MDBs. Keeping administrative expenses to a minimum helps generate extra net income while still keeping loan prices down. The trade-off in keeping administrative costs down is that a key part of an MDB's "value added" as a development organization is the expertise, knowl-edge, and technical support that come along with loans, which requires investment in qualified staff and policy-relevant research. This is one reason why many MDBs, including the European Investment Bank and the recently created Asian Infrastructure Investment Bank, do without expensive sitting boards of executive directors. For borrower shareholders, the US$115 million that the World Bank spent in 2020 on its sitting board seems like resources not well used, particularly when that same board recently imposed US$400 million in budget cuts across operational and research units.

Generating higher investment income from MDB treasuries is another little-understood option to increase net income. MDBs all invest and earn a return on a portion of their unused resources, and the returns on these investments can be sub-stantial. For example, the World Bank's IBRD Treasury generated between $100 and $230 million each year between 2018 and 2020 on its investments. However, shareholders are wary of potential investment losses, and have imposed policies directing MDB treasuries to invest mainly in low-risk, low-return assets. The risks of seeking greater investment income were illustrated when IDB posted a shocking

$1.6 billion loss in the book value of its investment portfolio in 2008, although that loss was subsequently mostly recovered (IDB 2013, 1). In the 2008, World Bank shareholders allocated US$1 billion in resources to create the "Long-Term Investment Portfolio," specifically to generate more net income—essentially creating a mini-investment bank within World Bank's Treasury that could take on slightly higher risks to pursue more returns than normal investment income. The fund was closed after four years, despite generating considerable net income, demonstrating the wariness of shareholders to give MDB treasuries too much investment authority.

External Funding

MDBs raise most of the resources they need to operate by borrowing from external lenders. For the large MDBs, these lenders are almost entirely bond market investors, while other MDBs fund themselves through a mix of bond issues, commercial bank loans, and official borrowing from bilateral or international agencies. This section first explores which MDBs borrow from which external sources and some of the trade-offs involved. Next, it looks in more detail at how borrowing patterns influence MDB policies, development strategies, and even membership.

Where do MDBs get their money?

For the MDBs backed by high-income member countries, such as the World Bank, the major regional MDBs, or the Asian Infrastructure Investment Bank, essentially all borrowing comes via issuing bonds on international capital markets. The World Bank floated its first bond in 1947 and has since become one of the most respected bond issuers in the world. The other legacy MDBs are not far behind in reputation and market presence. AAA-rated MDB bonds are highly sought after by investors seeking safe assets that can be sold quickly if needed (they are "liquid," in financial jargon). As a result, MDBs issue bonds at extremely low interest rates in multiple currencies and in just about any market conditions. In fact, AAA-rated MDB bonds often experience a "flight to quality" in financial crises, as investors seek particularly safe assets to park their money, bringing borrowing costs down even more. These attributes allow the major MDBs to pick and choose optimal timing and among different capital markets (Table 1.1).

The superlative access of the legacy MDBs to global capital markets keeps their cost of funding down. For example, in the first half of 2021, all five legacy MDBs issued benchmark five-year bonds denominated in U.S. dollars ranging in size from $2 billion to $5 billion, all at an interest rate within 10–25 basis points (0.1–0.25 percent) over comparable U.S. Treasuries issued at the same time

Table 1.1 Annual Bond Issues by Legacy MDBs (2020)

	AfDB	ADB	IBRD	IDB	IFC	EBRD
Bonds issued (US$ billions)	6.2	35	76	26.8	11.3	15.8
Number of currencies	13	22	27	13	29	22

Source: 2020 financial statements.
Note: IBRD and IFC is fiscal year 2020 (July 2020–June 2021), while others are calendar year 2020.
Does not include commercial paper of one year maturity or less.

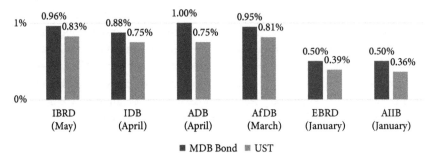

Figure 1.2 Interest Rate on Five-Year MDB Bonds (2021) vs. US Treasuries.
Source: ADB 2021, AfDB 2021, AIIB 2021a, EBRD 2021, World Bank 2021a, IDB 2021.
Note: Issue month in parenthesis. All US Treasuries are five-year bonds issued within a week of the MDB issue.

(Figure 1.2). This is extraordinarily inexpensive, among the best of any bond issuers in the world. As a result, these MDBs can offer loans for development projects at rates much lower than borrowers could get elsewhere, with enough of a financial margin over their own funding costs to cover MDB administrative expenses and generate additional net income each year. The newly-created Asian Infrastructure Investment Bank appears to be following in this same pattern, issuing a five-year dollar bond for US$3 billion in January 2021 at 0.5 percent, 14 basis points above a comparable U.S. Treasury bond.

Now consider the funding situation at lower-profile MDBs. Ecowas Bank for Investment and Development, East African Development Bank, and Pacific Islands Development Bank are three of the smallest MDBs currently operating, each owned almost entirely by low-income or lower-middle-income countries. Due to their shareholding structure, less established reputation and risky operating environment, these MDBs have no access to international bond markets. Instead, they borrow from official sources like bilateral aid agencies from wealthy

Table 1.2 Share of Total Borrowing: EADB, PIDB, EBID (2020)

	Official Agencies (Concessional terms)	Export Agencies (Semi-Concessional terms)	Bank Loans (Market terms)
East African Development Bank	92.4%	0%	7.6%
Pacific Islands Development Bank	100%	0%	0%
Ecowas Bank for Investment and Development	10.9%	58.3%	30.8%

Source: 2019 annual financial statements.

countries, larger MDBs, or export banks from other countries at below-market interest rates, supplemented by expensive loans or credit lines from commercial banks (Table 1.2).

This profile of funding sources restricts the operational capacity and autonomy of MDBs. While the official lending is usually at low interest rates, it can be cut off at any time. As well, external aid agencies or larger MDBs frequently mandate that resources lent to these MDBs be used to fund certain kinds of projects that suit their own interests, and not necessarily those of the MDB or its borrowers. In some cases, external agencies even require reforms to the MDB's internal policies and management structure in return for credit lines. Export–import banks are also problematic, as resources are often at near market rates and must be spent on goods or services from the export–import bank's home country. This can mean higher project costs and/or lower quality, and also shuts recipient country firms out of bidding on MDB project contracts. Borrowing from commercial banks gives greater freedom to the MDB in how the money is used but is expensive and usually must be repaid in the short term.

As a result, these smaller MDBs are less useful to their borrowers. Project loans are small in size, with higher interest rates and shorter repayment periods. The MDBs must keep their own administrative costs down to keep the interest rates they charge borrowers at a reasonable level, meaning they cannot easily invest in research departments or project staff able to offer meaningful technical assistance. For the same reasons, they cannot generate much if any net income, which could be used to build reserves and grow their financial capacity. And they remain dependent on the fickle largess of bilateral or export agencies (which have their own priorities) or commercial banks (which are expensive and not always available).

Considering the relative benefits and limitations of these two extremes, it should come as no surprise that most MDBs are working as hard as possible to move in the direction of the funding profile of the legacy MDBs and establish themselves as regular bond issuers on local and international capital markets. This trend has become even more pronounced since the 1990s, as international capital market investors have become more comfortable buying emerging market bonds and as local capital markets in several developing countries have gradually deepened.

The early leader among smaller MDBs to access capital markets was CAF, an MDB in Latin America owned by a group of borrower countries. Founded in 1970 and initially relying on credit lines from bilaterals, export agencies, and commercial banks, CAF's leadership reformed itself in the late 1980s after years of poor results and minimal growth. It received its first bond rating in 1993 and has since steadily improved its rating to A+ (Standard and Poor's)[8] and AA–/Aa3 (Fitch and Moody's). It is now major issuer in international capital markets, with US$26.5 billion in outstanding bonds at end-2020, compared to US$1.7 billion in bank borrowing. In 2020, CAF issued US$3.7 billion in bonds in eleven currencies. The entry of CAF into the bond markets coincided with the start of its extraordinary growth trajectory over the past thirty years (see Chapter 4 for more on CAF).

Other borrower-controlled MDBs are following the path that CAF blazed. Eleven MDBs majority-owned by borrower countries now have bond ratings from at least one of the three major rating agencies, and all except CAF were first rated after 2002. Almost all of those ratings are above investment grade—a crucial minimum level that allows a much broader range of investors to buy their bonds (due to regulations faced by many institutional investors like pension funds and insurance companies), substantially bringing down funding costs. These MDBs have gradually improved their ratings and increased capital market funding, tapping both domestic capital markets in developing countries as well as international markets. The recent period of low global interest rates has helped this process, as investors seek higher returns. Africa's Trade and Development Bank, for example, issued a US$500 million Eurobond in 2017 that was oversubscribed more than four times, leading to an additional US$200 million issued shortly thereafter, which was again oversubscribed (TDB 2018).

Accessing capital markets has greatly improved the financial terms at which these MDBs can lend and reduced their dependence on conditioned financing from official agencies and export–import banks. For example, Central America Bank of Economic Integration obtained essentially all of its funding in 1996 from bilateral and export agencies, but by 2020 70 percent of funding was from bond issues in sixteen currencies and only 13.5 percent was from official agencies. Another example is the Eurasian Development Bank, which in 2007 obtained 100 percent of its medium- and long-term resources from bank loans, but by 2020 about half came from bond issues in the Russian, Kazakh, and U.S. dollar capital markets. Access to capital markets gives MDBs a steady source of low-cost financing—less expensive and usually longer-term than bank loans, and without

---

[8] CAF was downgraded to A+ from AA– by S&P in early 2019, mainly due to CAF's loans to Venezuela (Standard and Poor's 2020a).

any of the strings that come with loans from official creditors like bilateral or export promotion agencies. This broader shift toward market financing by borrower-led MDBs could be the beginning of their growth to more developmentally relevant organizations, as the trajectories of CAF and TDB suggest.

Impact of bond market funding on MDB structure and operations

While bond market funding has many attractions for an MDB, it comes with trade-offs. Development per se is of little concern to the great majority of bond investors—what they care about is being repaid. Bond market actors focus on a few key aspects of MDBs, which are often quite different from those analyzed by academics, development specialists, and MDB member countries. Of particular importance are the views of the "Big Three" rating agencies of Standard and Poor's (S&P), Fitch, and Moody's, which collectively account for 95 percent of all global bond ratings at December 2020 (Securities and Exchange Commission 2022) and which guide the decisions of almost all bond market investors.[9] The way these rating agencies evaluate MDBs, as well as other factors related to accessing capital markets, deeply shape many aspects of MDB operations.[10]

The relationship between MDBs and capital markets has evolved considerably in the past decades. When the World Bank opened for business in 1946, the New York financial community was suspicious of this strange new international organization, the likes of which they had never seen. Overcoming this suspicion deeply shaped the early structure and operations of the World Bank (see Mason and Asher 1973, Kapur et al. 1997, and Humphrey 2016a). This included picking much of the early senior management from Wall Street, lending for what was considered to be "bankable" projects (mainly physical infrastructure), and systematically building financial reserves. The World Bank finally received the coveted AAA bond rating in 1959, and this eased bond market access for the other major MDBs. ADB, EBRD, and IDB were all granted a AAA rating immediately on their creation, as was AfDB once it accepted industrialized country shareholders in 1982.

From the 1960s through the early 2000s, capital market actors perceived the legacy MDBs as extremely safe investments. Bond rating agencies expended little effort in analyzing MDB finances in any detail, and did not even have a formal, detailed methodology for evaluating MDBs until the early 2000s. As a former top World Bank finance official put it in a 1995 book on MDB finances: "ratings agencies do not actually base their rating of the MDBs on the spurious sophisticated

---

[9] A number of other bond rating agencies exist, and although small, they are relevant to MDB access to certain markets. These include the Japan Credit Rating Agency, DBRS and—in China's fast-growing capital market—China Chengxin International Credit Rating and China Lianhe Credit Rating.

[10] See Abdelal and Blyth 2015 and Griffith-Jones and Kraemer 2021 for more on the power of rating agencies over sovereign governments.

and often confusing, if not almost irrelevant, financial ratio analysis they purport to impress their readership with" (Mistry 1995, 17). The key variable overriding all others was whether or not an MDB was backed by the G7 powers—if it was, it got a AAA rating, and if not, it did not. The only temporary exception was AfDB, which went through a period of financial difficulties and was downgraded to AA+ between 1995 and 2003 by S&P (although not by Moody's or Fitch).

This comfortable situation began to evolve in the 2000s, as MDB financial activities and financial markets themselves became increasingly complex, and accelerated dramatically in the wake of the 2008 global financial crisis, when regulators pressured rating agencies to make their methodologies more transparent. All three agencies have since published detailed and complex criteria for how they evaluate the bonds of MDBs. S&P has moved the furthest toward building a highly quantitative, replicable methodology based on a modified version of how they evaluate commercial banks. Fitch and Moody's take a more qualitative and less easily replicable approach, but also rely on an array of financial ratios. These methodologies differ in many details and are frequently revised and modified.[11] But in broad terms, they are similar in impacting MDBs in two key areas: membership and lending patterns.

Which shareholders join an MDB?

The composition of MDB shareholders is a key component to its bond rating. MDB shareholders contribute not just normal paid-in capital when they join, but also callable capital, a type of guarantee that shareholders commit to pay should an MDB ever face financial difficulties. Since callable capital has never actually been used and has no direct analogue in commercial banks, it is not entirely evident how ratings agencies should account for it, if at all. All three of the main ratings agencies take callable capital into account by giving a boost to the bond rating of an MDB. That is, the agencies evaluate an MDB's "intrinsic" bond rating based on standard financial metrics as well as an evaluation of an MDB's administration and policy relevance, and then increase the rating up to three notches depending on which countries have provided callable capital and in what amounts. The specific method for including callable capital is different in all three agencies, but the key similarity is that they all value callable capital from countries which themselves have a high bond rating (invariably wealthy non-borrower countries) much more than callable capital from lower-rated countries (which are predominantly developing borrower countries).

The result is that MDBs with substantial shareholding by high-income countries are rated AAA, while MDBs without high-income shareholders are unable

[11] See Standard and Poor's 2020b, Moody's 2019a, and Fitch 2020 for the most recent methodologies; and Humphrey 2018a for an overview and comparison from a policy perspective.

to obtain a AAA rating. The only MDB with a AAA rating that does not have any AAA-rated shareholders is Islamic Development Bank, due in large measure to Saudi Arabia's wealth and controlling capital share (along with the bank's very conservative financial management). This dynamic explains why African Development Bank accepted non-African shareholders in 1982, despite being founded as a proudly independent African institution in 1966 (Mingst 1990 and English and Mule 1996). Trade and Development Bank has made a similar calculus and has sought (as yet unsuccessfully) to bring in wealthy western nations as shareholders. As a top bank official put it, "The main obstacle to our rating is that our shareholders are poorly rated. Our capital, and especially our callable capital, is largely owned by poorly rated governments" (interview, May 16, 2017). It's no coincidence that the Asian Infrastructure Investment Bank—which includes several AAA-rated shareholder countries—was granted a AAA rating from the three major rating agencies soon after its launch in 2016. By contrast, New Development Bank—launched at the same time but without any AAA-rated shareholders—only obtained a AA+ rating.

The views of bond investors and rating agencies are not the only financial factors influencing MDB membership. Legal and regulatory access to capital markets plays a role as well. Countries invariably offer MDBs of which they are members favorable regulatory treatment and tax exemptions for bond issues on their capital market. MDBs as a result may be tempted to offer memberships of countries with capital markets that they consider useful for their funding programs, notably the U.S., European nations, and Japan, and increasingly also emerging nations like China (now with the third-largest bond market globally)—even though admitting these members could change governance dynamics.

Inter-American Development Bank experienced this in the 1960s, when its access to European capital markets was blocked. An internal study from 1965 noted that governments were "severely restricting access the markets of Austria, Belgium, France, Holland, Italy, and the United Kingdom; the only open market is Germany," and that "these countries give preference ... to international institutions of which the country is a member" (IDB 1965, 65, author's translation). The only substantial financing Europeans were willing to offer at that time were loans that had to be used to buy goods and services from companies based in the lender country ("tied" loans), which bank staff complained restricted the types of projects the bank could offer. The bank accepted nine European countries as members in 1976 explicitly to diversify its source of financing (Humphrey 2016a).

Why don't all MDBs bring on shareholders from high-income countries, to improve their access to finance? A number of MDBs limit shareholding to borrower nations, or with only a minority portion of shares open to non-borrower nations. The reason is directly linked to governance. Non-borrower members might bring financial advantages, but they also bring development agendas and policy preferences that do not always align with those of borrowers. This was the trade-off taken by the African Development Bank in 1982. By accepting non-borrower shareholders, it essentially converted from a borrower-led MDB to a legacy MDB. It obtained a AAA rating, but also many of the same policy impositions from G7 shareholders as the other legacy MDBs.

Which borrowers are offered loans?

MDBs have many reasons for lending given amounts to different countries, ranging from development need, absorptive capacity, borrower demand, or less noble factors like political allegiance or trade ties to major MDB shareholders. Financial factors are much less well understood but equally important in defining MDB lending patterns. From the point of view of ratings agencies, an MDB that makes loans to riskier borrowers or projects is more likely to face problems paying off its bond holders than an MDB that lends to less risky borrowers or projects. As a result, ratings agencies closely monitor the riskiness of MDB loan portfolios. The amount owed by each borrower is weighted by that borrower's perceived riskiness, and then all exposures are added up to arrive at an MDB's overall "risk-weighted portfolio." An MDB loan that is judged to be particularly risky uses up more lending headroom space than a loan that is less risky, because more of an MDB's own shareholder equity capital must be set aside to back up that loan. As a result, MDBs constantly face a choice between i) making riskier loans and using up lending headroom more quickly; ii) making less risky loans and being able to make more loans; or iii) making a lot of risky loans and accepting likely downward pressure on their bond rating.

The tension between these financial realities and an MDB's development mission is obvious. MDBs were created specifically to make riskier loans (i.e., for development projects that cannot easily obtain funding from commercial investors), yet they face financial incentives to lend more to safer borrowers, just like a commercial bank. An MDB can make loans several times larger to the government of a middle-income country like Mexico, China, or Indonesia than to a lower-income country, while using up the same MDB lending headroom. This embeds a strong financial incentive to lend less to lower-income countries and more to middle-income countries, regardless of development impact.

Loan portfolio concentration risk complicates the situation further. A bank that extends all its loans to just a few clients is in a riskier position than one with loans distributed across many clients, all else being equal. This "concentration risk" is a standard factor used to evaluate commercial banks. The problem is that MDBs lending mainly to government borrowers have by design only a very small number of clients (unlike private sector–focused MDBs like the World Bank's International Finance Corporation, which has many more borrowers). In 2020, for example, the World Bank's main lending window had a total of seventy-nine borrowers, compared to many thousands of borrowers for a commercial bank of comparable asset size. Regional MDBs have even fewer—Inter-American Development Bank's public sector window had twenty-six borrowers in 2020, and just three governments (Argentina, Brazil, and Mexico) accounted for 45 percent of the portfolio.

Concentration risk has taken on much greater urgency since 2012, when S&P began utilizing a calculation[12] that heavily penalizes MDB loan concentration. The calculation is particularly punitive when a large borrower is facing economic difficulties. For some of the regional MDBs with one or more large borrower country in an economic crisis, the concentration penalty can literally more than double the perceived riskiness of their portfolio—not because of any repayment problems, but simply because of the way S&P calculates portfolio concentration. The result is that the MDB ends up using twice as much of its lending headroom, leaving it facing the choice of reducing lending or facing a possible downgrade. Moody's and Fitch also evaluate MDB portfolio concentration, but using metrics that are less punitive than S&P's.

The loan concentration penalty represents a major restriction on the capacity of MDBs to help large borrowers facing a crisis. For example, when Argentina was in default to commercial creditors in the mid-2000s, and when countries in northern Africa faced political turbulence as part of the Arab Spring, the Inter-American and African Development Banks (respectively) had to reduce lending to those countries, even though none of them missed any MDB loan repayments. Egypt and Tunisia were cut off entirely in 2012–2014, exactly when they needed extra financing to face their crises. One African Development Bank official commented, "The North African countries were most efficient at using our resources and had a big portfolio. Then they got downgraded and we had to back off, arguably when they needed us the most ... The Egyptians were very upset" (interview, June 12, 2015). Argentina's executive director at Inter-American Development Bank noted that this led to "some pretty drastic cuts to our envelope ... due to the impact that more loans would have had in S&P's methodology" (interview, June 10, 2015). Hence, S&P is heavily penalizing the MDBs for doing exactly what they were designed to do and have done for decades without any threat to their financial stability: lend to a small group of country governments and lend countercyclically in times of need. The impact of S&P's concentration penalty has led the legacy MDBs to swap loan exposures amongst each other to diminish loan concentration (see Chapter 3), which though effective in the short term does pose questions about weakening the long-term relationship between borrower countries and MDBs—all in reaction to one poorly-designed aspect of one rating agency's methodology.

---

[12] The calculation is based on a paper written to assess the concentration risk of commercial banks (Gordy and Lütkebohmert 2013). The authors explicitly state that their methodology is not appropriate for banks with fewer than 500 exposures, but S&P has continued to use it, despite complaints from MDBs. See Humphrey 2015b and 2018a for details.

In short, the exigencies of bond markets and credit rating agencies—in particular S&P—has a substantial impact on where MDBs lend, and increasingly so in recent years. A vice president of operations at one of the legacy MDBs said, referring to the S&P methodology,

> You cannot overstate the impact that this methodology has had on our operations—it has in a way changed our entire business model. Formerly we assigned our resources strictly based on need and absorption capacity. But bit by bit the S&P methodology has become the main driver of our allocation decisions ... I can't simply push resources on smaller economies to improve our portfolio, they can't absorb it. And at the same time I have huge demands from countries that I cannot serve because of the impact on our capital ratio.
>
> (interview, September 11, 2015)

A treasury staffer from another legacy MDB put it more bluntly: "S&P has become the de facto regulator for us. Everything we do, we test immediately to see how it will impact the rating" (interview, June 12, 2015).

This dynamic is not necessarily the fault of the ratings agencies themselves. They are required by bond market regulators and their customers to evaluate MDBs with methodologies that are relatively quantifiable and replicable. But the agencies have no signposts to help them, as MDBs have no regulatory oversight like a central bank or the Basel Committee. How are ratings agencies supposed to quantify the official relationship MDBs have with borrowers, or their nonprofit development mandate, or their structurally concentrated loan portfolio? The agencies have attempted grappled with these questions (their MDB reports are excellent and highly educational), but are being forced to evaluate essentially political issues with financial metrics. As one ratings agency analyst put it, "We don't want to be a regulator" (cited in Humphrey 2018a, 22). In an effort to address this problem and provide official guidance to the ratings agencies, the G20 in 2021 created an independent commission of experts to review key aspects of MDB finances, including callable capital and concentration risk (G20 2021).[13]

Borrower Demand

A fundamental difference between MDBs and most other types of development organizations is that MDBs make loans that must be repaid, rather than offering grants. Developing countries are not required to take out MDBs loans—MDB projects and financial terms must be perceived as attractive enough

---

[13] The author is a panel member in the review. This book does not include any information from the panel's data gathering, deliberations, or conclusions.

for government officials to agree to take out the loan, since it will have to be repaid with interest. Without demand for their loans on the part of borrowers, MDBs cannot fulfill their mandate.

It is remarkable how little attention policymakers and academics pay to the importance of borrower demand. All too often policy papers propose that an MDB should reorient its lending to focus on certain sectors or to push types of projects based on the latest trends in development thinking or priorities among wealthy countries. NGOs, in turn, sometimes demand that MDBs refuse to fund certain kinds of projects or to mandate consultations with certain social groups in recipient countries. The oft-overlooked reality is that however well intentioned, if the proposals are objectionable to borrower governments, the MDB might find the door shut in its face, rendering them moot.

In academia, this blind spot is exemplified by attempting to analyze lending patterns by MDBs with the same approaches as the "aid allocation" literature, using mainly statistical methods to isolate factors such as developmental need, political influence, or commercial interests to explain aid flows. The assumption behind the aid allocation literature is that supply-side factors are the only variables of interest. This assumption makes sense for bilateral aid, which is mainly free grant resources (Bermeo 2017 is a recent example). It is also arguably justified for zero interest loans or grants from MDB concessional lending windows like the World Bank's International Development Association (Andersen et al. 2006). However, an assumption of constant and limitless demand by borrowers for regular MDB loans ignores the reality that borrower countries might choose not to take out an MDB loan for any number of reasons. This could be to avoid MDB-imposed policy conditions, reduce external dollar debt, prioritize investment in sectors that an MDB does not support, or a sudden influx of budget resources from a commodity boom. Studies taking this supply-focused approach to MDB lending (for example Frey and Schneider 1986, Neumayer 2003, and Dreher et al. 2009) run the risk of misunderstanding a more complex demand-supply dynamic between MDBs and borrowers.

A few examples illustrate this point. In its early years, CAF insisted on lending only for regional integration projects, but the lack of demand forced it to change its lending criteria to adapt to borrower needs (Humphrey 2016a). South Africa declined to take out loans from the World Bank for years after the fall of the apartheid regime, and the desire on the part of the World Bank to restart lending was an important factor in bending its rules to make massive loans for a controversial coal-fired power plant, against the wishes of some non-borrower shareholders. The Asian Development Bank is reacting to competition for projects from the new Asian Infrastructure Investment Bank as well as China's Belt and Road Initiative that impact demand for its loans (Kajimoto 2017).

One might argue that if a developing country does not take out loans from an MDB, then they don't really need the resources. MDBs shouldn't need to compete to make loans—if demand for their loans declines from a country, then that country has de facto graduated from needing MDB support. This argument is overly simplistic, for at least three reasons.

- Borrowers might be able to access other sources of finance, like private markets or nontraditional bilateral lenders like China, which are attractive in the short term but may not generate the same level of positive benefits to the borrower country or the international community. Problems with other lenders can include worse financial terms (and hence unsustainable debt loads), lower project standards and quality, or funding ill-conceived and unsustainable projects.
- Some of the issues that weaken borrower demand, especially at the legacy MDBs, are the result of policies imposed by a subset of non-borrower shareholders for reasons that at least in part respond to their domestic political interests rather than the optimal approach to development (see Chapter 3 for more on this).
- MDBs are cooperatives created by a group of countries to improve their ability to access development resources on financial terms better than they could get on their own. There's no inherent reason for that model not to provide useful services to countries that might also be able to access other sources of finance, as the huge portfolio of European Investment Bank loans to high-income European countries suggest, particularly for projects with positive public benefits.

What shapes demand for MDB financing? The answer varies from country to country, and over time within the same country, depending on far too many factors to systematically analyze here. It is nevertheless possible to outline a few key issues, based on 122 interviews with government ministerial officials that engage directly with external development financiers in sixteen countries in Africa, Asia, and Latin America between 2009 and 2020, and supplemented by other research in this area (including Greenhill et al. 2013, Prizzon et al. 2016, Gallagher et al. 2012, and Swedlund 2017). The main characteristics of an MDB that shape demand for loans on the part of borrowers can be reduced to five:

- *Financial terms* of MDB loans, including the interest rate, length of repayment period (maturity), currency of loan, and overall amount made available.
- *Developmental value-added* that comes with MDB financing, i.e., the perceived quality and usefulness of MDB staff expertise in helping design and implement the project.
- *Bureaucratic requirements and loan processing times* required to access MDB lending, including time spent negotiating with MDB staff, overall time to

approve and disburse loans, and stipulations like procurement rules or environmental and social safeguards.

- *Impositions from an MDB on a country's development priorities*, which can involve only supporting certain types of projects, pressuring governments to modify their development agenda, or requiring policy changes in exchange for loans.
- *Idiosyncratic personal relationships between individual MDB operations staff and government officials* in positions of authority to initiate development projects.

These characteristics are balanced against a number of factors on the side of borrowers, including how badly a borrower needs the loan, what other sources of financing might be available, the urgency to complete a project, a government's own technical ability to prepare and implement the project, and potential domestic political implications of working with an MDB.

For most borrower-led MDBs, financial considerations are a critical factor limiting demand. Because of their own more challenging access to funding, the interest rate on loans from borrower-led MDBs tend to be substantially higher than the AAA-rated MDBs, the length of time given to repay the loan is shorter, and the amount of resources available is smaller. As well, very few borrower-led MDBs have much in the way of in-house technical expertise in project design and implementation, meaning their developmental value-added tends to be limited at best. To offset these disadvantages, smaller MDBs highlight their ability to be extremely responsive to borrower government wishes and to provide financing very quickly with minimal hassles or impositions (see Chapter 4).

The situation is essentially reversed for the legacy MDBs. With their AAA bond rating and much higher capitalization, the legacy MDBs are able to provide substantial resources at excellent financial terms. The expertise and knowledge of staff—especially at the World Bank, but also at the regional legacy MDBs— is widely recognized as superlative, and many governments are eager to avail themselves of this even if they don't need the financing (China's ongoing demand for World Bank and Asian Development Bank loans is a case in point). On the other hand, the legacy MDBs are loaded down with a variety of rules, mandates, and bureaucratic processes that can make them much less attractive to borrowers. Loan negotiations are arduous and slow, require multiple in-country missions and consultations with headquarters, and must go through multiple levels of internal review and approval. And legacy MDBs are much more inclined to stipulate policy conditions, define project design based on their own criteria, and promote a vision of development favored by major shareholders rather than borrower governments.

Responding to borrower demand is much more important at MDBs due to their financial model, compared to trust funds or bilateral agencies that make mostly grants and as a result tend to be more supply-driven. While speaking of "clients" and being concerned about MDB "competitiveness" might make the development community uncomfortable, it is in fact one of the best traits of MDBs. Because they are lending organizations, MDBs must listen closely to borrowers and adapt to best suit their needs—precisely in line with what the international community has called for as part of the Paris Declaration on Aid Effectiveness (OECD 2005), Accra Agenda for Action (UN 2008), and the Busan Partnership for Effective Development Cooperation (OECD 2011). Some MDBs are better at this than others, but it is unavoidable for all. The key for MDB staff and management is striking the right balance between the mandates of shareholders—including non-borrower shareholders who have every right to promote their views on development—and the needs and desires of borrower countries.

Conclusions

The goal of this chapter has been to outline how financial pressures shape MDB policies and actions. The core argument is that the MDB model is extraordinarily powerful as a means of channeling financing (mostly private financing) to development goals, but that it also imposes certain imperatives and incentives that do not exist at budget-funded development organizations. By relying on external resources rather budget allocations, MDBs generate more resources and do not cost shareholder governments nearly as much as, for example, bilateral aid agencies. The trade-off is that MDBs must pay attention to considerations beyond pure development goals, including the perceptions of capital markets and the demands of borrowers. These trade-offs can be seen as having both positive and negative developmental outcomes, depending on one's views. The "discipline of the markets" might be seen by some as a salutary contrast to budget-financed organizations like the UN, and responsiveness to borrowers is well aligned with much recent international rhetoric on development. On the other hand, relying on bond market investors and ratings agencies might be seen as embedding a cold-hearted market logic that weakens or even undermines the ability of MDBs to address urgent social challenges. Whatever one's point of view, financial pressures are unquestionably a major influence on MDBs, and taking these pressures into account is essential to fully understanding how MDBs function and proposing realistic, viable reforms to improve them.

2

Who's in Charge? Governance across MDBs

Multilateral development banks are owned and governed by groups of national governments—this is what makes them "multilateral." All existing MDBs were created by an international treaty agreement among sovereign states. No authority exists that can regulate MDBs beyond that same group of countries that owns them. They are, to use the apt term employed by credit rating agencies, "supranational."

Governance and politics are fundamental to understanding MDBs, and national governments are a key set of actors shaping their policies and actions. It could hardly be otherwise, as MDBs are created and owned by, and mainly serve, groups of nation-states. MDBs are fundamentally political in nature. They are public agencies, and their goal is to serve a public policy purpose. How that purpose is defined and the ways by which it is pursued are deeply political. While many MDB staffers might prefer to think of their work as purely technical and apolitical, it is not. Even when considering how other factors such as the financial pressures described in the previous chapter, bureaucratic incentives, or development ideology shape MDB behavior, the political motives of the government shareholders are always a "framing constraint" as Woods (2006, 12) put it.

Government interests cannot explain everything about MDBs, but many aspects of how MDBs act cannot be fully understood without taking member government interests into account. This includes which countries receive MDB loans and which do not, a topic examined by numerous scholars over the years. Beyond individual loan decisions, and more the focus of this book, is the influence of governmental interests on underlying characteristics of an MDB, such as processes for approving loans, operational strategies, procurement and environmental rules, and financial policies. If the financial realities of the MDB model described in the previous chapter are a constant affecting all MDBs in similar ways, the governance make-up of an MDB—and in particular the interests and balance of power among different member countries—is the single most powerful variable explaining how MDBs differ from one another.

Member government interests enter into MDB activities first and foremost through mechanisms of governance: how the countries owning an MDB take decisions on policies and operations. The first part of this chapter proposes a theoretical framework to analyze how the interests of member countries explain

Financing the Future. Chris Humphrey, Oxford University Press. © Christopher Humphrey (2022).
DOI: 10.1093/oso/9780192871503.003.0003

MDB characteristics and to systematically compare how the dynamics of national interest and governance rules play out in different MDBs. The second section examines the governance mechanisms and procedures of how decision-making actually takes place and describes similarities and divergences across the universe of MDBs.

A New Analytical Framework for MDB Governance

Employing governance as a key variable to understanding MDBs, and international organizations more generally, is hardly a new idea. The "realist" school—which, in broad terms, posits that international organizations are created and controlled by states to suit their purposes—is perhaps the oldest tradition in international political economy, building on Machiavelli and Hobbes. To quote one of its earliest modern exponents, E.H. Carr (2016): "International government is, in effect, government by that state which supplies the power necessary for the purpose of governing."

Analyses grounded in part on realist theories of power politics among major shareholders have long been applied to research on MDBs, including Babb's (2009) study of how the U.S. has exerted its control over the World Bank and regional MDBs, Woods' (2006) volume on the World Bank and IMF, Krasner's essay on regional MDBs (1981), and Wade's (1996) article on ideological fights within the World Bank. Numerous researchers have sought statistical evidence for U.S. and G7 influence directing MDB lending toward allies and away from opponents (among others, see Vreeland and Dreher 2014 and Kilby 2006 and 2011). Many of these studies conclude that the World Bank and regional MDBs function essentially "as a tool of foreign policy by ... major stakeholders," i.e. G7 nations (Dreher et al. 2009, 27).

Realist-oriented research has generated convincing evidence demonstrating how the interests of powerful member states shape the actions of the World Bank and the major regional MDBs. The problem is that the application of the realist framework in these studies has focused not on the national interests of all MDB member governments, but rather on just one or a small handful of powerful members that are perceived to control MDB policies and actions. This approach might (arguably) have made sense when examining the legacy MDBs in the 1970s and 1980s, but it is questionable in a world in which U.S. power is less certain, the G20 has supplanted the G7, and China is rapidly expanding its influence across the globe. Just as important, this theoretical approach is much less useful for MDBs that are not obviously dominated by the U.S. or G7. What can a focus on the major western powers tell us about CAF or the West African Development Bank, which have relatively balanced governance among a group of developing countries? No single shareholder country or minority of countries is "hegemonic" in any analytically useful sense, and trying to use that kind of realist lens to understand them misses the point. The way member countries interact and take decisions is fundamentally different from the legacy MDBs.

Another shortcoming of this approach is that it tends to lump together the World Bank and four major regional MDBs as all controlled in essentially similar ways by the U.S., despite voting share differences. At end-2020 for example, the U.S. voting share ranged from a low of 4.4 percent at African Development Bank to a high of 30.01 percent at the Inter-American Development Bank, and the collective share of borrowing countries from a low of 13.8 percent at the European Bank for Reconstruction and Development to 55.3 percent at the African Development Bank. Are these variations irrelevant, just a smokescreen for U.S. dominance? That seems unlikely, and evidence discussed in Chapter 3 suggests that it is incorrect—these differences do indeed matter in differentiating the legacy MDBs.

As a result of the changing geopolitical and economic context in the first decades of the twenty-first century, both academic research and the policy world are starting to move beyond the singular focus on the legacy MDBs and to reevaluate the assumption of U.S./G7 dominance. In light of these shifts, it is also time to rethink how national interest impacts the governance of MDBs and of international organizations more generally. Lyne et al. (2009) point out that the U.S. and G7 are far from the only shareholder able to influence the World Bank. The authors highlight the "complexity" of principals and take seriously formal shareholding composition and governance rules of the World Bank as a means of explaining a shift in social policy lending through the collective preferences of all shareholding countries, not just the U.S. or G7. Gutner (2002) makes a similar point in her study of MDBs in Europe, as does Copelovitch's (2010) study of the IMF.

These contributions point the way to rethinking MDB governance beyond hegemonic great power politics rooted in the geopolitical realities of the past century. At the same time, following the lead of Lyne et al. (2009) of accounting for the policy preferences of all shareholders on each policy choice would be extraordinarily difficult to operationalize in even one MDB, much less thirty. How does one realistically aggregate and weigh the preferences of the World Bank's nearly 200 shareholders on the hundreds of decisions taken by the boards of governors and directors each year? And how can one compare that in a meaningful and analytically feasible way across MDBs with different (but sometimes overlapping) groups of shareholder countries?

This study proposes a conceptual framework for MDB governance that builds on the intuitions of the scholars mentioned above, but simplifies in a way that is analytically useful and tailored to the specific realities of MDBs. The framework conceptualizes governance at MDBs as a balance of power between two sets of MDB member countries: **borrowers** (lower- and middle-income countries eligible to receive MDB financing) and **non-borrowers** (high-income countries that contribute shareholder capital but are not eligible to receive MDB financing). The dichotomy between borrowing and non-borrowing countries in the context of an MDB defines two important groups of shareholders that tend to have aligned interests within each group, but divergent interests between the two groups.

What are the interests of national governments in MDBs, and how are these interests defined? This might at first seem obvious—the almost tautological answer is that a government's interest is for an MDB to have policies and act in ways that afford it the most benefits. For non-borrowing nations, that means that MDBs support its geopolitical position vis-à-vis other nations, promote its economic interests, and generate development outcomes that it (and other nations) benefit from, like greater global economic growth, reduced migration flows, or climate change mitigation. For borrower nations, that means MDBs provide financing and technical assistance at attractive financial terms to help address pressing investment needs that will result in improved economic and/or social outcomes for its citizens.

But of course, a nation's government is composed of individual bureaucrats and politicians, many of whom take into account domestic political realities and even sometimes personal interests when formulating policy toward an MDB or other IOs, not just higher-level concerns of national interest. Broz and Hawes (2006) discuss this in relation to the empirical case of U.S. banking interests and the IMF, concluding that "the evidence we found suggests that domestic politics may influence policy-making by international organizations," (103), while Milner (2006) considers the issue on more conceptual terms for multilateral organizations generally. Numerous scholars have highlighted the importance of domestic political considerations influencing U.S. policies toward the legacy MDBs, for example Wade's (1997) study of how nongovernmental organizations pressured the U.S. Congress to force MDBs to adopt stringent environmental and social safeguards and Babb's (2009) analysis of U.S. congressional interests on many aspects of MDB policy over decades. Although the domestic interests of borrower countries are much less studied, one can easily imagine that borrower government officials might want to quickly move ahead with an MDB-supported infrastructure project to help their prospects in an upcoming election, steer MDB contracts toward politically-connected domestic business interests, or avoid politically difficult policy requirements on an MDB loan.

The insertion of these types of interests may not align well with what might be considered the national interest of an MDB member country. To take the example of environmental and social safeguards, a cynical realist approach by the U.S. government would focus on directing MDB resources to allies and cutting off enemies, and issues like environmental or human rights protection would be a complicated distraction from that goal. Similarly, a borrower country official directing MDB financing to a project for political reasons could weaken the potential positive economic and social impact of MDB engagement, thus going against the national interest for more parochial or personal concerns. This sort of activity might be better viewed as an international extension of domestic interest group politics (such as outlined by Grande 1996 and Richardson 2000), or a variation of the public choice view of international organizations outlined by Vaubel (1986) or Frey (1997) that highlights how government officials make use of IOs for their own domestic political interests.

The dividing line between higher-level concerns of national interest and those more motivated by the political interests of government officials is of course a blurry one. Pushing MDB procurement policies in a way that benefits a country's industry might be in the national interest, a response to politically-connected lobbying, or both. Stronger MDB environmental safeguards might be in response to focused lobbying by a group of NGOs in a powerful shareholder country, or a better long-term approach to development that benefits the entire global community, or both. The main takeaway is simply the recognition that a country's policies toward an MDB come from a mix of motivations that are not always purely "realist" in the classic sense of pursuing a country's national interest.

The dichotomy between borrower and non-borrower shareholders plays out in numerous policy issues of relevance to MDB operations (Table 2.1), a dynamic amply documented in numerous studies.[1] As a result, the balance of power between these two groups of shareholders in the governance of each MDB can go a long way to explaining many aspects of its policies and operational characteristics. MDBs dominated by non-borrower countries are more inclined to impose conditions on lending, have more levels of bureaucracy and oversight, take longer to approve loans, and maintain more conservative financial policies. Borrower-dominated MDBs, on the other hand, are likely to give recipient governments a freer hand in how loan resources are used, follow national laws related to environmental and social issues, approve loans much faster, and seek to maximize MDB lending. MDBs with a more balanced split between borrowers and non-borrowers tend to fall between these two extremes.

The composition of shareholders also has an important role in defining the financial strength of an MDB, which in turn has an indirect impact on its developmental activities (as discussed in the previous chapter). Wealthy non-borrower countries can generally afford to contribute more capital to MDBs than lower-income borrower countries, which face tighter budgetary restrictions, meaning MDBs with more non-borrower shareholders tend to be better capitalized and thus have greater lending capacity. The presence of non-borrower shareholders also gives MDBs an image of solidity in the eyes of capital market actors, most notably credit rating agencies. The upshot is that non-borrower-controlled MDBs can offer more and cheaper loans to recipient countries for development projects compared to MDBs controlled by lower-income borrower countries.

[1] Among others, see Krasner (1981), Mingst (1990), Tussie (1995), Kappagoda (1995), English and Mule (1996), Kapur et al. (1997), IDS (2000), Gutner (2002), Sagasti and Prada (2006), Griffith-Jones et al. (2008), Humphrey and Michaelowa (2013 and 2018), Humphrey (2014, 2016a, and 2016b), and Park and Strand (2016).

Table 2.1 Borrower vs. Non-Borrower Priorities at MDBs

	Borrowers	Non-Borrowers
Loan Approval Process	Streamlined and fast	Quality control and oversight more important than speed
Environmental and Social Safeguards	Borrower country decides priorities and processes; national law and regulation predominates	Impose external standards over and above national laws—country systems only in limited cases
Independent Complaint Mechanisms	Opposed. No NGO role in MDB policies and operations. Complaints channeled via national governments	Strong and independent mechanism allowing NGOs and other parties to challenge MDB operations
Lending Priorities	Demand-driven, in response to government's development agenda	MDBs promote latest development thinking and encourage borrowers to utilize perceived best practices in development
Policy Conditionality	No conditions, or only minimal and country-led	Used as a tool to promote policy changes, at times against domestic opposition
Loan Pricing	Keep loan pricing down to benefit borrowers	Higher loan pricing to generate net income used to build equity (in lieu of a capital increase) and use for other shareholder causes
Graduation Policy	Unnecessary. All countries have right to borrow from the cooperative	Middle-income countries should become ineligible or have reduced and/or more expensive loans according to transparent rules
Capital	Increase capital to strengthen MDB lending capacity, including considering non-sovereign shareholders	Minimize capital increases; build lending capacity via net income retained earnings
Financial Policies	Loosen capital adequacy rules to allow expanded lending	Conservatively restrict lending to minimize any chance of financial problems

To be sure, borrowers and non-borrowers sometimes have aligned interests. Most members are likely to want to avoid having an MDB face financial collapse, or to restrain MDB administrative costs, or for an MDB to provide assistance following a natural disaster. Individual borrower countries might support policy positions generally backed by non-borrowers, and vice versa. For example, while borrowers tend to want to MDBs to be better capitalized, some may oppose a capital increase due to their own budgetary restrictions. Some borrowers may support environmental and social safeguards, while some non-borrowers may see safeguards as overly onerous and bureaucratic. Positions also diverge within each group. The African Development Bank, for example, is notorious for disputes over its history between English-speaking, French-speaking, and North African borrower county shareholders. The role of non-borrowers also varies substantially: the way the U.S. acts as an MDB shareholder is often quite different from Germany, the U.K., or Japan, even if their basic priorities are often similar. But in broad terms, tensions between borrowers and non-borrowers play out in similar ways at numerous MDBs.

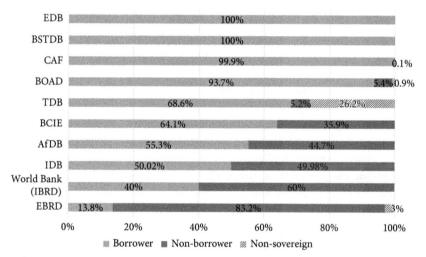

Figure 2.1 Voting Power, Selected MDBs (2020).
Source: 2020 MDB financial statements.

These tendencies implied by the relative power of borrower and non-borrower shareholders in MDB policy preferences and financial capacity form the basis for a framework for analyzing different MDBs by considering the balance of power between the two groups of shareholders (Figure 2.1). Other observers have also noted these tendencies—not coincidentally those few who have previously attempted to compare different MDBs—but stopped short of developing a more general model of MDB governance that could be applied systematically across the class of institutions.

To state the basic model succinctly:

MDBs fall along a continuum of governance arrangements based on the balance of power between borrower and non-borrower shareholders. As a result, many of the most important operational characteristics of MDBs can be expected to fall in a similar position along that continuum in parallel.

This governance model works well for most MDBs. However, a few MDBs don't fit so neatly into the framework, due to the ambiguous nature of one or more major shareholders. For example, both Islamic Development Bank and the Eurasian Development Bank have a dominant shareholder country (Saudi Arabia and Russia, respectively) that in some respects act as a "borrower" country (unlikely to impose policy conditionality or environmental safeguards) while at the same time supporting financial policies and directing lending in ways that support their national interests. Some borrower-led MDBs (Central American Bank for Economic Integration or ECO Trade and Development Bank, for example) are dominated by a subset of founding members rather than using a more balanced governance setup.

Hence, one can visualize a continuum of governance control:

- At one end are the legacy MDBs dominated by non-borrower shareholders. The World Bank and European Bank for Reconstruction and Development are at the extreme due to their strong control by non-borrowers, while non-borrower control is tempered by a greater influence of borrower shareholders at African, Asian, and Inter-American Development Banks.
- At the other end are borrower-led MDBs. CAF, FONPLATA, and Black Sea Trade and Development Bank follow a more classic cooperative bank model with no dominant shareholder, no non-borrower shareholders (thus far), and relative alignment of interests among members. Other MDBs such as Caribbean Development Bank, Trade and Development Bank, and West African Development Bank are also strongly controlled by borrowers, but are to a greater or lesser degree influenced by minority non-borrower shareholders.
- A third group of MDBs, led by borrower countries but with one dominant shareholder, occupies an ambiguous position along the continuum. MDBs like Islamic Development Bank, Eurasian Development Bank, and the Asian Infrastructure Investment Bank share some characteristics with borrower-led MDBs, but like the legacy MDBs are governed in a less egalitarian fashion.

Placing an MDB along this governance continuum cannot be done mechanically based only on voting shares. A number of other governance mechanisms discussed later in this chapter—notably special voting majorities on key issues—complicate the panorama. As well, the role of donor-funded concessional lending windows at the World Bank and major regional MDBs also play a role, as noted by Babb (2009) and Kapur (2002), giving donor countries greater leverage over the governance of these MDBs. For example, African Development Bank would appear on the face of it to be a borrower-led MDB, with a clear majority (55 percent in 2020) of voting power controlled by borrower countries. But its dependence on non-borrower member countries to fund the African Development Fund concessional lending window is one factor giving them more governance power than their voting share might suggest.

Access of an MDB to sources of borrowing to fund its operations is another key issue influencing governance dynamics, as discussed in the previous chapter. Again to take the example of African Development Bank, the bank's desire to maintain a top bond rating to access bond markets at low interest rates gives non-borrower shareholders considerable leverage beyond their voting power, since their participation as shareholders is critical to that goal. A similar dynamic appears to be at work at the China-led Asian Infrastructure Investment Bank, where European shareholders have influence greater than their voting share due to their importance to support the bank's bond rating. A third example is Africa's Trade and Development Bank, where China is a minority shareholder but provides substantial lines of credit that improve overall funding costs. Hence, China likely has more sway in Trade and Development Bank governance than its *de jure* voting power.

In short, this is not a watertight framework into which one can neatly plug all MDBs and always expect to generate the same results. It is rather intended to help observers understand how governance dynamics causally shape operations and policies across a diverse array of MDBs in a systematic and analytically useful way. The framework is robust over time, as it is based not on a specific geopolitical context (as is, to a degree, the focus on great power politics), but rather the broad interests of nation-states as members of an MDB and the particular mechanisms of governance built into the MDB model.

The dichotomy between borrower and non-borrower shareholders has begun to blur slightly with the economic rise of some developing countries, most notably China. If China were to graduate from borrowing at the World Bank,[2] as the U.S. has pushed for in recent years (Rappeport 2019), would that mean it would switch

[2] Only the legacy MDBs have a policy of "graduation" from lending, which are a topic of continual disagreement among shareholders and remain deeply political and subjective rather than using transparent criteria, like GDP per capita. Other MDBs—including those with high-income borrower countries like the European Investment Bank or the Nordic Investment Bank—do not have graduation policies.

into the "non-borrower" camp in this governance framework? The answer is no, at least in the medium term. China's overall approach to development (focused on infrastructure and economic growth, compared to poverty reduction and social indicators), antipathy to external policy impositions, and vocally stated allegiance with other developing nations and in opposition to the G7 all suggest that it will continue to hold policy positions closer to other borrower shareholders. The early trajectory of the Asian Infrastructure Investment Bank and New Development Bank bear this out, as explored in Chapter 5, and a similar dynamic can be seen in countries like Saudi Arabia, Korea, and Chile.

Ownership and Governance Mechanics

Before examining how this governance framework plays out in different groups of MDBs in Chapters 3–5, the rest of the chapter describes the mechanics of how MDBs are governed: who can be a member, how shares are allocated to members, how shares translate into voting, and different levels of decision-making authority within MDBs. This section is empirical and descriptive rather than theoretical, and has two main purposes. *First*, to understand how the split between borrower and non-borrower members plays out in practice, it is important to examine how a country's membership in an MDB translates into actual decision-making power. In most cases, simply looking at shareholding is insufficient, as several other mechanisms come into play. *Second*, it is interesting in and of itself to understand the diversity of governance arrangements employed across the range of MDBs, to appreciate the possibilities inherent in the MDB model and the choices made by different sets of member countries.

When considering MDB governance, the degree of uniformity in how MDBs are owned and how decisions are made is remarkable. In an almost literal sense, a template exists for drawing up MDB governance arrangements, based originally on the World Bank's Articles of Agreement.[3] Reading through the founding statutes of twenty-five currently operating MDBs that are publicly available, the broad outlines of how they are structured, owned, and governed are very similar, even down to sometimes nearly identical section titles and text phrasing in the statutes.

This governance template—along with the financial power of the MDB model outlined in the previous chapter—helps explain why so many MDBs exist, and why new ones continue to be created. They have an almost out-of-the-box set

---

[3] The IBRD's Articles, as drawn up at Bretton Woods in 1944, were based partly on an earlier proposal for an inter-American financial institution negotiated in the 1930s but never approved by the U.S. Congress. See Mason and Asher (1973), Helleiner (2014), and Bazbauers and Engel (2021) for details.

of rules that different groups of governments can tweak to fit their particular goals. No other type of international organization has such a clearly-defined and widely agreed set of ownership and governance rules. This common governance framework is a key reason why MDBs can be analyzed as a "family" of international organizations, despite the many differences in goals, operating characteristics, and scale.

Ownership

Ownership of all MDBs is divided into shares, like private stock corporations. When countries create an MDB, a specified number of shares are issued, each of which have a defined monetary value. When a member country joins, it does so by not only signing and ratifying the MDB's founding international treaty, but also by purchasing capital shares. Member countries can later agree to issue more MDB shares, either for a new member to purchase or so that existing members can increase the financial capacity of the MDB. The decision-making power of each member is in most cases (twenty-one out of twenty-five MDBs for which rules are available) directly tied to the number of shares it owns of the MDB's capital stock.

It is worth dwelling briefly on how odd this arrangement is, despite being for the most part accepted and unquestioned in the decades after Bretton Woods. MDBs—the most important international development organizations in existence—are formally owned in a very similar way to a private stock company. Shareholders can receive dividends from any profit the MDBs generate (although they almost never do). Should a member leave an MDB or the MDB cease operations, members have the right to receive back their capital share. So whatever else MBD shareholding membership might imply, it is also an actual financial investment.

This ownership structure is fundamentally different from other types of intergovernmental international organizations. The United Nations has no "owners" per se, but rather member countries that have agreed to create and fund the budget of the organization. The same is true for Interpol, the International Energy Agency, the Global Environment Fund, the Organization of American States, or the European Union. Even the International Monetary Fund, which makes loans to member countries like MDBs, is not "owned" by members in a formal sense— it is essentially a very large fund to which members contribute quotas and have certain drawing rights.

Examining precisely why MDBs have this ownership structure is beyond the scope of this book. One can hypothesize that it is linked to the fact that the World Bank and other MDBs were designed to intermediate private sector finance, and therefore require gaining the confidence of private investors, espe-cially bond investors. Using the familiar governance arrangement of a private corporation could help assuage concerns and bolster the appearance of finan-cial rectitude. It also establishes clear lines of financial responsibility and gives shareholders an incentive to protect the value of their shares. It is unlikely to be a coincidence that the only other major international organization formally owned by shareholders—the Bank for International Settlements—also engages regularly in financial markets (Bitterman 1971, 61 and 81).

Who can become MDB shareholders?

Who owns MDBs? The answer in almost all cases is straightforward: sovereign national governments. Of the thirty MDBs examined for this research, only six had any shareholders that were not national governments, and their shareholding stake is invariably quite small. The main exceptions are four African MDBs: West African Development Bank, East African Development Bank, Central African States Development Bank, and Trade and Development Bank. For these MDBs, the reason is financial. Many African nations face serious budget constraints and are unable to provide capital in line with their ambitions for the MDBs. Bringing in non-sovereign shareholders helps increase capital stock and expand operational capacity. Most of these non-sovereign shareholders are official actors, including other MDBs (African Development Bank and European Investment Bank), bilat-eral development agencies like Germany's KfW or Holland's FMO, and (in the West African Development Bank's case) the West African Monetary Union cen-tral bank. The other two MDBs with non-sovereign shareholders are European Bank for Reconstruction and Development, in which the European Union and the European Investment Bank each own 3 percent of shares, and Latin America's CAF with a tiny (0.5 percent) shareholding by a group of commercial banks dating back to its early years.

Trade and Development Bank is the only MDB thus far to take on institu-tional investors as shareholders. About 26 percent of its paid-in capital stock was owned by eighteen institutional investors (mainly regional pension and insurance funds) at end-2020, and Trade and Development Bank pays these shareholders a dividend. Other MDBs have been wary of taking this route to address capital con-straints, due to the need to pay out dividends and more fundamentally because it dilutes their official, public character. The formal government-to-government relationship within MDB governance and between MDBs and borrower countries is critical to the way they operate, and taking on private investors as sharehold-ers muddies that relationship. Bond rating agencies consider MDBs with private shareholders as less creditworthy: "the participation of private shareholders ... may also dilute [an MDB's] public policy role and affect its governance" (Standard and Poor's 2020b, 53).

Allocating shares among members

There is no obvious rule for how an MDB decides the amount of capital shares each member is eligible to purchase. Disagreements about how to allocate shares of MDB capital among member countries began with the early negotiations of the World Bank and have continued unabated ever since. One might intuitively think that the relative size of each member country's economy would be an appropriate metric to allocate shares, but there is no financial or technical reason why this should be the case. If a smaller country wants to contribute more to an MDB's capital compared to a larger one, it would have no impact on how the MDB functions. This contrasts with the IMF, where linking the size of a member's economy to its quota makes technical sense: the amount a country can borrow is linked to its quota, and the amount a country needs to borrow from the IMF in the event of a financial crisis is logically linked to the size of its economy (see IMF 2014).

A member country's economic weight is the sole formal criteria to define shareholding at only one MDB: the Nordic Investment Bank, the statutes of which stipulate that shares are allocated according to gross national income at market prices (NIB 2011, Section 3). Three other MDBs employ GDP by policy (not by statute) as a variable in determining shareholding allocation. European Investment Bank shareholding is determined by the relative size of GDP at the time a country joined (EIB 2015, 5), with an exception capping the shareholding of the three largest members—Germany, France, and Italy—at the same level (18.8 percent, as of 2020). After years of pressure, the World Bank has since 2010 employed a shareholding formula that incorporates GDP as a main variable with 80 percent weighting in the most recent iteration (World Bank 2018b).[4] Asian Infrastructure Investment Bank also has a GDP-based formula for determining shareholding of regional members, but it is only "indicative" for non-regional members.

Beyond these exceptions, share allocation at all other MDBs is a purely political decision. This is perfectly legitimate: when a group of like-minded countries get together to create a cooperative bank for specific purposes, there is no reason why they cannot divide up ownership in any way they wish, and for whatever reasons appropriate to their circumstances. The size of each member's economy is a relevant consideration, if only because wealthier countries are more able to afford the

[4] The other 20 percent relates to contributions to the World Bank's IDA concessional lending window. See Chapter 3 for details.

budgetary outlay required for a larger capital share. But that is only one of several potential considerations.

For the World Bank and the regional MDBs, geopolitical power was a prime consideration in defining the original shareholding. With the exception of the African Development Bank, the creation of these MDBs was dominated by the U.S. and other industrialized countries. The story of the initial shareholding negotiations for the World Bank at Bretton Woods neatly illustrates this dynamic. U.S. negotiator Harry Dexter White drew up a ranking of country shareholders for the World Bank and tasked one of his assistants to reverse-engineer a formula that would result in the desired ranking, simply to give the appearance of technical transparency (Conway 2014, 222–232). As the assistant put it later, "I tried to make the process appear as scientific as possible," he said, "but the delegates were intelligent enough to know that the process was more political than scientific" (ibid., 225).

After considerable haggling at Bretton Woods, the U.S. ended up with 39.5 percent of World Bank shares in 1945, while industrialized countries including the U.S. collectively accounted for 76 percent of shares (World Bank 1946). The U.S. had 43 percent of shares when the Inter-American Development Bank was founded in 1960, three times the amount of any other shareholder (IDB 1960). At the Asian Development Bank, the U.S. split control with its ally Japan, each having 20.6 percent of voting power when the bank was launched in 1966 (ADB 1967). This dominance is a direct expression of the U.S.'s desire to control these organizations, while at the same time offering sufficient shareholding to others to create a degree of legitimacy and buy-in, particularly for U.S. allies. Although the relative size of the U.S. economy as well as U.S. voting shares have declined in the intervening years, it remains the dominant shareholder in all these MDBs.

Powerful member countries also have large or controlling shareholding stakes in several smaller MDBs. Russia is by far the largest shareholder of the International Investment Bank and the Eurasian Development Bank, with 42.9 percent and 66 percent of shares, respectively. Saudi Arabia has the most shares (23.5 percent) in the Islamic Development Bank and Nigeria is the largest shareholder (31.2 percent) in the Ecowas Development Bank. The new Asian Infrastructure Investment Bank has taken a similar approach, using a GDP-based formula that gives China, its founding country, the largest shareholding stake—27.4 percent at end-2020, including Hong Kong's shares (see Lichtenstein 2018).

By contrast, most smaller MDBs founded by borrower countries take a more egalitarian approach. In several—including the ECO Trade and Development Bank, West African Development Bank, and the Central American Bank for Economic Integration—all the founding member countries have exactly the same shareholding stake, whereas newer and non-regional members have a lower share. The New Development Bank founded by the BRICS countries in 2016 also follows this pattern, with each of the five founding countries controlling the same share-holding and new members receiving a smaller share. This egalitarian division of governance power is appealing from a normative point of view, and has practical benefits as well in promoting a cooperative spirit and mutual commitment. The downside is that it reduces an MDB's capital (and hence lending capacity) to the contribution of the most budget-constrained member country. For example, the New Development Bank's capital is capped by the amount that South Africa can afford to pay for its membership stake, whereas China could have easily contributed much more (and reputedly wanted to, as discussed in Chapter 5).

In an effort to address this trade-off, a number of MDBs combine elements of both approaches to allocating shares. Wealthier countries have more capital shares, but are in some cases capped at a certain level such that several countries have the same capital share. This is the case for example at the European Investment Bank, where shareholding is mainly derived from economic size, but the largest member countries of Germany, the U.K., France, and Italy all have the same shareholding. A similar arrangement is used at the Black Sea Trade and Development Bank, FONPLATA, CAF, and the East African Development Bank.

In a few cases, MDBs have created multiple share classes, each with different voting power. This has been used only by borrower-led MDBs and has generally been employed as a means to bring in other shareholders from outside the region to contribute capital, but in a subordinate position so as not to dilute the governance control of the regional borrower members. Examples include Central American Bank for Economic Integration and CAF in Latin America, and Trade and Development Bank, West African Development Bank, and East African Development Bank in Africa.

Fourteen of twenty-five MDBs for which information is available have statutes mandating that the shareholding of certain groups of countries cannot fall below a certain level in any circumstances (Table 2.2). In most cases, this is designed to protect the ownership stake of the regional countries in which the MDB operates, although in one case—the Inter-American Development Bank—the rule is designed to ensure the veto authority of just one country, the U.S. In one other case—Trade and Development Bank—individual country shareholding is capped at 15 percent, to avoid dominance by any single member.

Translation of capital shares into governance control

At almost all MDBs, the level of a member's share capital is directly linked to its voting power in governance. Only three MDBs (Nordic Investment Bank, International Investment Bank, and FONPLATA) base voting power on the one country, one vote principle used in the United Nations, although a number of MDBs employ some variation of one country, one vote on a few key issues like admitting

Table 2.2 Special Shareholding Stipulations at MDBs

Legacy MDBs	**African Development Bank**	Regional members shareholding must result in 60% collective voting power
	Asian Development Bank	Regional members must collectively have at least 60% share capital
	Inter-American Development Bank	Shareholding must result in i) regional members having at least 50.005% collective voting power; ii) the largest member (U.S.) must have at least 30% voting power; iii) Canada must have at least 4% voting power
	European Bank for Reconstruction and Development	EU members plus European Investment Bank must have a majority of share capital
Regional or Subregional MDBs	**Black Sea Trade and Development Bank**	Founding members must collectively have majority of share capital; founding members have right (but not obligation) to equal shareholding
	Caribbean Development Bank	Regional members must collectively have at least 60% share capital
	Central American Bank for Economic Integration	Founding members must collectively have at least 51% of share capital
	East African Development Bank	Regional member states must collectively have at least 51% of share capital
	ECO Trade and Development Bank	Founding members have same shareholding; founding members much collectively have a majority of share capital
	North American Development Bank	Mexico and the U.S. (the only two members) must have exactly equal shareholding
	Trade and Development Bank	No member may have more than 15% of share capital
	West African Development Bank	Only regional members may have "A" shares (which dominate voting rules)
New MDBs	**Asian Infrastructure Investment Bank**	Regional members must collectively have at least 75% share capital
	New Development Bank	Founding members must collectively have at least 55% of share capital; non-borrowing members may not have more than 20% of share capital; no non-founding member may have more than 7% of share capital

Source: MDB founding statutes.

new members or suspending bank operations. Beyond those exceptions, a country's voice in MDB governance is tied to its shareholding—countries with more shares have more voting power, just as in a private corporation.

However, all MDBs also employ one or more mechanisms that dilute the direct link between shareholding and voting power. In some cases these mechanisms weaken the governance power of major shareholders vis-à-vis smaller shareholders, while in other cases they accentuate the power of larger shareholders. Their use is derived, on the one hand, from a desire to give an MDB greater perceived legitimacy to smaller shareholders, and on the other hand, from the desire of a subset of powerful shareholders to entrench their power. The two most common mechanisms—both used by all the largest MDBs—are basic votes and special majorities for certain governance decisions (see the following section for details).

These mechanisms are a tacit recognition that economic and political strength by itself is a unstable foundation on which to build a solid, long-lasting international institution. MDBs are cooperatives, and it is essential in both normative as well as practical terms that countries feel they have a meaningful role in governance, as noted by Woods (1999). Balanced against this is the fact that countries that contribute the most resources feel justified in having governance power commensurate to their contributions, or may simply want to exercise their power to control the MDB for their own purposes. At some MDBs one of these two factors is paramount, depending on the countries involved and the historical circumstances of its creation, while in others both are in play.

Decision-making structures

The decision-making structures of MDBs are remarkably uniform, regardless of the size of the organization or the group of countries involved. Of twenty-six MDBs for which somewhat detailed information is available, twenty-five utilize the same overall set of decision-making bodies.[5]

The highest authority for an MDB is the **board of governors (BoG)**, sometimes called a governing council. "Governors" are high-level representatives from each member country—often ministers of finance or central bank governors—and they meet once a year (BoG meetings can by statute be called more frequently, but almost never are). Formally, governors have the authority to take all decisions about an MDB, including policy as well as individual project approvals, but in practice many operational issues are delegated to the board of directors or management. In almost all MDBs, certain major decisions—such as changes to the capital

---

[5] The exception is the North American Development Bank, which alone among MDBs has only two shareholders—the U.S. and Mexico. This unusual ownership allows for a more streamlined governance structure with only a board of directors and management, and no board of governors.

structure, admitting or suspending members, or allocating net income from the previous year—must by statute be taken by governors and cannot be delegated.

Most routine operational decisions such as approving individual projects, budgeting matters, and many operational policies are delegated by governors to a **board of directors (BoD)**. The composition and meeting schedule of directors varies substantially among MDBs. At the World Bank and major regional MDBs, directors are designated by member governments but are formally employees of the MDB and sit in permanent session at the MDB's headquarters. At other MDBs, directors meet several times per year and are higher-level officials from member governments such as ministers or deputy ministers. At MDBs with many members, groups of countries are represented by a single director whose voting power is the sum of the voting power of all countries in their group.

Actual presence at the BoD is a contentious issue at several of the larger MDBs, because i) the constituencies have often been organized in a way that one or two countries monopolize the directorship and ii) some MDB voting rules stipulate that the director's vote cannot be split, even if the countries that the director represents have divergent views. This can in effect mean that the voice and vote of some countries are never represented at the BoD (see Strand 1999, 2001, and 2003). Currently, BoD chair votes cannot be split at World Bank, Inter-American Development Bank, African Development Bank, Caribbean Development Bank, and West African Development Bank. For all other MDBs that group directors into constituencies, a director can split the vote to allow dissenting views within individual constituencies to be accounted for at the BoD.

To give an extreme example of what the constituency arrangements at a BoD can mean in practice, consider the ED07 constituency at the World Bank's BoD. ED07 consists of fourteen countries, including Canada, Ireland, and twelve developing countries from the Caribbean region. In 2020, ED07 had a total voting power of 3.87 percent. Of that, Canada alone had 2.82 percent, while Ireland accounted for 0.35 percent and the other countries had tiny voting shares of between 0.04 percent and 0.16 percent. That means that Canada always wins the executive directorship and Canada's representative sits at the BoD, exercising the full 3.87 percent voting power of the entire constituency. Canada could ensure that the voices and opinions of the other thirteen countries in ED07 are never represented at the BoD. Being a consensus-oriented country, Canada generally consults other members to arrive at agreements on major votes with the other members of the constituency, but it is under no obligation to do so. As the World Bank's website states, "In the case of a constituency of countries, their constituency arrangements, including which country will nominate for the position of Executive Director, are regulated by internal constituency agreements. The Bank has no role in negotiating or administering these constituency agreements—they are matters for government shareholders within the constituency" (World Bank 2020a).

MDB administration and operations are overseen by **management**, led by an executive officer (almost always a president) appointed by the BoG or sometimes the BoD. In only one case—the New Development Bank—does an individual country have the right to nominate the president (on a rotating basis among the five founding member countries of the bank), while the Asian Infrastructure Investment Bank and Central American Bank for Economic Integration both specify that the president must be a citizen of a regional member country. Nonetheless, it is common practice that MDBs have unwritten agreements among members about nominating the president. The presidents of the World Bank and Asian Development Bank, for example, are invariably chosen by the U.S. and Japanese governments, respectively. The Inter-American Development Bank's president has traditionally come from Latin America with the tacit approval of the U.S. (although the 2020 nomination of U.S. national Mauricio Claver-Carone by the Trump administration violated that agreement), while the African Development Bank presidency tends to rotate between different regions within Africa. The executive is generally responsible for all staffing decisions, although most statutes mandate that the BoD approves the appointment of senior management such as vice presidents.

Basic votes

From the very beginning at Bretton Woods, negotiators were aware that a voting system based on capital shares went against the historical tradition in international relations of equality among sovereign nations (Gianaris 1990), as exemplified by the one nation, one vote approach of the United Nations. To address this issue, negotiators came up with the idea of giving each World Bank member country a certain number of "basic votes" regardless of their shareholding. Basic votes have the effect of diluting the voting power of the largest shareholders in favor of smaller shareholders. As noted by one analysis of voting at the World Bank and IMF, "The basic votes were included because of the concern that some of the less developed members with very small quotas would otherwise have no sense of participation in the organizations' functions" (ibid., 921).

Following the World Bank's lead, basic votes were included at the African, Asian, and Inter-American Development Banks (although not the European Bank for Reconstruction and Development) and is also utilized by the Islamic Development Bank. The reason why these MDBs use basic votes, while MDBs created mainly by developing nations do not, is the nature of the countries involved. These MDBs all have member countries with vastly different economic power. It makes sense that wealthier countries should provide large amounts of capital to the MDB, thus endowing it with a greater operational capacity, while smaller countries contribute what they can. But translating that shareholding directly into governance power would undermine the cooperative by effectively shutting some countries out of any meaningful voice in decision-making. Basic votes can help alleviate that problem, at least symbolically. This tension is much less problematic at smaller, borrower-led institutions where the economic difference between members is less stark.

The practical relevance of basic votes to governance has always been limited, and it has declined precipitously over time. The total amount of basic votes allocated ranged from a low of 3.2 percent of total votes (at Inter-American Development Bank) to a high of 20 percent (at Asian Development Bank) in earlier decades, but successive capital increases as well as the addition of new shareholders has diluted their weight. Only Asian Development Bank has maintained the 20 percent share of basic votes throughout its history, with basic votes account for a high of 0.3 percent of votes per member currently and between 0.001 percent and 0.05 percent at the other major MDBs.

Despite the limited practical significance of basic votes, they continue to be employed at the major MDBs as a relatively small concession of governance control from more to less powerful members to enhance the institution's legitimacy. For example, Asian Infrastructure Investment Bank opted to include basic votes as part of its voting rules when it launched operations in 2016 (Lichtenstein 2018), and an increase in basic votes remains an important part of the World Bank governance reform discussions (World Bank 2017a).

Special majorities

A second mechanism that complicates the direct translation of shareholding into governance power is the requirement of special majorities for major decisions at MDBs, rather than a simple majority vote. Special majorities are mainly reserved for votes on fundamental issues such as changing an MDB's capital structure, admitting new members, or modifying the statutes, whereas normal policy decisions and project approvals usually require regular majority voting. Most special majority voting occurs at the BoG rather than the BoD. While basic votes always help increase the voting power of smaller shareholders, special majorities can work to either accentuate or dilute the strength of powerful shareholders, depending on the shareholding composition of each MDB.

As with basic votes, special majorities were first created at Bretton Woods and have been since copied in various forms at every one of the other existing MDBs for which voting rules are publicly available. The historical record makes it clear that their original reason was to preserve the U.S.'s ability to veto decisions that it opposed at the World Bank and IMF, over the objections of the U.K.'s lead negotiator (Gianaris 1990, 920). The U.S. still retains *de jure* veto power over key votes at the World Bank and Inter-American Development Bank, and jointly with Japan at the Asian Development Bank (as discussed in Chapter 3). It has no *de jure* veto authority at European Bank for Reconstruction and Development or African Development Bank. Even in cases where the U.S. falls short of the *de jure* votes needed to exercise a veto, it has historically been relatively easy for the U.S. to bring along one or more other shareholders to control major decisions, as detailed by Babb (2009) among others.

The U.S. and other wealthy non-borrower shareholders have additional de facto voting power at the World Bank and African Development Bank because of their importance in donating to the "concessional" lending windows of both institutions—the International Development Association and African Development Fund, respectively. Because of the generous financial terms offered to borrowers, these concessional windows must be periodically replenished with donor contributions, unlike the core MDBs to which they are linked. The concessional funds are still critical to many low-income countries: seventy-four countries were eligible for World Bank concessional resources in 2020, and thirty-eight countries for African Development Bank concessional resources. These funds come for most part [6] from the budgets of donor countries, and donors have not been shy in using replenishment rounds to demand reforms at the non-concessional MDBs—despite the fact that they are actually separate treaty organizations.

Thus, the concessional windows have become "the tail that wags the dog" in the words of Kapur (2002, 62), giving greater control to non-borrowers over MDB policy. This helps explains why non-borrowers are so influential at African Development Bank, even though they collectively had only about 45 percent of its voting shares in 2020. As Woods (2003) recounts, the U.S. has repeatedly leveraged its contributions to the International Development Association as a means of imposing its policy priorities, for example by forcing the World Bank to cut Vietnam off from lending in the 1970s and creating the Inspection Panel in 1993. This helps explains why the three-yearly replenishment rounds for the concessional windows are so time consuming and contentious: the negotiations invariably involve policy issues at the main MDBs, not just the concessional windows themselves. The concessional windows at World Bank and African Development Bank act as a de facto special majority accentuating the governance power of non-borrowers. In past years, the concessional windows of the Inter-American and Asian Development Banks also provided additional governance leverage to non-borrower shareholders, although this has been much reduced since recent reforms discussed in Chapter 3.

China has followed the model of the legacy MDBs in allotting itself similar veto power on special majority votes at Asian Infrastructure Investment Bank. At end-2020 China had 27.4 percent of voting power (including the votes of Hong Kong), while special majorities of 75 percent voting are required to appoint the president, modify the BoD, change the capital structure, allocate net income, admit

[6] Concessional windows are also partly funded by allocating net income from the regular MDB lending windows, and as of 2016 the International Development Association has raised some resources from bond issues (see Chapter 3 for details).

or suspend members, and suspend operations. President Jin Liqun said in a public event (at Boston University on October 18, 2019) that China was willing to lower its shareholding under the 25 percent threshold in the near future, although in light of China's influence over numerous Asian members this is unlikely to threaten its de facto veto power.

While special majorities at the legacy MDBs and Asian Infrastructure Investment Bank give veto authority to the most powerful shareholder, at other MDBs it can improve equity in voting power. For example, Russia is by far the largest shareholder at the Eurasian Development Bank, with 66 percent of capital and voting. However, voting rules stipulate a three-quarters majority of voting power to change the capital structure, amend the articles of agreement, or suspend operations. This gives the only other significant shareholder—Kazakhstan—formal veto power over major decisions, even though it has much less voting power than Russia. Similarly, voting rules at the ECO Trade and Development Bank ensure that the three major shareholders (Iran, Turkey, and Pakistan) each can block major changes in capital structure or membership.

Several other MDBs without any single dominant shareholder also use special majority mechanisms. One example is the use of double majorities—a majority of voting power as well as a majority of member states. In seven MDBs (African Development Bank, CAF, Council of Europe Development Bank, European Investment Bank, FONPLATA, International Investment Bank, and Nordic Investment Bank), special majorities of some type are required for all decisions taken by the BoG (and in four MDBs by the BoD). In one case (Nordic Investment Bank) all decisions must be taken by a unanimous vote. In several of these MDBs, special majorities accentuate the vote of regional borrower members over shareholders from outside the region, while others enhance the voting power of smaller shareholders. But in all cases these rules dilute the power of larger members, as no single country has even close to sufficient votes to wield effective veto power.

The upshot is that special majorities can cut both ways. At the World Bank, Inter-American Development Bank, and Asian Development Bank, they have helped ensure that the U.S. retains certain veto authority. As numerous studies have shown,[7] the U.S. has not been shy to make use of that—in particular, holding hostage any increase to an MDB's capital—as a means of ensuring its policy priorities are upheld. China's voting power at Asian Infrastructure Investment Bank looks to follow a similar pattern, although time will tell if China makes use of this in a similar manner to the U.S. At many other MDBs, on the other hand, special

---

[7] See, for example, Babb 2009 on how the Reagan administration halted capital increase at the IDB in the 1980s until it forced through major policy changes to "tame" the IDB and Kapur et al. 1997 on several instances of U.S. pressure on the World Bank during capital increase discussions.

majorities combined with a relatively equitable voting power distribution promote more consensus-oriented decision-making on major issues and ensure that no single country or minority of countries dominate.

Conclusion

As organizations created and owned by governments and designed to implement public policy goals, MDBs are inherently political organizations. That is not a criticism, but a statement of fact. A thorough analysis of the way MDBs take decisions via their governance arrangements is a fundamental building block to understanding their behavior. The chapter has proposed a new framework for evaluating governance arrangements based on the balance of power between borrower and non-borrower shareholders, which helps explain differences in many MDB operational characteristics and actions. This framework has the advantage of moving beyond the prevailing focus in the literature on the role of a few powerful shareholders at the World Bank and four major regional MDBs to encompass the variety of membership compositions across the range of MDBs operating today.

All MDBs build from a remarkably uniform set of governance rules embedded in their founding statutes—shareholding allocation, boards of governors and directors, and voting rules for specific decisions—but assemble these parts in different ways according to the unique constellation of member countries and their goals. And individual governments have idiosyncratic interests and approaches at the MDBs to which they belong. As such, the borrower vs. non-borrower framework proposed here cannot be applied in a simplistic, cut-and-paste fashion. Rather, the framework is intended to serve as a lens that helps frame the way governance is analyzed, a conceptual point of departure that is applicable to all MDBs, and encourages consideration of the interests of all shareholders rather than just a small subset. This book argues that such a governance framework—combined with a deeper understanding of the financial imperatives of the MDB model discussed in the previous chapter—goes a long way to explaining the behaviors and policies of different MDBs.

3

The Legacy MDBs

World Bank and Major Regionals

When most people think "multilateral development bank," the World Bank is the first to come to mind, closely followed by the four major regional MDBs: the African, Asian, and Inter-American Development Banks, and the European Bank for Reconstruction and Development (AfDB, ADB, IDB, and EBRD). For decades, these five MDBs have dominated international development cooperation (Table 3.1). They have set the global development agenda, channeled hundreds of billions of financing for development projects, and helped coordinate the activities of the major bilateral donors. With thousands of staff spread across almost every developing country on the planet, these MDBs have amassed a tremendous body of experience and knowledge on just about all facets of development.

Collectively, the five MDBs are an unparalleled asset in the world's efforts to improve the living conditions and economic prospects of our population. The practical expertise of their staff and relationships built up over decades with developing country governments make them essential tools to face ongoing and future global development challenges. These traits are combined with impressive financial firepower, built on their AAA bond rating and superlative access to international capital markets. In an era of fragmented international leadership and with a growing awareness that the markets themselves cannot solve many social problems, the legacy MDBs represent one of the best sets of tools to help move the planet to a more economically, socially, and environmentally sustainable growth path.

The world has changed dramatically in the decades since these five MDBs were created. Despite their many strengths, they have struggled to keep up, and this has limited their operational effectiveness and international legitimacy. A few of the main reasons behind this are:

- Many developing countries are more self-confident, with capable government officials and a clear view of their own development path. The heavy-handed, top-down style associated with the legacy MDBs no longer fits this reality (Greenhill et al. 2013, Prizzon et al. 2016, Humphrey and Michaelowa 2019).
- Options for external finance available to borrower countries have proliferated, from new official sources like China and India to philanthropic

Financing the Future. Chris Humphrey, Oxford University Press. © Christopher Humphrey (2022).
DOI: 10.1093/oso/9780192871503.003.0004

Table 3.1 Overview Legacy MDBs (2020)

	Launch Year	Sovereign Members	Borrower Voting Power	Disbursed Portfolio (US$ million)	2020 Approvals (US$ million)	Borrowers
African Development Bank (AfDB)	1964	81	55.3%	32,004	5,314	17 middle-income African country governments (80%) and private sector borrowers (20%)
African Development Fund (ADF)	1974	31	0*	19,549	1,352	37 low-income African governments (zero interest loans and grants)
Asian Development Bank (ADB)	1966	68	39.3%	132,054	28,232	47 developing member country governments in Asia (95%) and private sector borrowers (5%). 14 low-income country governments eligible for zero interest loans or grants
Inter-American Development Bank (IDB)	1959	48	50.02%	104.8	13,948	26 country governments in Latin America and the Caribbean. 3 governments eligible for concessional lending
IDB Invest	1985	47	52.3%	4,177	6,782	Private sector borrowers in Latin America and the Caribbean
European Bank for Reconstruction and Development (EBRD)	1991	69	13.8%	40,519	13,304	38 country governments in Eastern Europe, Central Asia, and North Africa (18%) and private sector borrowers (82%)

Table 3.1 *Continued*

	Launch Year	Sovereign Members	Borrower Voting Power	Disbursed Portfolio (US$ million)	2020 Approvals (US$ million)	Borrowers
World Bank Group						
International Bank for Reconstruction and Development (IBRD)	1944	189	40.0%	204,231	27,976	70 middle-income country governments
International Development Association (IDA)	1960	174	45.02%	160,961	30,365	74 low-income country governments eligible for zero interest loans or grants
International Finance Corporation (IFC)	1956	184	35.1%	44,309	11,135	Private sector borrowers in developing countries
Multilateral Investment Guarantee Agency (MIGA)	1988	181	48.8%	22,600	3,961	Financial guarantees for investments made in developing countries

Source: Annual reports and financial statements.
Notes: World Bank Group data is for Fiscal Year 2020 (July 2019–June 2020); all others are for calendar 2020. Disbursed portfolio and annual approvals include project loans, trade financing, guarantees and equity investments. * AfDB as an institutional shareholder has 50% of ADF voting power.

organizations to international and even domestic capital markets (World Bank 2021b, UN 2021). The legacy MDBs find themselves in a competitive dynamic to which they are unaccustomed.

- Development finance has become increasingly sophisticated and often works in partnership with private sector actors (McHugh 2021, Hussain et al. 2019, Humphrey 2018b). MDB staff, management, and administrative systems designed for traditional public sector loans are finding it difficult to adapt.
- The five MDBs have built up multiple layers of bureaucratic practices, administrative systems, and staff cultures that are inefficient and resistant to change (Birdsall and Morris 2016, Humphrey 2016b).

Underneath it all, the foundational problem faced by all five of the legacy MDBs is governance. These MDBs were built around a set of geopolitical and economic power arrangements and relationships that are coming apart before our eyes. The authors of a major report on the World Bank and regional MDBs termed them the "legacy" MDBs (Birdsall and Morris 2016), and indeed they are—the legacy of a global order that is fast disappearing. The governance arrangements, decision-making processes, and approach to development operations of the legacy MDBs have not yet fundamentally changed in response to this shifting context. This has hampered their ability to face the challenges posed by the emerging global order of the twenty-first century. Instead, they are saddled with unclear or even contradictory mandates, insufficient resources, and all manner of unrealistic proposals for how they should reform.

This chapter is not a general overview of the legacy MDBs, which can be found in the existing academic and policy literature as well as strategic documents from the MDBs themselves. Rather, it outlines how these MDBs are reacting to the evolving global context in which they find themselves. The chapter focuses on i) the politics surrounding MDB capitalization and financial capacity and ii) business practices that impact the relevance of the major MDBs to borrower countries. In each of these two areas, the chapter draws a causal link to governance tensions and the pressures resulting from the imperatives of their financial model. The aim is to better understand how governance and financial factors have led them to the position they are in, as a first step toward considering realistic ways that they can be reformed.

What Are the "Legacy" MDBs?

Can the five legacy MDBs be meaningfully analyzed as a single group? They are, after all, legally separate institutions, each created by an international treaty negotiated with a distinct group of member countries and with their own historical trajectory. The World Bank was created in 1944 while World War II still raged, the AfDB was founded by proudly independent African nations in the wake of decolonization in the early 1960s, and the EBRD was established in 1991 in the wake of the collapse of the socialist economies of eastern and central Europe. They all have different organizational cultures, operational procedures, and staff backgrounds, as amply illustrated by numerous studies.[1] IDB and the World Bank's International Bank for Reconstruction and Development (IBRD) lend entirely to public sector borrowers, AfDB and ADB have lent about 20 percent and 5 percent respectively of their current loan portfolio to private sector borrowers, whereas about 80 percent of EBRD's loans are to private sector borrowers (see Box 3.1). Certainly, the MDBs themselves resist being lumped together as a single MDB "system," as evidenced by the repeated failure of efforts by external policymakers to establish some kind of division of labor and formal coordination among them.

Box 3.1: MDB Lending to the Private Sector

This chapter includes EBRD with the other legacy MDBs, although it is in many ways substantially different. It was created much later than the others (1991) and was designed to address a specific goal: facilitate the transition of formerly socialist countries to market democracies. It is mainly focused on private sector financing, which accounts for about 80 percent of its portfolio, in line with the market-focused ethos embedded in its statutes. The transition EBRD was created to support is largely completed—or at least as completed as it is likely to be—and EBRD now finds itself in the curious position of a financially strong MDB looking for a purpose. This helps explain EBRD's move into North Africa in the wake of the Arab Spring, and proposals to partner with AfDB in sub-Saharan Africa or possibly join forces with European Investment Bank (Comte and Hay 2021). It also explains why EBRD has not received fresh paid-in capital since 1996—shareholders do not appear entirely sure about its current mission. One possibility that shareholders do not seem to be contemplating is shifting EBRD to provide more public sector financing in its core European and Central Asian countries, although the Ukraine crisis and eventual reconstruction needs could prompt consideration of that (Humphrey 2022).

The International Finance Corporation (IFC) and IDB Invest, the dedicated private sector lending windows of the World Bank and IDB respectively, are not included in this chapter. They, as well as bilateral development finance

---

[1] Among others, World Bank: Kapur et al. (1997); Mason and Asher (1973), Mosley et al. (1995), Stiglitz (2002), Mallaby (2004), Woods (2006); IDB: Tussie (1995); AfDB: Mingst (1990), English and Mule (1996); ADB: Kappagoda (1995); regional MDBs: Culpeper (1997), Gutner (2002), Griffith-Jones et al. (2008), Babb (2009), and Park and Strand (2016).

institutions like Germany's KfW, Agence Francaise de Developpement, or the Entrepreneurial Development Bank of the Netherlands, merit a separate study of their own due to their growing role in development finance and sophistication of their operations (see Attridge and Gouett 2021 for a recent study on the topic). IFC has become increasingly important as a shaper of development agenda, with new ways to engage the private sector with both individual projects as well as platforms to channel resources by major institutional investors. While these activities hold out potential for bringing in substantial resources, they also raise questions about development additionality, competition with the rising class of commercial impact investors, and the incentives these MDBs face to "make deals" and operate at scale (see for example Dreher et al. 2019).

The key characteristic that unifies the legacy MDBs and differentiates them the other MDBs is governance. All five are effectively controlled by the G7 nations, and in particular the U.S. This governance control is a "legacy" of postwar power relations that are fast receding from view but remains in place because of entrenched voting power. This is not to say that the legacy MDBs are simple pawns for the U.S. and G7 to manipulate as they wish. But when key interests are at stake, the major non-borrower nations can enforce their will at the legacy MDBs.

Looking at the breakdown of voting power among member countries, the dominance of non-borrower shareholders stands out (Figure 3.1). This dominance has held steady over recent decades, with only small changes, despite massive shifts in the global economy during that time. The share of the global economy accounted for by wealthy western nations has declined steadily since the 1990s and the proportion by emerging and developing countries (EMDCs)—most notably China—has risen sharply. Yet, this has not been reflected in the relative shareholding and voting power of legacy MDB shareholders. The continued dominance of G7 and European nations in legacy MDB governance in the face of this shifting global economic panorama calls into question their representative legitimacy.

The World Bank's IBRD highlights these inequities. India's economy in 2020 in purchasing power parity (PPP) terms was three times the size of its former colonial master the U.K. as a share of the global economy (7% compared to 2.4%), but it had only 3% voting power at the IBRD compared to 3.9% for the U.K. Even more galling is the case of China, which accounted for 17% of global economic output but had only 4.7% of IBRD votes in 2020 (due to rise to 6% in coming years). To give a sense of perspective, China's economy in 2020 was larger than all six G7 countries apart from the U.S. combined, yet those six G7 countries controlled a total of 25% of IBRD voting power—five times that of China. Collectively, the twenty largest non-borrower shareholders of controlled over 56% of IBRD

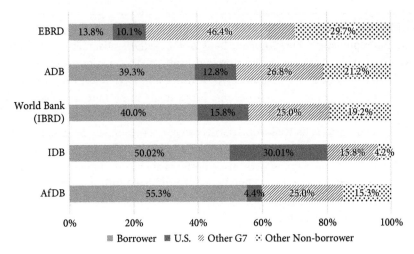

Figure 3.1 Share of Voting Power Controlled by Country Groupings (2020).
Source: 2020 MDB financial statements.

votes in 2020, despite accounting for only 40% of global GDP. By contrast, the twenty largest borrower shareholders controlled only 25% of IBRD votes even though they represent 46% of global GDP and a substantial majority of the global population.

Some efforts have been made to rectify these voting imbalances, but progress has been minimal due to the simple fact that non-borrowers have been unwilling to relinquish their power. An EBRD management official described efforts in 2014 and 2015 to rebalance shareholding to give borrowers more voting power: "There was blood on the walls. The process took two years and was incredibly divisive. And in the end it amounted to nothing," with shareholding remaining essentially unchanged (interview, January 18, 2021). The "voice and voting" reform at the World Bank's IBRD has made more progress, but not by much (World Bank 2020b). Former World Bank and IDB vice president Otaviano Canuto noted that efforts to increase the voting power of the BRICS countries increased after the 2008 global financial crisis, "but there was a limit. Because this could only happen if there was a reshuffle of the capital of these institutions, that started to create a resistance from the major shareholders" (Canuto 2020).

The worst offenders in terms of overrepresentation at IBRD are European nations like Belgium, Denmark, Finland, France, Switzerland, and the U.K. These countries have held onto their voting power by arguing for a shareholding formula that benefits them. They have opposed using purchasing power parity (PPP) to calculate economic size, despite being more commonly used by economists, as this would disproportionately benefit borrower countries (Vestergaard undated, 23). The most recent formula uses PPP GDP for 40 percent of the calculation and

GDP at market prices for 60 percent (World Bank 2020b, 2)—a rearguard action to prolong the entrenched power of non-borrowers that will almost certainly be chipped away in future IBRD shareholding reviews.

Non-borrowers have also argued that 20 percent of the shareholding formula should be based on contributions to the World Bank's concessional lending window for the poorest countries, the International Development Association (IDA). While this might seem to make emotional sense to non-borrowers—giving them credit for their contributions to poor countries—in fact it has little justification. IDA is a legally separate organization from IBRD, created with a separate international treaty and with its own balance sheet.[2] Contributions to IDA should and do result in a higher voting power at IDA, but there's no reason why these contributions should impact the shareholding of IBRD, which is a separate treaty organization. Non-borrowers have nonetheless employed this argument to entrench their voting power, and since they currently have enough power to decide the rules themselves, there is little that borrowers can do about it. Some countries are still underrepresented even with the current flawed IBRD shareholding formula, most notably China, as the World Bank's own analysis shows (World Bank 2020b, 4).

Despite the dominant position of non-borrower shareholders, the situation varies substantially among the legacy MDBs. The governance of the World Bank's IBRD and IFC, ADB, and especially EBRD are thoroughly dominated by non-borrowers. On the other hand, borrowing country members have a slim majority of voting power at IDB, and at AfDB borrowers have by statute a guaranteed 60 percent of shares (although only 55 percent of subscribed shares at end-2020) compared to 28 percent for the G7. How can one argue that IDB and AfDB are controlled by non-borrowers when they don't command a majority of voting power? As well, while the U.S. is the largest single shareholder at all the major MDBs, its share ranges from a high at 30 percent at the IDB to only 4.4 percent at AfDB. How can the U.S. by itself have such influence over all the MDBs?

The first mechanism is special majority voting rules. For a few key decisions, notably increases in an MDB's capital stock, changes to the statutes, or admitting new members, a higher voting threshold beyond a simple majority is required. These rules give formal veto power to the U.S. by itself over changes to the capital structure at the World Bank's IFC and IDB, and in conjunction with its close ally Japan at ADB (Table 3.2). Hence, whenever one of these MDBs needs more capital from shareholders, the U.S. can effectively hold the MDB hostage until it receives whatever policy changes it desires—a power it has not been shy to use, as Babb (2009) and Woods (2003) illustrate in detail.

---

[2] When IDA was first created, IBRD management insisted on a strict legal separation between the two, for fear that IBRD's strong financial standing would be "contaminated" by the concessional IDA (World Bank 1961).

Table 3.2 U.S. *De Jure* Veto Power at Legacy MDBs

	Change Capital Structure	Amend Articles of Agreement	Admit New Members	Suspend Operations	Modify Board of Directors
IBRD	No	Yes	No	No	No
IFC	Yes	Yes	No	No	No
IDB	Yes	Yes	Yes	Yes	Yes
ADB*	Yes	Yes	Yes	Yes	Yes

Source: MDB articles of agreement and (from financial statements) 2020 voting power.
Notes: *Jointly with Japan.

Examples abound, from the Reagan administration forcing out IDB's president and enacting a series of internal reforms in the 1980s to the Trump administration pushing the World Bank to wind down lending to China as part of the 2018 capital increase. As a U.S. Treasury report to Congress states, "As part of the [2018] capital increase, shareholders, with leadership from the United States ... negotiated a set of transformational reforms that closely align with U.S. national security, foreign policy, and economic priorities" (U.S. Treasury 2019, 9). In situations where the U.S. does not by itself have veto power, it has historically been able to assemble a blocking coalition of allies to enforce its policy priorities with relative ease. Even at AfDB, where borrower nations have a clear majority of votes, non-borrower shareholders are critical to maintaining the bank's strong access to capital markets, giving them important leverage. Non-borrower concerns about AfDB's leadership and strategic direction put a hold on a new capital increase for several years until it was finally agreed in 2019. "We need their [non-borrower] support, there's no way to move ahead with a capital increase without them," said a senior AfDB official in 2017, at the height of the impasse (interview, December 6, 2017).

The second mechanism is the role of wealthy countries in contributing to the concessional lending windows for the poorest countries at AfDB and the World Bank. Because the concessional windows offer zero interest loans or grants, they must be replenished regularly with donations from wealthy countries. These replenishment rounds have become key pressure points for non-borrower nations to push internal reforms at the regular lending windows of the MDBs, as Babb (2009), Kapur (2002), and others have described. Concessional windows remain major parts of the World Bank and AfDB, financing projects in seventy-four and thirty-seven borrower countries respectively in 2020. IDB and ADB each had concessional windows that also provided leverage to non-borrowers historically, but these were shut down in 2016 (IDB) or merged into the regular balance sheet (ADB), as discussed later in this chapter.

The dominance of the legacy MDBs by non-borrower shareholder nations is not to suggest that the differences in voting power among the legacy MDBs are irrelevant. There is no question that the greater governance power of borrower country shareholders translates into a different set of policies, procedures, and operational style more amenable to borrower countries, as illustrated by Humphrey (2014 and 2016b) and Humphrey and Michaelowa (2019) in the cases of the IDB and AfDB, respectively. This comes about not just through greater voting power of borrower shareholders, but also from the preponderance of MDB staff from regional borrower countries (often ex-government officials) as well as a more nuanced and sympathetic understanding of borrower country culture and political contexts.

Nor do the legacy MDBs do everything that major non-borrower countries wish. In the multilateral forum of MDB decision-making, the U.S. and other G7 members pick their battles. If the U.S. put its foot down on every policy discussion and directed all loans purely in line with its own interests, the legacy MDBs would quickly lose all international legitimacy. It is impossible to micro-manage the MDBs, as they execute hundreds of projects and their staff take thousands of operational decisions each year across the globe. Major shareholders use their voting power and leverage mainly on key issues of MDB policy that are relevant to their national interests, while also pushing loans to specific allied countries on occasion, as several researchers have shown (among others Vreeland and Dreher 2014 and Kilby 2006 and 2011).

Sometimes it's less about specific policies or projects, and more the symbolism of G7 dominance that grates on borrower member countries. The Ukraine conflict led the World Bank and EBRD to shut down all operations in Russia, a move supported by many shareholders appalled by Russia's actions. But borrowers remember in 2005 when the U.S. appointed Paul Wolfowitz as World Bank president. Wolfowitz was widely reviled in the development community not only for his leading role in orchestrating the Iraq invasion and subsequent years of violence in the region, but also because his appointment nakedly revealed both U.S. attitudes about the bank and its decision-making power. Even World Bank staff—normally accustomed to accommodating the realities of power—protested his appointment and helped ensure his early resignation. As one World Bank staffer put it at the time, "We all know that the U.S. has a lot of influence here. But this makes us look like puppets."

The Quest for Capital

One of the most fundamental policy issues facing the legacy MDBs—but also one of the most conflictive and least understood—is their capital. Shareholder countries are happy to saddle the legacy MDBs with all sorts of mandates to achieve global development goals, but they are much less enthusiastic about contributing sufficient capital to turn those mandates into reality. The seemingly technical topic of capital is in fact deeply political, and the tensions over it are having spin-off effects on the ability of the legacy MDBs to pursue international development goals. This section considers four aspects of shareholder capital at the legacy MDBs:

- Capital increases from shareholders
- Net income policies
- Capital adequacy and lending capacity
- Efforts to overcome insufficient capital

Increasing MDB capital: Mexican soap opera

Convincing non-borrowing shareholders to increase the capital of the legacy MDBs has never been an easy task, despite the relatively small amounts of money involved. The U.S. in particular has since the 1980s resisted increasing the capital of MDBs, due to a generalized suspicion of multilateral institutions, opposition to foreign aid in the U.S. Congress, and a belief that MDBs are wasteful, inefficient, and market-distorting. Even under the relatively "internationalist" Clinton and Obama administrations, Congressional opposition to MDBs made approving new capital a difficult proposition.

In testimony to the U.S. Congress in late 2018, U.S. Treasury official David Malpass (subsequently World Bank president) listed eleven policy priorities for the U.S. at the MDBs, and the first one is to "Create lending limits that will end the cycle of capital increases" (U.S. House of Representatives 2018). Malpass went on to discuss how the 2018 capital increase for the World Bank's IBRD was only done on condition that it implement mechanisms to ensure future operations "without the World Bank having to approach the United States and other shareholders for a capital increase," and he further noted U.S. opposition to capital increases at the other legacy MDBs (ibid.).

Other major non-borrower shareholders have been less dogmatically opposed to MDB capital increases, but are generally not willing to pick a fight with the U.S. on the issue, and some may be relieved to avoid politically difficult requests for funding from their own legislatures. One G7 official said in a 2017 interview, referring to the World Bank capital increase debates then underway, "If it's clear that there's no appetite from the largest shareholder [the U.S.], there's enough other shareholders who are not convinced enough to make this go forward. It won't be forced through" (interview, March 20, 2017). A top legacy MDB finance official concurred, saying "I've been here twenty years, and generally where the U.S. goes, the other industrialized countries will follow. The U.S. can block it [a capital increase] if it wants" (interview, March 10, 2017).

It is possible to selectively increase MDB capital, whereby some shareholders contribute while others do not. China, for example, has repeatedly expressed a willingness to contribute more capital to the legacy MDBs. But if China contributes at a level sufficient to address capital constraints while the U.S. and other large shareholders do not, it would change relative voting power in MDB governance. One legacy MDB treasury official commented, "For this to happen, the U.S. and other major shareholders would have to agree to dilute their shares. And up to now, they have not been willing to do so" (interview, March 15, 2017). This is extremely frustrating for other shareholders, including some non-borrowers who might be open to a capital increase: "The U.S. stance on additional capital for the core MDBs has been particularly vexing for other countries, because the United States has been willing neither to contribute more MDB capital nor to allow other countries to contribute" (Morris 2016, 14).

A related obstacle to increasing legacy MDB capital has been the long-standing practice of the U.S. and to a lesser extent other G7 governments to use capital increase negotiations as a lever to force through reforms to MDB policies and procedures that suit their interests. Capital increase requests are a key opportunity for the U.S. and G7 powers to shape MDB policies to their liking. This has involved everything from environmental and social safeguards, procurement rules, administrative budgets, financial policies, reporting requirements, external audits, policy conditionality, sectoral and geographic focus, and development priorities. As a result, capital increase negotiations are, as one World Bank treasury official put it, "like a Mexican soap opera" (interview, September 15, 2010)—complex and time-consuming affairs that invariably end up imposing new policies on the MDBs.

Not only are capital increase negotiations conflictive and interminably long, but the result is minimal actual paid-in capital. The round of capital increases in 2010 in the wake of the global financial crisis ranged between 0 and 6 percent paid-in capital, with the remainder on call (Table 3.3). The pattern continued in the 2019 capital increase for AfDB, finally approved after three years of hard lobbying. While the headline number of US$115 billion sounded impressive, only US$7 billion (6 percent) is actually in cash (paid in over 10 years, no less), while the remainder is callable capital.

Table 3.3 2010 Capital Increases at Legacy MDBs

	IBRD	IADB	AsDB	AfDB	EBRD
Date agreed	April 25, 2010	March 23, 2010	April 29, 2009	April 23, 2010	May 14, 2010
Total capital increase	US$86 billion	US$70 billion	US$110 billion	US$66.5 billion	US$15 billion
Paid-in portion	US$5.1 billion	US$1.7 billion	US$4.4 billion	US$3.8 billion	0
% Paid-in	5.9%	2.4%	4%	5.7%	0

The reason why MDBs have so much callable capital is easy enough to understand: it has no cost to shareholders, since it has never been called and very likely never will be. Callable capital is essentially a guarantee of financial support should an MDB face an emergency and be unable to repay its bondholders. But MDB borrowers have an excellent track record of repaying their loans, meaning none of the legacy MDBs have ever even come close to needing to make a capital call, even in the worst global and regional crises of past decades. Governments are as a result much more inclined to offer callable capital rather than paid-in cash capital that must come out of their annual budgets. Callable capital does help support MDB bond ratings, and it also ensures headroom under the statutory lending limits written into their articles of agreement. But the main limitation on MDB lending is their capital adequacy limits, and for that callable capital might as well not even exist—only paid-in capital counts in how MDBs calculate their capital adequacy (explained in more detail below).[3]

As a result, the recent MDB capital increases are much less operationally useful than one might imagine with the eye-popping headline numbers. When the Covid-19 crisis hit, for example, AfDB was so starved of capital despite its recent capital increase that it actually had to reduce lending in 2020, while capital limitations meant that IBRD and IDB could barely increase their lending despite the worst global economic crisis since the MDBs were founded (Humphrey and Prizzon 2020).

Building equity capital through the back door: net income and reserves

If an MDB cannot obtain more capital from its shareholders when it runs up against its lending limits, what can it do to increase lending capacity? The answer is to retain its annual net income and accumulate financial reserves. The legacy MDBs do not distribute profit to shareholders (they are technically permitted to, but in practice never do) but rather keep it as reserves, otherwise known as retained earnings. In financial terms, reserves function exactly like paid-in capital, and together reserves and paid-in capital make up shareholder equity. Reserves form the majority of shareholder equity at all the legacy MDBs except AfDB, far more than capital provided directly by shareholders. At the IBRD, for example, shareholders have contributed a total of $18 billion in capital since the bank was created in 1944, but by 2020 the bank had accumulated $22.3 billion in reserves from net income (Figure 3.2).

[3] A G20 commission created in July 2021 was among other tasks asked to consider whether MDBs should change their capital adequacy policies to include a portion of callable capital (G20 2021 and Humphrey 2021b), but the commission's work was not completed as of book publication.

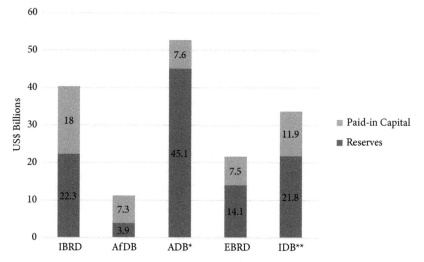

Figure 3.2 Shareholder Equity of Legacy MDBs (2020).
Source: 2020 MDB financial statements.
Note: "Reserves" are the difference between paid-in capital and total shareholder equity as listed on the balance sheet. This includes reserves, retained earnings, and other accounting adjustments.* Includes US$30.8 billion in reserves from ADF concessional window merger in 2017 (discussed later in this chapter).** Includes US$5.3 billion in paid-in capital from FSO concessional window merger in 2017 (discussed later in this chapter).

Retained earnings are a normal way for financial institutions to grow without asking shareholders to contribute more capital. Generating net income is relatively easy for MDBs, since unlike commercial banks they do not pay dividends to shareholders and can more easily generate income due to their very low funding costs. This suits the large shareholders, who would rather see MDBs build equity through reserve accumulation instead of asking for more capital. It also suits MDB management, who would much rather avoid conflictive capital increase negotiations that invariably end up with new rules imposed by non-borrower shareholders. Discussing a 2009 increase in loan prices, a senior World Bank official stated the dynamic bluntly: "This generates greater net income, which is allocated to reserves and hence can be used for lending ... We try to minimize capital increases as much as possible, because of the political difficulties involved" (cited in Humphrey 2014, 626).

The difference with commercial institutions, however, is that the development mandate of MDBs would suggest that loan interest rates and fees charged to borrower countries should be kept as low as possible, rather than raised to generate net income in lieu of shareholder capital. Borrower countries argue that shareholders should capitalize the MDBs through a direct capital increase instead and keep the interest rates and fees on development loans low. As Chinese official Jin Liqun (future president of AIIB) put it in a 2000 speech at the World Bank: "It is neither fair nor acceptable to put all financial burdens on part of developing countries ... IBRD borrowers, including blend countries, have already made their contributions to the Bank's net income; we therefore oppose the option to further raise IBRD loan charges" (World Bank 2000).

Not only is the practice of increasing loan prices to generate net income developmentally questionable, it also has governance implications. At a commercial bank, increasing loan prices are borne by external borrowing customers. At an MDB, however, the customers paying these higher loan prices are a subset of the shareholders. Hence, they are in effect paying for a capital increase through higher loan prices, but not receiving the voting benefits that would come along with a normal capital increase. If even a portion of the $22.3 billion in retained earnings at IBRD were to come with voting rights attached, the role of borrower countries in IBRD governance would be substantially higher.

But with voting control, non-borrower countries inevitably carry the day. At the World Bank, for example, IBRD loan prices were increased three times between 2008 and 2014, and a new pricing scheme was introduced in 2018 specifically with the aim of generating net income (World Bank 2018c, 30). Similarly, ADB justified its loan price changes in 2019 explicitly with the need to generate more net income (ADB 2019). Facing capital restrictions, AfDB raised loan prices in 2016 for the same purpose, over the resistance of borrower shareholders. "This increased allocable income by around 45 million per year going forward," said an AfDB treasury official. "But it's not realistic to do it again, the last time was quite a bruising fight. The borrowers didn't like it at all" (interview, June 6, 2017). At IDB, a senior strategy official commented that a 2016 loan price increase to build reserves "made a lot of the borrowers unhappy" (interview, March 15, 2017).

The second major issue with net income policies is that a large chunk is not put in reserves at all, but is instead allocated to causes that serve the interests of non-borrower shareholders. By far the largest allocations are to the concessional windows that provide zero-interest loans or grants to the lowest-income countries, the World Bank's IDA and AfDB's ADF. Created in 1960, IDA was originally funded entirely by contributions from wealthy donor countries. In its early years, when IBRD had particularly high net income in a given year, non-borrower shareholders voted to siphon off a portion of that as a contribution to IDA, which conveniently reduced the amount non-borrowers needed to donate from their own budgets to support the fund that they had created. Over the years this became increasingly institutionalized, to the point where net income transfers are an integral part of the three-yearly cycle of IDA replenishments. The World Bank now commits to shareholders ahead of time to transfer an agreed amount to IDA and sets loan charges to generate sufficient income to meet those targets.[4] Through

---

[4] In 2017, IBRD shareholders agreed to a formula that linked the amount of IDA transfers to IBRD's financial performance for the year, "ensuring that most allocable income is retained to grow IBRD's

2020, IBRD had contributed a total of US$16.1 billion in net income to IDA, and IFC a further US$3.6 billion. AfDB engages in a similar practice to support the concessional ADF, though on a smaller scale (US$1.1 billion through 2020), as does ADB for the Asian Development Fund (US$2.8 billion through 2020).

From the point of view of borrower member countries, this is a misuse of the resources of their cooperative. The concessional windows are by treaty financially separate institutions at IBRD and AfDB, and there is no justification for net income to be taken out and given to another institution that was created by donor countries and intended to be funded by them. Net income transfers to reserves might not be borrower countries' preferred way to increase MDB equity, but at least it benefits the overall cooperative by increasing lending capacity—concessional window transfers do not. For borrowers, this looks like a "transfer from one set of developing countries to another" (Mohammed 2004, 12), mandated by non-borrower countries to ease their own fiscal burden. This was spelled out by Russian Economic Development Minister Maksim Oreshkin in a 2019 World Bank Development Committee speech: "It might be argued that massive transfers to IDA practiced by the IBRD for many years were effectively a form of unacknowledged contribution of middle-income borrowing countries who were overcharged to make for these transfers" (World Bank 2019a). Needless to say, these IDA contributions do not count in IBRD's formula for allocating voting power discussed earlier.

Even more galling for borrowers is the use of MDB net income to cover programs linked to the geopolitical interests of non-borrowers, like support for West Bank/Gaza (IBRD and EBRD) or former Yugoslavia reconstruction (IBRD). Here again this is most egregious at the World Bank, but also occurs at the other legacy MDBs. It is not difficult to imagine the views of countries like Indonesia or Brazil when they are told that resources from their cooperative bank are being spent to support causes that they have nothing to do with, and may not even agree with. As a former Brazilian World Bank executive director put it, "Developed countries don't realize the importance of the institution to global governance—they want to milk it like a cow, to take the place of bilateral contributions" (interview, December 12, 2011). A senior treasury official at one of the legacy MDBs agreed, saying "These transfers have been considerable, even in years when we've had losses ... Shareholders are prioritizing themselves and their causes to our financial strength" (interview, March 10, 2017).

The amount of resources transferred to concessional windows and other purposes favored by non-borrower shareholders are substantial—US$25.4 billion from IBRD through FY2020, and US$13 billion from the other legacy MDBs

reserves" (IBRD 2020 Financial Statement, 17–18). Nonetheless, the amount of IBRD (and IFC) net income that is expected to be transferred to IDA remains a standard part of the IDA replenishment negotiations, and is a major factor in setting IBRD loan pricing.

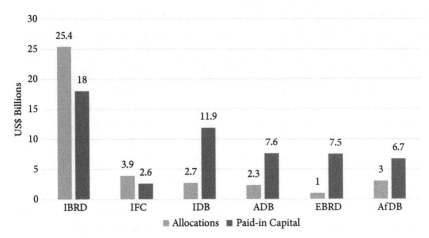

Figure 3.3 Cumulative Net Income Allocations vs. 2020 Shareholder Capital, Legacy MDBs.

Source: 2020 MDB financial statements.

Note: Includes transfers to concessional windows and other shareholder-established funds, as well as (in the cases of IBRD and IDB) "special programs" listed in administrative expenses. Does not include transfers to project preparation funds such as EBRD's Special Shareholder Fund and ADB's Technical Assistance Special Fund.

(Figure 3.3). This could have meant considerably lower loan charges—and hence debt burden—for borrower countries over many years. Alternatively, it could have been plowed into MDB equity, giving the MDBs a major boost in lending headroom without the need for capital increases. Based on current capital adequacy ratios, if these transfers had instead been retained as equity reserves, IBRD could carry an additional $130 billion in development loans on its books—a massive boost in lending capacity. The transfer of net income to shareholder causes was clearly not planned when the MDBs were founded. As Kapur et al. point out (1997, 938), the original Articles of Agreement of the IBRD indicated that net income should be used only for three purposes: accumulating reserves, reducing loan charges, or distributing to shareholders. Shortly after IDA was created and non-borrowers thought to make use of IBRD's net income to alleviate their own contributions, IBRD executive directors made a "formal interpretation" of the articles to permit grant transfers out of net income (Shihata 2000, 85–86).

Capital adequacy at the legacy MDBs

One might imagine that shareholders would encourage the legacy MDBs to maximize their lending to make the most of their capital contributions for development. In fact, they have highly conservative financial policies, far more restrictive than commercial banks. Like all banks, MDBs have "capital adequacy" policies to decide how much loans they can carry on their balance sheet in relation to their shareholder capital without threatening their financial stability. The models used by the MDBs to evaluate their capital adequacy are highly complex and are not public. A simple metric puts MDB approaches to capital adequacy in perspective: the equity to loans (E/L) ratio, which compares an MDB's equity (shareholder capital plus reserves) to its loan portfolio.[5] In 2020, the World Bank's IBRD had an E/L ratio of around 23 percent, while the four regional MDBs were between 32 percent (IDB) and 53 percent (EBRD) (Figure 3.4). This is strikingly well capitalized compared to commercial financial institutions, which typically have E/Ls in the 10–15 percent range, and all the more surprising in light of the superlative loan repayment record of MDBs. Government borrowers treat MDBs as "preferred creditors" and almost never stop repaying their loans. In the rare cases when they do go into arrears, those arrears have always been repaid eventually, as MDBs have a policy of never writing off loans.[6] On top of that, the legacy MDBs have hundreds of billions of dollars of guaranteed callable capital of the MDBs, designed to give them even more financial security.

Why do the legacy MDBs not lower their E/L ratios, thus freeing substantially more resources for lending? "We have been asking about this for years," said a World Bank executive director from a major borrower country. "They always come back to us with 'We will lose our AAA rating if we do'. And we don't know ourselves, so we can't really argue with that" (interview, January 25, 2012). An IDB executive director from a borrower country said, "It's like a religion with management, protecting the AAA. It seems to us that we could be lending a lot more, but they say we can't, and the U.S. seems to think the same so there's not much we can do about it" (interview, January 13, 2012). The importance of holding onto a AAA rating is stated repeatedly in MDB documents. For example the IDB's 2018 financial statement notes, "The Bank shall establish regulations, policies, guidelines, and related initiatives, including the definition of appropriate capital buffers, to maintain its firm financial footing and ensure a long-term foreign-currency credit rating of triple-A (or equivalent) level, with all major credit rating agencies" (IDB 2018, 59).

Having a AAA rating is unquestionably useful for the legacy MDBs, as it allows superb access to capital markets, which substantially reduces funding costs and, in the end, the interest rates charged to borrowers. But it also is evident that the

---

[5] The E/L ratio does not take into account the riskiness of each loan, and hence is a rough and imprecise comparative metric.

[6] The exception is MDB participation in debt relief, like the Highly Indebted Poor Countries initiative or the Multilateral Debt Relief Initiative. This debt relief has been driven by shareholders for developmental purposes, not by MDBs for financial considerations, and much of the financial hit has been borne by donor countries rather than MDB finances. Preferred creditor status is an important element underpinning MDB's AAA bond rating, which is the major factor behind their policy against any debt forgiveness—including opposition to participating in the G20's 2020 Debt Service Suspension Initiative (DSSI) in response to the Covid-19 crisis (Humphrey and Mustapha 2020).

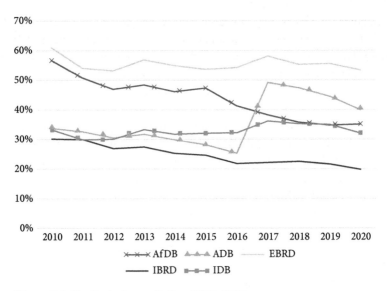

Figure 3.4 Equity-to-Loans Ratios, 2010–2020.

Source: 2020 MDB financial statements.
Note: Includes all loans as well as guarantees and development-related equity
investments. IBRD reports a slightly higher E/L in its financial statements due to
differing calculation methods. The spike for ADB is the result of a boost in equity in
2017 (discussed later in this chapter), rather than a change in financial policy.

legacy MDBs could substantially increase their lending portfolios and still maintain a AAA rating. As S&P itself pointed out in a research note (Standard and Poor's
2016), legacy MDBs could lend hundreds of billions more without any additional
capital under a AAA rating, simply by taking a portion of callable capital committed by the wealthiest shareholders into account in their capital adequacy models.
Calculations by Settimo (2017), Munir and Gallagher (2020), and Humphrey
(2018a and 2020a) arrive at similar conclusions.

But legacy MDBs refuse to include any callable capital in their calculations. One
senior treasury official at a legacy MDB said, "None of the shareholders have bud-
geted for it, and it's not certain that if you had a problem that you could get the
money. So we can't take it into account in our headroom calculations" (interview,
March 10, 2017). Ironically, MDB officials themselves appear to have less faith
in callable capital than the major bond rating agencies. This position has long
been backed up by the major shareholders, in good part to avoid even the most
remote possibility that they have to pay any of their callable capital. As one World
Bank executive director put it in the 1970s, "Management and the Board should
think about callable capital as a Christian thinks about heaven, that it is a nice
idea but no one wants to go there because the price of admission is death" (cited
in Kapur et al. 1997, 991). A top World Bank finance official said that this situation had not changed materially since then. "A call on capital is something they

[major shareholders] want to avoid, because it's not something in their budget, it would come out of nowhere. So the history of the Bank has always been to manage its finances to avoid a call on capital" (cited in Humphrey 2014, 624). A top IDB Treasury official agreed: "Ultimate[ly] we are trying to protect—in our case it's not bankruptcy, its callable capital. The main non-borrowing shareholders, especially the U.S., do not want to get called on" (ibid.).

Some non-borrower shareholders seem to be coming around to the idea that the MDBs could push their capital adequacy. "We've never suggested that they take a cut to their AAA, but there does seem to be scope for extra lending," said one official from a G7 European nation, adding that MDB treasury and risk teams "have been incredibly resistant to any overtures about this" (interview, March 20, 2017). Rather than take any action that could undermine their relationship with rating agencies and bond markets, MDB management prefer that shareholders stump up more capital, build equity through net income transfers to reserves, or increase lending headroom by other means, as discussed in the following sections. The U.S.—as the country with by far the most callable capital at stake—has long supported the MDB management position. But recent calls for MDBs to scale up lending in response to the Covid-19 crisis and to address climate change seems to have led to a softening in the Biden administration: in July 2021 it agreed to a G20 initiative calling for an independent review of MDB capital adequacy (G20 2021). Whether this review leads to actual change in MDB financial policy remains to be seen.

Creative financial engineering to expand capacity

The legacy MDBs find themselves in a bind created by contradictory directives from their major shareholders. On the one hand, they are being asked to achieve daunting global development goals that require massive investment. On the other, shareholders are not giving them adequate new capital and are pushing them to follow highly conservative capital adequacy policies. To try to square this circle, the MDBs are exploring new techniques to build financial capacity without more capital, partly with the involvement of private investors.

Transferring risk off the balance sheet
The legacy MDBs generally make very long-term loans—up to twenty years or more in some cases. This eases the debt burden of borrower governments and is aligned with the long-term nature of many projects (particularly infrastructure), but it also means that these resources are locked up for a long time on the MDB's balance sheet. MDB staff have begun thinking about ways to "recycle" these loans more quickly, freeing space for future loans. The idea is to transfer the risks embedded in these loans off the balance sheet to some external party, creating room to support new loans instead. EBRD, ADB, and IFC have sold individual loans to

private sector borrowers off their books to investors (mostly commercial banks) for several years, but on a small scale. New ideas are percolating to scale this concept up.

A first move in this direction was by ADB and Sweden's development agency SIDA in 2016, when SIDA guaranteed a portion of ADB's outstanding private sector loans. If the loans are not repaid for any reason, Sweden would repay the ADB. This guarantee essentially removed the risk of these loans from ADB's balance sheet (although ADB still legally owns and administers the loans), freeing more space for future lending (ADB 2016a). The World Bank concluded a similar operation at the end of 2016 covering loans to Iraq, with guarantees from the governments of Canada and the U.K. (World Bank 2016). Future operations are possible (and as of early 2022 were in discussions related to Ukraine reconstruction), but are limited by the willingness of donor countries to take on these risks.

MDBs have also turned to private investors. AfDB launched two operations in 2018, both of which transferred the risks that AfDB faced on part of their loans to investors (Hay 2018a and 2018b). While the loans stayed legally on AfDB's balance sheet and are administered by AfDB, the investors agreed to pay up if any of the loans were not repaid, in return for a fee paid to them by AfDB. One of the deals was a type of securitization with a private impact investment firm, while the second involved buying insurance from private insurance companies to cover part of AfDB's loan portfolio, but the result was the same—AfDB freed up space to make more loans. These deals sparked considerable interest in the development finance community. Risk transfer deals could dramatically accelerate the ability of MDBs to recycle their shareholder equity into new loan projects, rather than keep it locked up for years or decades as at present. This could be done on a rolling basis, with MDBs making loans, transferring risk to private investors, and making further lending without requiring more capital from shareholders.

Another technique MDBs have employed is "exposure exchanges," whereby two or more MDBs exchange the risks embedded in particular loans with each other. The actual loans remain on the balance sheet of the originating MDB, but the responsibility for taking any potential loss on the loan is shifted to another MDB. The reason is essentially to game the rating methodology of Standard and Poor's, which heavily penalizes an MDB when it has a high concentration of loans in small number of borrowers. The first exposure exchange occurred in 2015 between the World Bank, AfDB, and IDB, and resulted in several billion in additional lending headroom for the latter two MDBs (Humphrey 2017b). In 2020, ADB and IDB announced a second exchange (IDB 2020).

Co-financing and syndication
The legacy MDBs have also sought to "stretch" their capital by finding outside investors willing to pair their money with MDB loans, thus giving projects more financing without requiring more MDB capital. Co-financing and syndication are

two terms for essentially the same thing, with the former involving official agencies and the latter bringing in private investors. MDBs develop a loan project and the external financier lends additional funding on top of the MDB loan. Thus, the financier does not have to do any of the hard work of developing or administering a loan, and—because of the official relationship between MDBs and borrowers—feels more confident about being repaid. These arrangements are generally for loans to private sector borrowers, rather than developing country governments. This is because the external financier earns the same return on the loan as the MDB. Since MDB loans to private sector borrowers are closer to market rates, they are much more attractive to investors compared to the below-market public sector loan rates offered by MDBs.

Co-financing and syndication are not new, but in recent years these arrangements have ramped up dramatically. ADB reported financial approvals of US$31.6 billion on its own account in 2020, and another US$16.4 billion from various types of partnering. IDB's public lending window and private sector IDB Invest approved a combined US$19.5 billion on their own account, and another US$4.5 billion in from partnerships, while the World Bank's private sector IFC approved US$11.1 billion in own account investments in FY2020 and another US$10.8 billion in private sector mobilization. Particularly dramatic is IFC's Managed Co-Lending Portfolio Program (MCPP), which involves not individual projects, but rather large pots of money committed by external financiers that IFC matches with its project pipeline on an ongoing basis. MCPP has brought in US$4 billion from the Chinese official sources (People's Bank of China and Hong Kong Monetary Authority) and another US$3 billion from institutional investors like Swiss Re, Allianz, and Munich Re (IFC 2020). IDB Invest set up a similar arrangement in 2018, and other MDBs are likely to follow suit. China also created co-financing funds with IDB and AfDB, each for $2 billion (Humphrey and Chen 2021).

Reforming concessional lending windows
Another initiative to maximize financial capacity has been via "mergers" of concessional and non-concessional lending windows at ADB and IDB. The concessional windows for low-income countries are funded by donations and net income transfers from the regular MDB lending windows (as discussed in the previous section). By far the largest concessional window is the World Bank's IDA, set up in 1960. AfDB, ADB, and IDB also had concessional windows, while EBRD has never had one.

The concessional windows of the ADB (Asian Development Fund, or AsDF) and IDB (Fund for Special Operations, or FSO) began losing their relevance in the 2000s, due to the declining number of very low-income countries in Asia and Latin America. But because concessional loans are paid back over decades, these funds still had a substantial portfolio of outstanding loans on their books from large formerly eligible countries like Brazil, China, and India. Rather than let those loans sit there unused until they were paid off, ADB and IDB "merged" the portfolio of outstanding loans into the balance sheets of their regular MDB lending windows. Because these loans imply a future revenue stream (the repayments that borrowers will make in future years) they could be merged into the shareholder equity of the regular lending windows. The results of the 2017 mergers were impressive—a boost of US$34.6 billion, nearly tripling ADB's shareholder equity (ADB 2015a), and $5.2 billion for IDB (IDB 2017). These one-time operations created very substantial additional lending headroom for ADB and a sizeable boost for IDB, without requiring a capital increase.

A concessional window merger could have a huge impact at the World Bank (IDA's outstanding portfolio is over US$150 billion) and smaller but still useful at AfDB (US$13 billion in the ADF portfolio). However, both IDA and ADF are legally independent entities with their own international treaty, unlike AsDF and FSO, which were legally part of ADB and IDB. As well, IDA and ADF both serve a higher number of countries that still depend on concessional finance, especially in Africa. As a result, mergers make less financial and developmental sense and would be more complicated legally for the World Bank and AfDB.

World Bank shareholders instead chose to allow IDA to get a bond rating of its own and start issuing debt to fund part of its operations (World Bank 2017b, 59). Although the move does nothing to increase lending headroom at IBRD, it does reduce the need for wealthy countries to contribute to IDA (World Bank 2019b, 28). This "paradigm shift in IDA's financing model" (ibid.) as the bank optimistically put it is once again a workaround to the limited generosity of donors to address the needs of the world's poor, and it may have long-term, unforeseen impacts. IDA's donor funding model was designed specifically to keep costs low for borrowers and to focus purely on development projects, and not be distracted by the need to attract bond market investors. Starting to depend on capital markets could in the medium term increase the costs of IDA loans and gradually shift its approach to development, especially if (as is likely) future replenishment rounds call for a greater share from market borrowings and less donations (see Landers 2021). In short, IDA could gradually become just another MDB.

Conclusions

The legacy MDBs are caught between countervailing tensions. Member countries are happy to task the MDBs as the main agencies in charge of achieving ambitious development goals, but disinclined to supply the shareholder capital needed to achieve those goals. At the same time, the interests of non-borrower shareholders are holding back the ability of MDBs to make better use of the capital and income they do have. Rather than supply new capital, non-borrowers prefer to push through loan price increases to build equity on the backs of borrower countries and redirect a chunk of net income for their own interests. Nor have non-borrowers been willing to relax the extremely conservative financial policies of the MDBs to allow them to lend more, out of excessive concern that their callable capital might one day be called.

The result is an ever-increasingly clamor for the major MDBs to use their balance sheets more creatively and bring in external resources—mostly from the private sector—for development. This reality lies underneath the endless conferences about blended finance, financing for development, the World Bank's "cascade" approach (World Bank 2017c), and much more: how MDBs can achieve more development impact without more shareholder capital. This drive is further supported by the ideological bent of some major shareholders to focus more on leveraging private investment rather than funding public sector projects (see for example CSIS 2013).

External finance always involves trade-offs that can impact the ability of MDBs to pursue development goals. This is most obvious with private investors—their goal is profit. MDBs already balance the views of credit rating agencies and bond markets with their development mandate with their traditional funding model. Bringing investors directly into project lending takes this dynamic to another level. Investors in syndication or risk transfer deals with MDBs will only be interested in projects that they view as financially viable, like revenue-generating infrastructure facilities. That represents a subset of the projects and investments needed to achieve global development goals, even just in the infrastructure sector. This could incentivize MDB staff to start targeting projects that they know investors are likely to find attractive—the safest and most profitable ones, not necessarily those with the greatest development impact.

Arrangements with official co-financiers run similar risks. For example, when Sweden guaranteed a group of ADB loans, it picked the loans according to Sweden's particular developmental priorities. Ramping up official portfolio guarantees could lead to donors using guarantees to support their own priorities, which weakens MDB collective governance in a way similar to what has occurred with the proliferation of trust funds (Reinsberg et al. 2015). The case of China is even more potent. China has dropped close to US$10 billion in co-financing resources across the legacy MDBs. This increases the overall influence of China within these MDBs, despite its limited formal voting power (Humphrey and Chen 2021).

Bringing in external financing and engaging in more sophisticated balance sheet engineering also has the potential to eat away at the unique relationship MDBs have with borrower countries. Borrower governments know that MDBs are always there for them, even in times of crisis when other sources of financing dry up. This underpins preferred creditor treatment, which means borrowers prioritize repaying MDBs and is a key component of MDB financial strength. If borrowers feel that their MDB loans are being offloaded to private investors or a different MDB, this official relationship could erode. The legacy MDBs might begin to be perceived less as development partners and more as deal-makers for other investors.

The original legacy MDB model—using a small amount of capital from share-holders to borrow from capital markets at excellent terms, and then on-lending for development projects—has worked extremely well for decades. But rather than contribute additional capital to align financial capacity with development man-dates, major shareholders are instead pushing the legacy MDBs to reinvent their business model by using their operations and balance sheets to leverage external financiers. Bringing in external sources of finance will change how MDBs oper-ate and could weaken their legitimacy and development effectiveness. This is not to say that MDBs should not move ahead with these innovations, but rather that MDB shareholders and the development community should be clear on what is driving them and the trade-offs involved.

Beyond the Money: Business Practices of the Legacy MDBs

While the supply of finance from the legacy MDBs is constrained for the reasons described in the previous section, demand for lending is also restricted, due to business practices that in some cases offset attractive loan terms and high-quality technical assistance. Borrowers face lengthy and complicated review and approval processes, safeguards on environmental and social issues that often surpass laws in wealthy countries, and a sometimes overbearing approach to dictating develop-ment priorities and policies to borrowers. The result is that some countries prefer to use other financing sources altogether. High project quality and developmental best practices are a key value-added of the legacy MDBs. But if process require-ments become such a burden that countries are willing to pay a higher financial cost to avoid them, they are no longer having their intended impact. The evidence suggests that the legacy MDBs may be losing this delicate balance, particularly the World Bank.

As with the financial problems facing the legacy MDBs, the reasons behind onerous business practices stem for the most part from the interests of major non-borrower shareholders. It is easier for non-borrower governments to add on rules and layers of oversight to placate domestic interests rather than defend organizations that don't have much domestic support and the benefits of which are not easy to articulate to skeptical legislatures. Borrower governments have in many cases used their voting power, alliance-building with some amenable non-borrower shareholders, and informal influence (especially through the staff of the regional MDBs) to shape business practices in ways that better suit their interests. Nonetheless, as noted in a 2016 report, "The legacy MDBs have become overly bureaucratic, rigid, and rule-driven in large part because of shareholder governance" (Birdsall and Morris 2016, 26).

This section explores the details and causes of legacy MDB business practices, with a particular focus on i) the interests of non-borrower countries in establish-ing these practices and ii) how they impact the demand for MDB lending on the part of borrower countries. Evidence is derived from 122 in-person interviews in sixteen African, Asian, and Latin American countries with borrower country government officials engaging directly with MDBs and other development financiers, as well as scores of interviews and informal discussions with executive directors and high-level staff at all the legacy MDBs and ministry officials of non-borrower countries between 2007 and 2020. Further evidence was culled from secondary sources, including the views of borrower government officials in nine countries in Africa and Asia (Greenhill et al., 2013 and Prizzon et al., 2016); a survey of borrower country views of AfDB (AfDB 2012), a series of stakeholder consultations by (ADB 2016b–f), and three rounds of client survey data from the World Bank (World Bank 2018d).

Project approval and implementation bureaucracy

A key complaint voiced by government officials about working with the legacy MDBs is the procedural hassles they must navigate to design, negotiate, approve, and disburse project financing. The MDBs are perceived to be extremely bureaucratic, with an array of time-consuming and complicated procedures that borrower government officials find extraordinarily frustrating. Ministry officials must learn Byzantine (and frequently changing) MDB policies, commit substantial time to hosting staff missions, and navigate special MDB finance, procurement, and safeguard requirements. On top of that, agreements made with project teams are sometimes rendered obsolete when projects are reviewed by other internal MDB teams.

The average time required for a project at the legacy MDBs to move through the entire approval process to the first disbursement of resources was over two years in the case of the World Bank and ADB, and not much less for AfDB and IDB (Figure 3.5).[7] This is far longer than the few months or even weeks needed to obtain resources from the private sector—without any addition requirements related to policies, safeguards, or procurement—and also much slower than borrower-led MDBs like CAF or Trade and Development Bank or nontraditional bilateral sources of finance such as China. The process times reported here are *averages*—approval times for major infrastructure projects can be much longer due to greater complexity in project design, social and environmental safeguards, and procurement. It is telling that, after years of almost no improvement, the World Bank stopped reporting project processing times in its Corporate Scorecard after 2017. The most recent report (2019) includes 101 different indicators but excludes

---

[7] The inconsistency in delivery time data is reported by the legacy MDBs is itself suggestive that the MDBs are loath to highlight their poor performance in this area. Only IDB—which has performed by far the best—has consistent and comparable time series data each year.

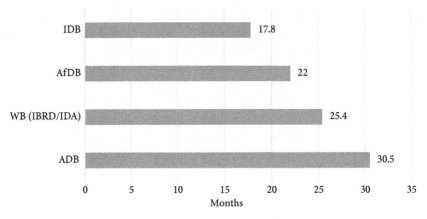

Figure 3.5 Average Loan Processing Time to First Disbursement.
Sources: World Bank 2017d; ADB 2020; AfDB 2020; IDB 2019.
Notes: EBRD not available. Public sector projects only. Data is not precisely comparable due to different definitions of project start.

one of the most critical issues for borrower countries—how long it takes to approve and disburse a loan.

Borrower country officials consider the time it takes for MDB projects to move ahead absurdly long. As one Panamanian official put it

> We've got a lot of big investment projects, and every politician wants to be there to cut the ribbon when it's done. The IDB and World Bank take too long for that, by the time the project is done the election is already passed. I need to get a no-objection to putting a turbine here, or authorization from some bureaucrat in Washington who doesn't know anything about the project
>
> (interview, November 14, 2013, author's translation)

Comparing the World Bank and AfDB to Chinese financing, a Tanzanian official said,

> People want to go with these export-import banks or even commercial banks because of the procedures that are involved. From the project design, appraisal, until you get the money, it takes a long time with the World Bank. For example with the gas pipeline project, we wanted to finish it as soon as possible. We thought that if we went to the World Bank it would take more time than the government wanted. So we went to the Chinese.
>
> (interview, 18 October 2016)

Complaints about bureaucracy and slow project approvals are voiced repeatedly by borrower government officials in interviews as well as secondary sources

(Greenhill et al., 2013 and Prizzon et al., 2016) and MDB client consultations and surveys (ADB 2016b–f, AfDB 2012, and World Bank 2018d).

Some of this bureaucracy is a function of the size and institutional culture of the MDBs and some delays are caused by borrower governments themselves. A large share, however, stems from requirements imposed by non-borrowing shareholders. One high-level World Bank official said,

> The World Bank is majority-owned by Part 1 countries like the US, Japan, France, Netherlands, and the Nordics. So every time there's a screw up, another rule gets written and process gets added, formal or informal. Unfortunately that's the way the place works ... These ideas come from the Part 1 countries, they're certainly not the borrowers' ideas—they didn't come to the Board asking for tighter restrictions on how we do things
>
> (interview, September 7, 2011).

The project cycle at all legacy MDBs has numerous required review steps. At the World Bank, most loans involve four separate country missions (identification, pre-appraisal, appraisal, and negotiations) as well as four formal internal reviews (World Bank 2020c). Considering the need to organize the project staff team (many of whom work on multiple projects in different countries), coordinate schedules with government officials, circulate documents two to four weeks before all review meetings, and find a slot in the Board of Directors (BoD) agenda, the lengthy approval process comes as no surprise. The regional MDBs follow a generally similar process. Until 2015,[8] the AfDB had twenty formal review and approval steps between the initial request for financing and board approval (AfDB 2013). For each step, documents must be written and circulated in advance of meetings, and the appraisal report must be officially translated prior to the board meeting, adding further weeks of delay. Four or sometimes five country missions are required throughout this process.

Perhaps the most clearly politicized level of the approval process is the final vote at the MDB boards of directors (BoD). Each individual project must be formally approved by the BoD at all the legacy MDBs,[9] despite the fact that staff have already dedicated time and budget on its preparation for over a year in many cases. The EDs themselves rarely make operationally useful suggestions and either rubber stamp the projects or make political statements. Directors often require staff to give extensive briefing, using up staff time, as a former ADB vice president lamented: "the amount of staff time devoted to briefings on the ninth floor (BoD offices) has been increasing at exponential rates over my seven years and is just not sustainable ... There simply must be a better way and a clearer demarcation between Management's responsibilities and the Board's oversight

---

[8] AfDB staff said in interviews that this has been streamlined, but more recent data is unavailable.
[9] Some of the legacy MDBs have instituted non-objection BoD procedures for certain types of loans, accelerating the process somewhat.

function" (quoted in Morris 2019). Many other MDBs, including the European Investment Bank and newly created Asian Infrastructure Investment Bank, give more authority to management to move ahead with many projects without BoD review. The tight control of BoD at the legacy MDBs is an expression of the distrust non-borrowers have for MDB management and staff.

Interviews with MDB staff and borrower officials indicate that the regional MDBs—with more influence of borrower countries in governance and representation in senior management—are somewhat less bureaucratic than the World Bank. This includes fewer and shorter in-country missions, faster turn-around times between review levels, shorter documents, less conflict between project teams and other internal staff, more authority in local offices, and more flexibility to adapt to country needs and circumstances. Speaking about the AfDB, an Ethiopian official noted that "it's controlled by the same countries as the World Bank, so the policies are basically the same, but AfDB is a bit more understanding and easier to work with for us" (interview, October 13, 2016). A Dominican Republic Planning Ministry official had a similar reaction regarding IDB: "Because of the nature of the IDB, there's a greater understanding of the political realities here, and that translates into more flexibility. The World Bank has more stakeholders involved so they are more restricted" (interview, November 20, 2013, author's translation).

Environmental and social safeguards

The legacy MDBs mandate the use of "safeguard" policies that in many cases supersede borrower country laws and regulations to avoid or mitigate negative project impacts on the environment and vulnerable social groups. Safeguards were first instituted at the World Bank in the 1980s and the other legacy MDBs in subsequent years. The World Bank's safeguards are still the most comprehensive and rigorous, but the safeguards of the ADB, IDB, and AfDB have been tightened over the years such that the differences between them are relatively small, particularly on the hot-button issues of environmental assessment and resettlement.

All projects are screened to determine if they trigger any of the MDB safeguards, and if so, what level of risk they pose. Depending on the outcome, a series of procedures are required before a loan can be approved and disbursed. The most frequently triggered safeguards in the case of the World Bank relate to environmental assessment and involuntary resettlement (World Bank 2010a). Procedures mandated under the safeguards are extremely detailed, and in many cases difficult for borrowers and even staff to fully understand, according to a study commissioned by the German government (Von Bernstorff and Dann 2013, 19). Requirements vary between MDBs and other development financiers, and have changed multiple times over the last decades, meaning government officials have a hard time keeping track of what they are required to do and for whom.

In practical terms, safeguards impose substantial financial costs and add to the time required to get projects up and running, particularly for any kind of infrastructure project. Borrowers are required to hire external consultants at their own cost to produce studies following specific guidelines, despite the fact that most borrower countries have their own agencies with experts overseeing these issues. A World Bank study from 2010 found that in a sample of sixty World Bank projects, safeguard costs to borrowers averaged US$13.5 million, rising up to US$19.2 million for projects classified as Category A (the most stringent level) (World Bank 2010a, 75). These studies take months to produce and must be publicly disclosed in some cases for up to six months to receive comment before the project can move ahead. Government officials point to resettlement safeguards as the most problematic, leading to high costs and lengthy delays.

A World Bank safeguard staffer acknowledged the problem.

> There are quite significant costs, and most are related to safeguards. One is preparing all the environmental and social instruments, resettlement action plan, indigenous peoples plan, all of those instruments ... All of the responsibility for that rests with the borrower, they have to pay for the consultants, for all consultations they go through in country, and then they have to disclose everything publicly.
>
> (interview, January 12, 2012)

A World Bank executive director from a Latin American borrower country pointed out the ultimate impact. "If your costs are too high, your largest clients, the ones most in need of that partnership with the Bank, will go elsewhere ... . If the Bank says ex ante 'I want you to do twenty-eight conditions and take two years to do the analysis,' I don't want to be your partner" (interview, December 12, 2011).

Many borrowers also object to safeguards on more fundamental grounds. All countries have their own laws and regulations covering environmental and social issues, based on their own historical trajectory and socioeconomic realities. The safeguards of the legacy MDBs require that governments set aside their laws when borrowing from the MDBs, and instead follow rules imposed from outside and obeying priorities set by wealthy countries. This amounts to, in the words of an IDB executive director from a borrower country, "an extra-territorial imposition, and does not fit the treaty we signed when we joined the bank" (quoted in Humphrey 2016b, 2–3).

This materializes in many ways during actual projects. Several officials mentioned cases when the legacy MDBs pressured them to pay for the resettlement of illegal squatters, which they objected to on principal. In one road project in Uruguay, an official said that the IDB insisted on moving people working as street vendors without permits. "This was totally illegal, it would have validated them [the street vendors] breaking the law," complained the official. "We are happy to consult with people there legally, but not the other ones. If they [IDB] don't sort this out, we shake their hands and say goodbye, and we go with CAF" (interview, November 12, 2013, author's translation). In other cases, the legacy MDBs require governments to negotiate with NGOs in the project-affected region. "I've been involved in some discussions with NGOs that have no legal status, we don't know who they are or who they represent," said one borrower country World Bank executive director. "They get together a handful of people from the area and stop a project that can benefit hundreds of thousands of others. There has to be some balance" (quoted in Humphrey 2016b, 3).

In Africa, the safeguards on indigenous peoples creates major problems, as the concept of an "indigenous person" is not at all clear in the African context, and also because many African countries have undergone very serious ethnic violence and are working to build a national as opposed to ethnic identity. One Tanzanian Finance Ministry official put it,

> They [World Bank] wanted to trigger that policy for a project. But here in Tanzania we don't have indigenous people, so we had to argue with them for almost three years, and then they gave waivers for that particular project, but they said they would consider triggering the policy for other projects. They were very difficult in understanding our positions, that in Tanzania we don't want that.
>
> (interview, October 18, 2016)

The official went on to say he had been in a meeting of officials from across Africa where the World Bank safeguard policy was universally panned. "You want to bring in an indigenous people's policy to a country like Rwanda, with where they've come from?" the official asked rhetorically. "I remember the minister of finance from Rwanda that day, he said if they implement that policy you can forget about Rwanda knocking on their door for assistance" (ibid.).

Many borrower officials acknowledged that they found the safeguards to be useful in providing quality control in complex environmental and social situations where the government could see potential problems and lacked the capacity to address them on its own. They frequently noted the high quality of advice on environmental and social issues provided by the legacy MDBs and the strong commitment of MDB safeguard experts. In some cases officials said they found it useful to use the MDB safeguards as political cover, deflecting potential problems related to domestic NGOs and affected communities away from them and onto the MDB. On the whole, however, borrower country officials repeatedly stated a preference for using their own national laws instead of MDB safeguards.

Safeguards policies at the major MDBs were implemented at the behest of non-borrower shareholder countries, especially the U.S. with the support of several European nations, and against the wishes of borrower countries. Environmental and social safeguards were first created in the mid-1980s at the World Bank (Wade 1997 and Shihata 2000). The push began by a number of activist environmental NGOs, appalled at a few high-profile disastrous World Bank projects, notably the Narmada Valley Dam in India and Polonoroeste Project in Brazil. The NGOs adopted the innovative and effective tactic of pressuring legislators with power over government appropriations, first in the U.S. and later in Europe. By 1986, one study reports, "the executive directors of several major Part I countries, such as Canada, the Netherlands, Australia, the Nordic countries, and the United Kingdom, were also actively pressing for environmental reforms in the Bank similar to those that the U.S. executive director had been urging for a long time" (Wade 1997, 669).

From the start, borrower countries opposed safeguards at the World Bank. Wade writes, "Many of the borrowing governments, however, especially the big and important ones like Brazil and India, remained strongly opposed to the Bank's assertion of environmental criteria" (ibid., 670). A European G7 country advisor at the World Bank said in an interview that the situation had not materially changed. "What most borrowers would tend to say is that they don't want to be subjected to a set of standards that almost wouldn't apply to investment projects in developed countries" (interview, January 30, 2012). As one recent study put it, "Safeguard issues have sometimes led to borrower resentment because they are seen as imposed by U.S. and European shareholders concerned with reducing reputational risk without attention to associated costs and delays" (Birdsall and Morris 2016, 25).

The IDB began addressing environmental and social issues as part of the negotiations over the eighth capital increase in 1994 (IDB 2005, 6–7). In 2003 IDB's safeguard policies were tightened substantially, and then again revised further in 2006, resulting in a jump in the number of projects going through compliance review from 480 in 2007 to 775 in 2009 (IDB 2011). A top environmental staffer at IDB said in an interview, "It was the U.S. and the other donors, no question about it" (cited in Humphrey 2016b, 155). A European representative at the IDB added, "I can't see any non-borrowing country wanting to weaken safeguard procedures. That's the basis on which the Americans can support a capital increase" (ibid., 156). Environmental policies were first enacted at AfDB in 1990, revamped in 2000, and unified into a full safeguard framework in 2013 (AfDB 2014). ADB began implementing safeguards in 1995 and introduced a revised and integrated set of safeguards in 2009 (ADB 2009).[10]

Despite the overall similarity in safeguards across the legacy MDBs, greater influence of borrower countries at the regional MDBs has led to a more "borrower-friendly" approach compared to the World Bank. While policies are similar on paper, borrower officials say that the regional MDBs tend to be less legalistic and more sensitive to country circumstances and interests. A Tanzanian finance ministry official said,

---

[10] EBRD and IFC, which work mainly with private sector borrowers, have avoided using ex ante safeguards and instead take a more results-oriented approach (see EBRD 2014 and IFC 2012).

AfDB is more flexible compared to the World Bank with the safeguards. The policies look the same, but AfDB tries to see the challenges we are facing in a project. For example the Masaai [Tanzanian ethnic group] have their own way of living, and the AfDB understands that you have to manage that. But the World Bank, they are rigid, it has to be their way.

(interview, October 20, 2016)

An Ethiopian official agreed, speculating also that the World Bank's higher visibility led it to face much more lobbying pressure from NGOs compared to AfDB (interview, October 12, 2016).

Borrowers do not face the additional delays, costs, and impositions occasioned by legacy MDB safeguards when accessing resources from private lenders or export banks from China, India, or Brazil. An Ethiopian finance ministry official recounted how the World Bank wanted to support a hydroelectric project: "But because of the safeguards the government refused, they said 'No, we don't want your money.' They knew the World Bank would cause problems about local people, about the ecosystem, so they are financing it on their own along with Chinese banks" (interview, October 14, 2016). Similarly, an IDB staffer recounted discussions about a proposed hydroelectric plant in Brazil.

There was a point when some folks at the IDB were trying to court Brazil to finance that project, and the immediate response from the Brazilians was, "Not on our life, you'll come running in here with your safeguards" ... That set off a moment of reflection for the bank. The moment our safeguard become a turnoff for governments, we've lost the possibility to have an influence of the outcome.

(interview, December 7, 2011)

Similarly, Cambodian officials reported steering infrastructure projects away from the World Bank and toward other financiers specifically because of problems posed by resettlement safeguards (Greenhill et al. 2013).

Sectoral allocation, project design, and policy conditionality

Another major area of contention is the tendency of the legacy MDBs to impose their views of development and project design on borrowers, despite repeated MDB pronouncements on promoting "country ownership." This is in part driven by the educational and professional background of staff as well as the institutional culture of the legacy MDBs, as noted by, among others, Woods (2006) and Weaver and Leiteritz (2005) in relation to the World Bank. At a deeper level, though, it is evident that the more top-down, supply-driven approach to legacy MDB activities derives in large measure from desire of non-borrower shareholder governments to direct these institutions in a way that they consider most in line with their own views on development.

Turn away from infrastructure

A key borrower country complaint is that the legacy MDBs allocate lending more in line with the views of non-borrower countries than the priorities of borrower governments. For most borrowers, too much financing is directed to social sectors and capacity building, and too little to projects with direct economic and job-creation impacts, especially infrastructure. In former years, the World Bank was renowned for its focus on major infrastructure projects, but starting in the 1970s the emphasis began to shift more toward poverty reduction (Kapur et al., 215–268). Infrastructure lending declined sharply from 78 percent of World Bank lending in the 1960s to under 30 percent in the first decade of the 2000s, before rebounding slightly in the past few years (Figure 3.6). This pattern is mirrored at the other legacy MDBs, although ADB has notably maintained infrastructure lending above 50 percent of total.

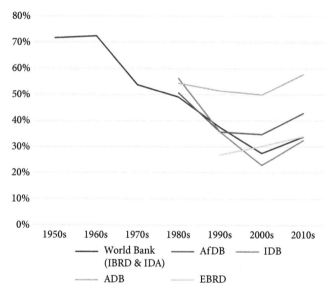

Figure 3.6 Average Annual Infrastructure Lending as Percentage of Total by Decade (to 2018).

Source: Compiled by author based on statement of annual project approvals.
Notes: EBRD data 2004–2017 and AfDB data 2016–2018 are aggregate numbers taken from MDB annual report, due to lack of project-by-project approval data. "Infrastructure" includes only financing for physical facilities, not policy loans, institutional reform, privatizations, resource extraction, or industry.

The lack of support for infrastructure is a constant source of frustration for government officials, particularly in African countries that have huge infrastructure gaps. A Tanzanian finance ministry official asked rhetorically, "You have been here since independence, World Bank, but where are your projects? A lot of money went to reforms, and we might have improved our capacity building or financial management, but there's nothing on the ground. We wanted to open up the interior, to connect the country, stimulate economic activity, and they have not helped with that" (interview, October 18, 2016). In Malawi, a finance ministry official lamented, "Institutions like the World Bank, they should invest more in the productive sectors to help this country boost its economic activity ... But we still find that the [World] Bank wants to invest in HIV/AIDS, even though the global funds of this world and the bilaterals would mostly want to spend there too" (interview, October 25, 2016). One Ethiopian finance ministry official put it bluntly, "We have been aggressively working with the World Bank and saying, 'Please invest in roads.' They say, 'What about capacity building, or something else?' but we say, 'No, roads'" (interview, October 14, 2016).

The result is that the major MDBs are increasingly marginalized in infrastructure, leaving borrower countries seeking other options like Chinese export finance. One study reported that nontraditional financiers like China were "better aligned with government priorities because of their focus on infrastructure, energy and growth-promoting sectors. These are often underserved by traditional donors, which focus more on the social sectors" (Greenhill et al. 2013, 27). In Africa between 2000 and 2014, more than 70 percent of China's financing commitments were directed to physical infrastructure, compared to about 35 percent of the World Bank's (Humphrey and Michaelowa 2019). Lending priorities driven by non-borrowers, coupled with the bureaucratic hurdles and safeguards that particularly impact infrastructure projects, have kept infrastructure to a minority of overall legacy MDB lending.

Imposition of development agenda

Another complaint is the tendency of legacy MDB staff to impose their own vision for project design. Government officials acknowledge and value design support provided by the MDBs, but say that this often slides into trying to dictate how the project should be done. In particular, the World Bank is perceived as both the most technically excellent of the legacy MDBs and at the same time the most likely to push its own views on borrower government officials. As an example, a Panamanian official told of how a World Bank staffer pushed to make a large sanitation project loan. "We had an agreement among three municipalities to deal with this problem of solid waste, which was a great opportunity. But this guy in D.C. thinks he knows everything and wants to impose a first-world solution. There's 30,000 people there, how can I spend US$100 million on that?" (interview, November 14, 2013, author's translation).

A degree of this is derived from the expertise of the MDB staff itself—a tendency to focus purely on their view of technical perfection, ignoring the country's circumstances and interests. But it is accentuated by a lack of service ethic to borrower countries, who are meant to be the main clients of the MDBs. Especially at the Washington-centric World Bank, staff easily lose sight of this reality, and instead focus on pushing projects that will win praise from non-borrower shareholders and their peers in the international development community.

The regional MDBs, by comparison, are perceived as closer to borrower countries and more willing to adapt projects to suit country circumstances. A former vice-minister of finance in Peru said, "With the World Bank I had the feeling that a lot came down from above, from the board. The board would say that they wanted to start working in some area, and all the lending then had to be oriented around that. The IDB was more like, 'where can we help?' They didn't have an agenda in the same way" (interview, June 7, 2009). An Ethiopian official made a similar comment about AfDB: "They are Africans too. It's true that the rich countries have a big influence on their policies, but the staff understand what we need and try to help. Because they are a regional bank, maybe they sympathize with us more" (cited in Humphrey 2019, 22).

Budget support and policy conditionality

Budget support loans are an injection of financing directly into the government budget, not allocated to any specific project or sector. Borrower governments favor budget support, as it gives them freedom to use resources as they see fit and disburses immediately after approval, unlike the lengthy disbursement of project loans. Budget support was not originally meant to be an important instrument of the legacy MDBs, which as an IDB report noted "were created under the premise that they would mostly finance specific expenditures related to investment projects. Policy-based loans, which provide budget support, were originally perceived to be at odds with this premise" (IDB 2016a, 17). But the World Bank and the other legacy MDBs began to ramp up budget support lending in the 1980s as a way to quickly transfer resources to countries in crisis and use as a lever to push governments to change policies—the so-called structural adjustment loans.[11] Budget support lending continues to form a substantial portion of annual lending by the legacy MDBs (Figure 3.7).

Although borrower country officials generally favor budget support lending, the legacy MDBs limit the amount they offer. The World Bank's IBRD tries to limit budget support to 25 percent of total lending (with exceptions during crises), while the ADB aims for 20 percent of total public sector lending and the IDB 30 percent of total lending over a four-year cycle (IDB 2016a). These limits are imposed by

---

[11] See Mosley et al. (1995) for a nuanced analysis of negotiating dynamics of World Bank budget support operations. For two examples of the policy conditions in classic World Bank structural adjustment loans, see Bolivia's 1991 SAL (World Bank 1991, 63–69) or Peru's 1992 SAL (World Bank 1992, 56–70).

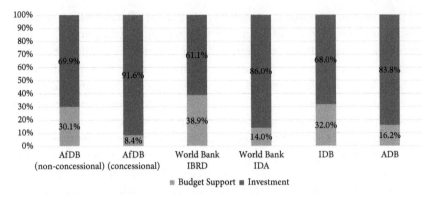

Figure 3.7 Budget Support vs. Investment Loan Approvals, 2010–2020 Average.

Source: Annual reports 2010–2020.
Notes: Results-based lending are included in investment lending, despite having characteristics similar to budget support lending. EBRD does not offer budget support lending.

non-borrower shareholders, who—as a World Bank executive director from a borrower country put it—"feel like they lose control with budget support" (interview, December 12, 2011). ADB consultations with the U.S. and Canadian governments reported that these countries are only cautiously in favor of budget support lending: "There is nothing wrong, in principle, with providing policy-based and results-based lending to DMCs [developing member countries]. However, such support should not be seen as 'easy money' ... The use of budget support instruments should be clearly justified based on ... a strong and substantive policy reform agenda" (ADB 2016b, 3).

Numerous officials in Africa and Latin America felt that the World Bank tended to push for more difficult reforms compared to the regional MDBs. "There is more flexibility to find a solution with the AfDB," a Tanzanian official said. "With the World Bank, these people come from Washington and just say, 'You have to get this done, or you won't get the money'" (interview, October 18, 2016). This finding is supported by the results of a client survey in Africa by the AfDB (2012), which reported that AfDB conditionality is perceived to be less onerous than with the World Bank. In some cases officials reported that the World Bank had even tried to impose loan conditions about passing laws, which is constitutionally the responsibility of the legislature, not the executive branch. "They [World Bank officials] told us we had to pass a law to get the money," said a Dominican Republic official. "We had to tell them, 'That's not possible, we can't commit to that, it doesn't depend on us.' The IDB wouldn't do that, they understand these issues better" (interview, November 21, 2013, author's translation).

The situation in larger middle-income countries is substantially different. As one senior IDB operations staffer put it, "Conditionality really depends on the country. With the big countries, you can't impose anything, they do what they want to do. India, Brazil, they are too important to the MDBs, they can dictate the rules ... In small countries like Central America, it's a different ballgame, you can really have influence" (interview, January 24, 2012). This reality, combined with the need for non-borrower shareholders to feel that the MDBs have "bought" something with budget support lending, has led MDB staff and middle-income borrowers collude to design policy conditions that the government already wants to do anyway and staff know will appease the MDB boards of directors. As one Panamanian finance ministry official put it:

> In the [budget support loan] policy matrix, we try to put things that we've already done, because that makes the loan a lot faster. The World Bank and IDB staff can sometimes push us, not because they want to, but because they know their boards can be very difficult. The teams will tell us, "No, the board won't like that, better to work in this area."
>
> (interview, November 18, 2013, author's translation)

Halting attempts at reform

The management and staff of the legacy MDBs—especially the front-line operational staff who engage directly with borrower governments—are well aware of the many problems that limit their attractiveness as a development partner. As far back as 2001, a World Bank report from the tellingly named Cost of Doing Business Task Force noted bluntly, "Bank safeguard and financial requirements and other business practices tend to be more comprehensive, more stringent and more consistently enforced and are perceived by clients to add costs" (World Bank 2001, 10). The report noted that these costs were most problematic with infrastructure projects: "IBRD borrowers articulated an explicit hierarchy of preference for official borrowing in these infrastructure subsectors: domestic resources, bilateral donors, Regional Banks and lastly, the World Bank" (ibid., vii).

In response, the MDBs have promoted a number of reforms in recent years to reduce bureaucracy, streamline project processes, and make greater use of client countries' own rules. As one World Bank management official put it: "We have a very slight competitive edge on the interest rate, but only if processing does not become too onerous ... All these MICs [middle-income countries] have alternative sources, and some just won't put up with extra processing requirements. The idea is to recapture that clientele" (interview, October 4, 2011). In designing reforms, management have tried to strike a delicate balance between reducing bureaucratic burdens and responding to borrower demand, while at the same time placating non-borrowers wanting to retain tight control over MDB activities. Evidence suggests that despite their efforts, a few powerful non-borrower shareholders—especially the U.S.—have successfully resisted meaningful reform.

This lack of significant progress is obvious in overall project processing times, which have shown minimal improvement in recent years. ADB, for example, undertook a thorough review of their approval process, culminating a series of measures to improve process efficiency, but the expected impact would only be of sixteen to forty-two days (ADB 2015b). The World Bank piloted simplified processes starting in 2011 to accelerate approval for lower-risk projects, but risk aversion led staff to limit its use, and average World Bank times to board approval remain largely unchanged on average since 2013. An earlier effort called the Investment Lending Reform in the early 2000s at the World Bank was also largely unsuccessful, for similar reasons. As an official involved in these efforts said, "There hasn't been a whole lot of progress speeding up the process ... The incentives really aren't there. Senior management doesn't want to order people to simplify because they'll get caught in a trap and there'll be some scandal with the shareholders" (interview, October 4, 2011).

Reforming safeguards has also been fraught with problems. The legacy MDBs have made repeated attempts to move toward a risk-based approach that makes greater use of country systems. The World Bank launched a pilot for country systems use in 2005, with the vocal support of borrower countries in Board of Governor speeches (see for example World Bank 2005a and 2006a). Non-borrower shareholders, however—spurred by the NGO community (see for example CIEL 2008)—were much less enthusiastic. U.S. Treasury Secretary John Snow said his country looked "with concern at efforts to rush to use country systems that do not meet the highest international standards" (World Bank 2006c). Other statements of caution, expressing fears that country systems could weaken bank fiduciary and environmental safeguards, can be found in speeches by representatives of Switzerland (World Bank 2004), Germany (World Bank 2005b), the Nordic countries (World Bank 2006b), and Canada (World Bank 2007), among many others.

As a result, the country systems pilot was scaled back and more requirements were put in place. A World Bank procurement staffer in Latin America said, "We picked Brazil, Colombia, and Panama, and none of them met the minimum requirements. So we couldn't apply whole country systems. At the end of the day they [the countries] considered that the whole thing was not worth it" (interview, April 24, 2012). One European executive director (ED) at the World Bank said, "It was only normal that it failed, the design was a monster. It was more difficult to try to have 'sound' country systems than to blindly adopt the Bank's standards" (interview, January 25, 2012). A World Bank report on safeguards came to a similar conclusion: "client expectations that Bank safeguard responsibilities would be transferred to the borrower did not occur. Management clarified that this was never the intention of the pilots" (World Bank 2010, 85). One could forgive borrowing countries from wondering what the intention was, then. The experience of the regional MDBs with country systems on environmental and social issues has followed a similar unsuccessful path. More progress has been made using country systems for procurement—an issue less likely to catch the attention of the NGO community, and no longer so relevant for the non-borrower country business community since non-western firms increasingly dominate MDB project procurement tenders (see for example World Bank 2020d).

In the wake of the failed country systems efforts, World Bank management turned toward reforming the safeguard policies directly. The torturous process of this overhaul is a case study in how difficult it is for the legacy MDBs to undertake meaningful reform, particularly on an issue that mobilizes civil society organizations. The process began with discussions at the World Bank's Executive Board in July 2010, and internal discussions to arrive at an acceptable "approach paper" (World Bank 2012b) lasted until October 2012. That was followed by three rounds of consultations, focus groups, and workshops that involved 8,000 participants from sixty-three countries as well as hundreds of detailed comment submissions from all variety of stakeholders that lasted until March 2016. The new policy did not come into effect until October 1, 2018, and is being phased in over seven years, meaning that the system will not be fully in place until fifteen years after the reform process began.

As might be expected with such an unwieldy process, no one was happy with the outcome. Borrowers had hoped for reduced bureaucratic burden and greater use of their own laws and regulations, while many major non-borrowers as well as the NGO community pushed fiercely to avoid any dilution of the existing safeguard framework. One public comment from a grouping of 360 NGOs from 2014 is scathing: "We, the undersigned organisations, strongly object to the World Bank's safeguards draft since it falls far short of the rules needed to protect the environment and respect the rights of affected communities, workers and indigenous peoples. The draft derogates from well-established international standards and would effectively dismantle 30 years of policy evolution" (NGO statement 2014).

Far from easing the burden on borrowers, the U.S. government trumpeted that the reformed policy added new requirements related to human rights, LGBT rights, labor protection, indigenous heritage, climate change, consultations with affected people, and expanded safeguard oversight budget (U.S. Treasury 2016). On the potential use of borrower country systems in some areas, the U.S. was highly skeptical, stating that "the World Bank should be conservative in its use of borrower frameworks" (ibid., 3). Continued pressure from the U.S. to not relax the safeguards is evident from a highly critical U.S. position note related to an initial draft of the ESF's Guidance Notes for Staff (U.S. Treasury 2017).

Unsurprisingly, borrower countries voiced strong opposition to the direction of the reform. A statement by the World Bank executive director for India notes that his and six other borrower-led chairs believe that "the proposed environment and social standards (ESS) make doing business with the Bank more and more difficult and costly for the borrowers" (World Bank 2015a, 1). The statement says that the second draft policy had been pushed away from the initial intention of making greater use of national country systems, "even if such frameworks are substantially compliant with the standards," and decries the broadening of safeguards to new areas that was cited approvingly by the U.S. statement. He concludes bluntly: "If we go ahead with this kind of imposition of standards, the Bank is likely to go out of business" (ibid., 3).

A close reading of the new safeguards (World Bank 2017e) makes it evident that they do not represent a substantial shift toward giving greater respect to borrowers' own national priorities and easing the bureaucratic burden imposed by the World Bank. Simply the amount of text gives it away: the safeguard policy is over 120 pages, then each of the ten safeguards has their own detailed "guidance note to borrowers" running another thirty to forty pages. Watching this drama and aware of U.S. views (see for example U.S. Treasury 2013 and 2014 related to AfDB and EBRD safeguards, respectively), the regional MDBs considering reforms to their policies will no doubt proceed with caution.

Conclusions

The World Bank and four major regional MDBs are tremendous resources for providing global public goods that our world urgently needs and which no other type of organization can supply. They are a legacy not just of Cold War era geopolitics, but also of a time when wealthy western nations were willing and able to commit political and financial resources to multilateral institutions capable of tackling global challenges. The core of their operational model remains solid. Even if undercapitalized, all five of the legacy MDBs have strong balance sheets, AAA ratings, and a steady stream of investors across the globe eager to buy their bonds. Their network of in-country offices, depth of country knowledge, and relationships with developing country governments are unparalleled. The practical expertise of their staff to address critical development issues built over decades is a precious asset for helping shape the future of our planet for the better.

Despite these strengths, all five of these MDBs are held back by the same issue: governance. This is the other side of their legacy—of a time when a few powerful countries, led by the U.S., ruled much of the world with little challenge or question. That postwar era is gone, but the governance dynamics of the legacy MDBs have not kept pace. The U.S. and some other major shareholders are no longer committed to supporting the legacy MDBs as they had in the past, and all too often allow domestic concerns and interests to outweigh shared development priorities. A group of powerful shareholders have grown accustomed for forcing through policies favored by domestic constituencies, regardless of what that might do to the functional capacity and legitimacy of the MDBs. This approach to governance is a key weakness of the legacy MDBs, complicating their efforts to be seen as honest brokers trying to help promote development rather than as pawns of the G7.

The situation is most critical at the World Bank, which at first blush may seem surprising. The World Bank is still by far the largest of the legacy MDBs, with global reach, world-class expertise on just about any development topic, and a stellar reputation in financial markets. But pressured on all sides by shareholders and civil society organizations and with senior management trapped in the Washington D.C. echo chamber, the World Bank has to a degree lost its sense of purpose as a truly cooperative bank. The situation is less extreme at the regional MDBs. The U.S. and other major shareholders can still force through their policy preferences, but the impact of these policy impositions on the operational characteristics of the MDBs is softened through greater borrower country voting power and the significant presence of staffers from borrower countries. The regional MDBs tend to be more responsive to borrower development agendas, more flexible in how safeguards and other requirements are implemented, and able to keep financial policies more in line with borrower interests.

The mix of non-borrower and borrower country members has many beneficial aspects for the legacy MDBs. Wealthy non-borrower countries bring financial and fiscal strength, their own experiences on development, and legitimate concerns related to quality standards, sustainability, and impact measurement. Borrowers, in turn, bring their own unique experiences and perspectives on development to inform MDB operations and exchange with each other, and bolster the international legitimacy of the MDBs through their active membership. Borrowers also play a major role in the financial strength of the MDBs by granting preferred creditor treatment to help sustain their high bond ratings and generate net income. But as this chapter has demonstrated, in critical areas of financial and operational policy, the parochial interests of a few major shareholders are unbalancing governance and undermining financial capacity. The legacy MDBs are, in the end, cooperative banks for all their members, and finding a better governance balance more aligned with current geopolitical, economic, and developmental realities is essential to improve their effectiveness in facing the daunting challenges of the coming decades.

4

Borrower-Led MDBs

Developing Countries in Charge

The World Bank and four regional MDBs described in the previous chapter are by far the best-known and most visible development finance institutions, but at least twenty-five other MDBs are currently operating around the world. Most of these MDBs—including, for example, the Development Bank of Latin America (CAF), the Black Sea Trade and Development Bank (BSTDB), and the East African Development Bank (EADB)—are majority-owned by and operate entirely within lower and middle-income developing countries.

These borrower-led MDBs are, for the most part, considerably smaller in scale than the legacy MDBs. To take the two extremes, the World Bank's main lending window had an outstanding loan portfolio of US$204 billion in 2020, about 1,300 times larger than the US$150 million loan book of EADB. Despite these and many other differences, borrower-led MDBs have exactly the same basic organizational model as the legacy MDBs.

Although borrower-led MDBs are mostly overlooked in academic and policy circles, they face many of the same challenges as their larger siblings. And precisely because of their smaller size, the efforts of borrower-led MDBs to resolve the tensions built into the MDB model can be seen in sharper relief. Their experiences and trajectories are highly revealing about the functioning and structure of this particular type of international organization, which is sometimes obscured by the high-flowing rhetoric and institutional complexity of the legacy MDBs.

Many borrower-led MDBs have in recent years begun growing in size and policy relevance. CAF is the prime example, evolving from a functionally irrelevant and financially unstable organization in the 1970s to a Latin America–wide MDB with nineteen members that lends as much in most years as the World Bank and Inter-American Development Bank (IDB) in its countries of operation. Other smaller MDBs in Latin America, Africa, Eastern Europe, and Asia are following a similar path, as shareholders and management overhaul their administrations and find new sources of funding—especially bond markets—to turn them into much more developmentally useful organizations. Just since 2008, the twelve MDBs analyzed in detail in this chapter have seen asset growth of 150 percent (Figure 4.1), and some like Trade and Development Bank (TDB), FONPLATA, and International Investment Bank (IIB) have grown even faster.

Financing the Future. Chris Humphrey, Oxford University Press. © Christopher Humphrey (2022).
DOI: 10.1093/oso/9780192871503.003.0005

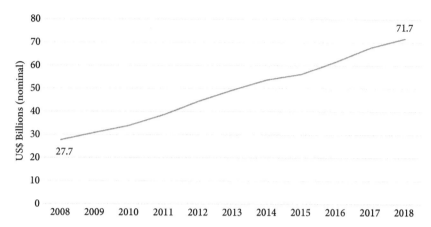

Figure 4.1 Asset Growth of Borrower-Led MDBs (2008–2018).

Source: Annual reports, 2008–2018.
Note: Includes CABEI, BDEAC, BOAD, BSTDB, CAF, EADB, EBID, EDB, ETDB, FONPLATA, IIB, and TDB.

Another reason why these MDBs are increasingly relevant is that they are controlled by developing countries themselves. In a world of shifting geopolitical alignments with U.S. power in retreat, international organizations dominated by emerging market and developing countries (EMDCs) assume an increasingly important role. Since the Paris Declaration on Aid Effectiveness (2005), Accra Agenda for Action (2008), and Busan Partnership (2011), the development community has promoted greater ownership of the development agenda by EMDCs themselves. The legacy MDBs have loudly espoused this rhetoric but have been much slower to implement it in practice. For borrower-led MDBs, country ownership is baked into their DNA. Their governance arrangements may prove better suited to the political and economic realities of the coming decades than that of the legacy MDBs.

This chapter begins with an overview of borrower-led MDBs, followed by an in-depth examination of the characteristics of a set of twelve borrower-led MDBs (Table 4.1). The subsequent section takes CAF as a case study, reviewing its evolution from obscurity in the 1970s to a major development institution now.

Overview

The key characteristic that differentiates the group of MDBs considered in this chapter from other MDBs is that decision-making power is in the hands of the same countries that borrow from them. This has major implications for governance dynamics, developmental priorities, operational policies and practices, and access to the financial resources needed to operate. Borrower-led MDBs are fundamentally different from the legacy MDBs in all these areas, despite having

Table 4.1 Overview of Twelve Borrower-Led MDBs (2020)

	Launch Year	Sovereign Members	Borrower Voting Power	Disbursed Portfolio (US$ million)	2020 Financing Approvals (US$ million)
Africa					
Trade and Development Bank (TDB)	1985	24	82.5%	5,363	3,657
West African Development Bank (BOAD)	1976	15	93.4%	4,363	485
Ecowas Bank for Investment and Development (EBID)	1979	15	100%	793	408
East Africa Development Bank (EADB)	1967	6	87%	381	184
Central African States Development Bank (BDEAC)	1975	10	51%	796	320
Americas					
Development Bank of Latin America (CAF)	1970	19	100%	28,321	14,147
Central American Bank for Economic Integration (CABEI)	1960	15	64.1%	7,948	3,459
Financial Fund for the Development of La Plata Basin (FONPLATA)	1974	5	100%	1,237	537

Continued

Table 4.1 *Continued*

	Launch Year	Sovereign Members	Borrower Voting Power	Disbursed Portfolio (US$ million)	2020 Financing Approvals (US$ million)
Eastern Europe/Central Asia					
Eurasian Development Bank (EDB)	2006	6	100%	2,730	1,336
Black Sea Trade and Development Bank (BSTDB)	1999	11	100%	1,973	933
International Investment Bank (IIB)	1970	9	100%	888	186
ECO Trade and Development Bank	2005	6	100%	514.8	Unavailable

Source: Annual reports and financial statements.
Notes: Disbursed portfolio and annual approvals include project loans, trade financing, and guarantees.

the same basic operational model, driven at the end of the day by different country shareholder composition.

This chapter brings to bear evidence from twelve borrower-led MDBs distributed across the globe: five in Africa; three in Latin America; and four in Eastern Europe/western Asia.[1] Those in Latin America and Africa were created alongside regional trade agreements, mostly in the 1960s and 1970s with the encouragement and support of the United Nations. Of the MDBs in Eastern Europe and Central Asia, IIB is the oldest, originally created in the Soviet era and encompassing Eastern bloc countries from Europe as well as Vietnam, Mongolia, and Cuba. The other three were founded after the collapse of communism in the region.

Research on borrower-led MDBs is thin compared to the reams of literature on the World Bank and major regional MDBs. An initial path-breaking study undertaken by the Institute for Development Studies (2000) was the first to systematically consider the entire range of MDBs. Although written as a policy study, it contains valuable insights on how MDBs differ from one another and what this means for the operational characteristics. More recent work in this direction includes Sagasti and Prada (2006), Griffith-Jones et al. (2008), Prada (2012), Humphrey and Michaelowa (2013 and 2019), Whitol (2014), Zappile (2016), Rosero and Rosero (2018), Delikanli et al. (2018), Kellerman (2019), Ray (2019), Humphrey (2014, 2016a, and 2019), and Bazbauers and Engel (2021).

Previous studies have tended to categorized the universe of MDBs in geographic terms—global, regional, and subregional. While a geographical categorization might arguably have made sense in past years, it is increasingly inappropriate now. CAF, for example, lends across all of Latin America and the Caribbean, so can hardly be termed a "subregional" MDB. Yet it would also not make sense to group it with "regional" MDBs like the Inter-American Development Bank (IDB), as it would miss the fundamental difference derived directly from different patterns of governance control. It is also hard to know how to characterize the geographically disparate shareholding of the IIB across former socialist countries and the New Development Bank (NDB) founded by the BRICs. This chapter instead focuses on their governance attribute of being led by borrower shareholders, rather than by a geographical category.

---

[1] Development Bank of the Central African States (BDEAC), West African Development Bank (BOAD), East African Development Bank (EADB), Ecowas Bank for Investment and Development (EBID) and Trade and Development Bank (TDB); Central American Bank for Economic Integration (CABEI), Development Bank of Latin America (CAF) and FONPLATA; Black Sea Trade and Development Bank (BSTDB), Economic Cooperation Organization Trade and Development Bank (ETDB), Eurasian Development Bank (EDB) and International Investment Bank (IIB). One important MDB not considered in this chapter is the Islamic Development Bank (IsDB), in part because its Islamic financing approach makes it difficult to easily compare with other MDBs. See Iqbal 2007 and Meenai 1989 for more on IsDB. The chapter also does not examine the Arab Bank for Economic Development in Africa (BADEA), which only lends to countries that are not shareholders. And the tiny Pacific Islands Development Bank is excluded as it is entirely dependent on the U.S government for all its funding, although the U.S. is not a shareholder.

What Makes Borrower-Led MDBs Different

The lessons of CAF's rapid growth in the 1990s and 2000s, recounted at the end of this chapter in more detail, have not been lost on other borrower-led MDBs. On the one hand it spurred existing MDBs to reform their approaches to replicate (with varying degrees of success) CAF's growth trajectory. On the other hand, it pointed the way to creating new borrower-led MDBs like BSTDB (launched 1997), EDB (launched 2006), and ETDB (launched 2008). The overall trend is clear: borrower-led MDBs as a group are growing quickly. None have yet reached the scale of CAF, but several are moving in that direction. The goal of this section is to show how the governance arrangements and the imperatives of their financial model have shaped the efforts of a group of twelve borrower-led MDBs to become relevant development institutions, and how that differs from the experiences of the legacy MDBs.

Governance: Variations on a theme

For all MDBs considered in this chapter, borrower member countries control a majority of regular votes as well all special majority votes on key issues like admitting new members, changing the capital structure, or reforming the articles of agreement.[2] At the same time, borrower-led MDBs are far from homogenous in their governance arrangements. These variations do not prevent analyzing borrower-led MDBs are a relatively coherent set of MDBs—especially in contrast to the legacy MDBs—but they are worth noting (see also Ray 2019).

The first and most obvious split is between MDBs that are entirely controlled by borrowers and those with some participation of non-borrowers. In Africa, four of the five functioning borrower-led MDBs have some non-borrower shareholding, including European donor nations such as Belgium, France, Germany, and Holland, emerging nations like China, India, and Kuwait, and other development finance institutions like African Development Bank and European Investment Bank. In all cases, non-borrowers are by statute limited to a minority position and can only purchase shares with reduced voting power. The only borrower-led MDB in Africa with no non-borrowing members is Ecowas Bank for Investment and Development (EBID), created in 1979 at the height of the oil price boom, and

[2] As noted in the previous chapter, AfDB formally fits this definition as well. However, AfDB depends on non-borrower donor nations to fund its concessional lending window (African Development Fund), which gives non-borrowers effective veto power over key aspects of AfDB governance. Similarly, borrower countries have a majority of votes in Caribbean Development Bank, but four major non-borrowers (Canada, Germany, Italy, and the U.K.) collectively can exercise *de jure* veto power over key decisions including membership, capital structure, electing the president and changes to the articles of agreement.

with Nigeria as by far the largest shareholder—a time when Nigeria wanted to use its newfound oil wealth to build regional influence.

By contrast, the two of the three borrower-led MDBs in Latin America and all four in Eastern Europe and Central Asia are 100 percent controlled by borrowers, with no non-borrower shareholders. These regions are historically less aid-dependent than Africa and with greater economic and fiscal capacity, making it more feasible to fund an MDB without external help. The exception is the Central American Bank for Economic Integration (CABEI), with 19 percent of shareholding by Taiwan, Korea, and Spain. As with the African MDBs, this likely had much to do with the reduced fiscal and economic strength of Central American nations when CABEI was founded. CABEI also restricts ownership of the more powerful "A" shares to borrower countries, thus benefiting from the presence of non-borrower shareholders (particularly to access financing) without giving up governance control.

A second major split is how governance power is distributed among borrower members. Three distinct groups are apparent:

- At one extreme are FONPLATA in South America and West African Development Bank (BOAD) and Central African States Development Bank (BDEAC) in Africa, all with exactly equal voting power among borrower members. TDB in Africa, BSTDB in Eastern Europe, and CAF also have relatively balanced governance among members, although a degree of differentiated shareholding and voting power.
- Several borrower-led MDBs concentrate power in a small group of shareholder countries. For example, Turkey, Iran, and Pakistan each control 30.9 percent of ETDB's voting power, while Azerbaijan, Kyrgyzstan, and Afghanistan divide up the remaining 7 percent. Central America's CABEI has reserved governance dominance to the five original founding countries, while other borrower and non-borrower shareholders have a minority shareholding status.
- A final set of MDBs are controlled mainly by a single member country much more economically and politically powerful than the other members. Examples include IIB and EDB (with Russia as the dominant shareholder) and EBID (Nigeria).

The internal governance dynamics of borrower-led MDBs are thus far from uniform. In-depth studies on individual cases—within regions, along different governance arrangements as outlined above, or in comparison with the legacy MDBs—is a rich potential vein of research for the future. For example, three of the more dynamic borrower-led MDBs—CAF, TDB, and BSTDB—all have relatively balanced governance arrangements, while three others with more unbalanced governance—IIB, EDB, and ETDB—have had less success in lending growth and access to finance. Whether this correlation is causal would be interesting to explore.

Funding

The financial terms at which an MDB funds itself is critical to its usefulness to borrowers. The search for funding has a major impact on the operations, strategies, and membership composition of borrower-led MDBs.

The AAA-rated legacy MDBs can raise resources via bond issues on international capital markets with ease. Borrower-led MDBs do not have this luxury. With no or only minimal shareholding by major industrialized countries, a much smaller loan portfolio, and lower international profile, they have to work hard to access bond markets at reasonable terms, or take more expensive loans from commercial banks. Borrower-led MDBs supplement relatively expensive commercial financing by seeking out other, less expensive sources of finance, including export banks or aid agencies from wealthier countries, to keep funding costs down and offer reasonably-priced loans to their borrowers. Borrower-led MDBs have a wide range of approaches to funding, depending on membership, track record, and perceived risk (Figure 4.2).

The impact of funding costs on the ability of borrower-led MDBs to offer competitive loan terms is a mentioned repeatedly in their internal strategies[3] and other

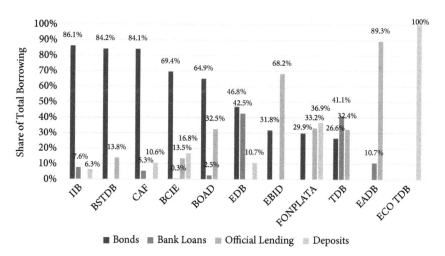

Figure 4.2 Sources of Borrowing, Selected MDBs (2020).
Source: 2020 MDB financial statements; 2019 for EADB, EBID, and ETDB.

---

[3] Publicly available strategies consulted for this chapter include: CABEI (2020), EBID (2016), BSTDB (2018), IIB (2017), EDB (2017a), and ETDB (2018b).

institutional documents. As ETDB's 2017 Annual Report states, "Obtaining the highest possible credit rating and the best possible financing terms for our members would be the essential targets of the coming period" (ETDB 2018a, 12). TDB's head of strategy noted that "we are not a AAA rated bank, that limits us on the cost of funding and our ability to compete for regional infrastructure projects that demand very competitive rates" (interview, May 15, 2017). An Ethiopian Finance Ministry official made the same point about TDB from the borrower point of view: "Our priority right now is financing big infrastructure projects. The government is not willing to borrow from TDB for that, because the volume is too small and interest rate too high" (interview, October 12, 2016). Addressing this obstacle was a key reason behind TDB's efforts to arrange $835 million in concessional financing from the World Bank for infrastructure, announced in 2020 (World Bank, 2020e).

Because of these challenges, it is no exaggeration to say that borrower-led MDBs are obsessed with their access to funding. The institutional strategy of EBID gives a sense of the array of different funding sources pursued by borrower-led MDBs:

> Efforts to strengthen the Bank's ability to contract debt are all geared towards mobilizing resources from the regional as well as foreign money and capital markets ... the Bank will issue debts on the U.S. capital market; the Nigerian capital market; the Chinese money and capital markets, among others. Resources will also be mobilised from Afreximbank; Eximbank India, OFID [OPEC Fund for International Development], ETC [Italy's Export, Trade and Cooperation agency] and China Eximbank.
>
> (EBID 2016, 73)

Borrower-led MDBs in Latin America and Africa relied in their early years mainly or entirely on official sources, and still do, to a degree. This has included credit lines from bilateral aid agencies of wealthy countries like Germany and France or from legacy MDBs, export promotion agencies from countries like China, India, and Korea, and global trust funds especially related to environmental and climate issues. Official funding is less expensive than market-based funding, which makes it easier for an MDB to be able to on-lend for development projects at reasonable financial terms.

However, official funding has downsides. First and foremost, it is unreliable, depending on the budgetary situation of official sources as well as the political leanings of donor governments. Second, official funding is in most cases "tied" in some way. In the case of export agencies, the tie is clear: resources must be used to purchase goods or services from the export agencies' home country companies. Aid agencies often have their own "ties," such as mandating that funding is used in certain sectors like health and education or requiring the MDB to follow certain rules related to environmental protection or gender. This is the case, for example, for the growing number of borrower-led MDBs seeking to access low-cost international funds like the Global Environment Facility or Green Climate Fund. While these requirements might be commendable in the eyes of many, they also limit the independence of the MDB and end-borrowers to make their own decisions on how to best use the resources—restrictions not imposed by commercial financiers.

Deposits supply a portion of the funding of at least seven borrower-led MDBs. Deposits are essentially the only source of borrowing for ETDB and account for about one-third of FONPLATA's total liabilities, while they are a smaller share at the others. MDBs in Latin America and Africa take deposits mainly from the central banks and government ministries of member governments, while the newer MDBs in Eastern Europe and Central Asia appear to mostly accept deposits from private corporations (although detailed information is not available). Regardless of the source, the main drawback of accepting deposits is that they can be withdrawn at short notice, meaning that MDBs tend to use these resources mainly to support short-term loans to borrowers, such as for trade financing, rather than long-term project loans.

While official funding and bank deposits can be useful, market funding is what has made the legacy MDBs such a remarkably powerful set of development institutions and has fueled the rapid growth of borrower-led MDBs like CAF, CABEI, and TDB. Being able to borrow regularly from commercial banks or bond markets at reasonable rates gives MDB operational autonomy and financial strength. Commercial resources come with no "ties" on how the money can be spent or on an MDB's development agenda and policies—only that the resources be repaid on time at a given interest rate. This frees an MDB from having to go hat in hand to fickle official lending sources and gives it the freedom to chart its own growth trajectory based on the wishes of its shareholders and the demand of its borrowers.

Market borrowing comes from two sources: an MDB can either take out a loan directly from a commercial bank or it can issue a bond on capital markets. In most cases, the interest rates on a bond are lower than on a bank loan. This is especially true of bonds issued in hard currencies like U.S. dollar, Euro, Swiss franc, or Japanese yen, which can draw from a huge pool of investors. However, issuing bonds on international capital markets requires a good rating from one of the major credit rating agencies, which is not easy to come by for borrower-led MDBs. As a result, most have begun their market financing by first borrowing from banks before attempting to obtain a credit rating and issuing bonds.

Accessing bond markets is a top priority for all borrower-led MDBs, as noted repeatedly in strategy documents, annual reports, and investor presentations. For example, EBID's most recent strategy states that an MDB's "ability to easily tap into capital markets, at attractive rates, is of prime importance for its medium to long-term sustainability" (EBID 2016, 49; see also CABEI 2020, IIB 2017, and BSTDB 2018, among others). CAF was the first borrower-led MDB to receive a rating from one of the three major agencies (S&P, Moody's, and Fitch), but by 2020 ten of the twelve MDBs examined in this chapter had a rating from at least one of the

Table 4.2 International Bond Ratings for Borrower-Led MDBs (2020)

	Moody's	S&P	Fitch
FONPLATA	A2	A–	N.R.
TDB	Baa3	N.R.	BB+
CABEI	Aa3	AA	N.R.
CAF	Aa3	A+	AA–
BOAD	Baa1	N.R.	BBB
EADB	Baa3	N.R.	N.R.
BSTDB	A2	A–	N.R.
EDB	Baa1	BBB	BBB+
IIB	A3	A–	A–
EBID	B2	N.R.	B

Source: MDB investor information.
Note: N.R. = not rated.

agencies (Table 4.2). Nine of the ratings were "investment grade" or better by at least one rating agency—a key threshold allowing major institutional investors to buy the bonds. Only ETDB had no rating, and EBID had a sub-investment grade rating.

The trend has been to move increasingly toward bond markets and away from official lenders and bank loans. For example, in 1996, CABEI relied on bank loans for 83 percent of its borrowing, but by 2020 that share had fallen to only 13.5 percent, while 69 percent came from bond issues in eighteen currencies. BSTDB, founded in 1997, was able to arrange its first syndicated bank loan in 2004, issued its first local currency bond in 2009, and by 2020 had eight bonds outstanding worth over US$1.3 billion in six currencies. After decades of relying mainly on official credit lines, BOAD obtained an international credit rating in 2015 and by 2020 relied on bond markets for two-thirds of all funding. The IIB, founded in 1970 to support socialism across the Soviet bloc, now obtains 86 percent of its funding by borrowing from capital markets in Russia and Central Asia.

While raising funds from bond markets offers tremendous funding potential, it also brings operational pressures and limitations. The difficulties begin with country membership. By definition, borrower-led MDBs have no or only small shareholding by wealthy non-borrower countries. The bond rating of an MDB's shareholders is a major factor in how ratings agencies evaluate the financial strength of the MDB (see Chapter 1 for an overview). Of the twelve borrower-led MDBs considered in this chapter, four have no share capital from member countries rated above A–, and the remainder range between 1 percent (BDEAC) and 18 percent (IIB). None of their members have a AAA or AA+ rating, which carries the most weight for how the credit rating agencies evaluate MDBs, compared to about one-third of the member shareholding of the legacy MDBs.

Beyond membership, borrower-led MDBs face a number of other ratings obstacles that are more problematic compared to the legacy MDBs, including:

- **Capital**: Capital adequacy is a key ratings factor, and borrower-led MDBs have a more difficult time getting capital from their shareholders due to member government budget constraints.
- **Riskiness of loan portfolio**: Some (but not all) borrower-led MDBs have had historically spotty track records of being repaid on time by their borrowers.
- **Administration**: Borrower-led MDBs are in many cases perceived by ratings agencies as not having strong internal systems for managing risks and ensuring loan quality compared to the legacy MDBs.
- **Policy importance**: Ratings agencies assess how important an MDB is to shareholder governments, and borrower-led MDBs invariably score worse than the legacy MDBs.
- **Governance**: All three major ratings agencies explicitly consider an MDB's governance to be inherently weaker when it is controlled by the same countries to which it lends (see for example S&P 20120b 53).

As a result, borrower-led MDBs find it impossible to achieve a AAA rating. The highest-rated is CABEI, at AA (two notches below AAA on S&P's scale), followed by CAF at A+, and BSTDB, FONPLATA, and IIB at A-.[4] While these ratings compare well with many sovereign country ratings as well as major corporations, they still result in a considerably higher cost of funding—and hence higher loan prices—compared to the legacy MDBs.

Membership

Membership of the twelve MDBs considered in this chapter range from a low of five countries (FONPLATA) to a high of twenty-four (TDB)—far fewer than the legacy MDBs. Having few member countries can be advantageous in agreeing on MDB policies, but it has drawbacks related to financing. Fewer members mean less share capital (which limits lending capacity) and a much smaller pool of borrowers (which makes it harder to find viable projects). A loan portfolio with fewer borrowers is perceived as riskier by ratings agencies, since an economic crisis in one country can lead to repayment problems for a large share of an MDB's outstanding loans. Having fewer members reduces an MDB's policy relevance and potential development impact, weakening its international reputation and standing.

[4] IIB was downgrade sharply as a result of the Ukraine crisis in spring 2022. See Humphrey 2022.

Most borrower-led MDBs explicitly include membership expansion as a key element of their strategies. IIB's most recent strategy puts it clearly: "A strategic vector for the Bank's development is to expand the IIB's historical footprint by drawing in new participants. The principal objectives of admitting new members are: Gaining access to new markets and clients; Obtaining new financial resources and other forms of support; Growth of assets and the loan portfolio; Gaining professional skills and expertise; Improving Bank's credit ratings" (IIB 2017, 13). Similarly, CABEI's strategy states that "attracting new member countries will help meet the growing financing needs of the region, improve the terms of financing, expand the credit capacity of the institution, provide new capital and improve the credit rating" (CABEI 2019, 12, author's translation).

Membership expansion can come through three main routes. The first is to bring in new borrower countries in the same geographic region as existing members. For example, CAF has incorporated ten additional countries in Latin America and the Caribbean since it began expanding, while TDB increased the number of regional member countries from fifteen in 1996 to twenty-two by 2020. The most advantageous members to bring in from an MDB's perspective are stable middle-income countries, as they offer the best prospects for making larger loans with lower risk and bringing in more highly-rated shareholder capital, both of which work in favor of an MDB's image in financial markets. IIB's institutional strategy states, "As priority candidates for full-fledged membership, the Bank primarily considers rapidly expanding and politically stable medium-sized and small countries" (IIB 2017, 21).

Attracting new borrower members requires convincing prospective countries that the benefits of membership are worth the shareholder capital investment. This is not always obvious, as borrower-led MDBs cannot offer as good financial terms or technical assistance as the legacy MDBs. Another important disincentive can be governance. Several borrower-led MDBs are dominated by one or a few countries, and new members might not like the prospect of being in a subservient position. This was a lesson learned by CAF in the 1990s: the original five founding member countries decided to give up special rights in CAF governance, which quickly led to a rapid increase in membership. Similarly, CABEI reformed its articles of agreement in 2016 to reduce the control of its original five founding members. Since that reform, three new countries (Cuba, Belize, and Korea) have joined, and two existing non-founding members (Panama and Dominican Republic) have increased their capital shares.

The second approach is to attract non-borrower countries to take a small capital stake. The backing of non-borrower shareholders gives a major boost to the credibility of a borrower-led MDB and brings in highly-rated shareholder capital (which helps an MDB's bond rating) and potential access to lines of credit from development or export agencies. Targeting new non-borrower shareholders is a stated strategic priority of BOAD, EBID, CABEI, and TDB. CABEI's strategy states that it seeks to "incorporate highly-rated and industrialized country shareholders" for the explicit purpose of increasing its own rating from AA to AAA (CABEI 2019, 17).

The trade-off is that non-borrower country shareholders have their own views on development and operations that can constrain the MDB. This might include requiring stricter environmental, social, gender, or procurement policies than favored by borrower shareholders, encouraging lending to certain sectors or countries based on the priorities of non-borrowers, or requesting changes in the policies and administration of the MDB itself. The delicacy of this trade-off is reflected in CABEI's strategy: "The incorporation of new members brings with it new opinions about CABEI's medium and long-term trajectory. As a result, it is important to establish a capitalization process that reflects the relevance of CABEI to its [new] partners and vice versa" (ibid., 17, author's translation).

Borrower-led MDBs have taken different approaches to incorporating non-borrower members:

- In **Africa**, BOAD, BDEAC, and EADB have a mix of traditional donor countries such as Germany, France, Holland, and Belgium as shareholders, along with rising middle-income countries like China, India, and Kuwait. TDB also has China as a shareholder. The advantage of shareholders like China and India is that they bring access to new sources of finance like export credit lines and do not have the same type of policy agendas of traditional donors, but the downside is that they are less helpful in boosting the MDB's credit rating due to their own lower sovereign rating.
- In **Latin America**, CAF and CABEI both have opted to take on Spain—which has obvious historical links to the region—as well as Korea and Taiwan (for CABEI) and Portugal (for CAF). These countries provide useful financial support through capital and credit lines and have been circumspect about trying to influence MDB policies.
- In **Eastern Europe and Central Asia**, none of the borrower-led MDBs have or are pursuing non-borrower members. These MDBs clearly prioritize governance independence over a quicker route to a higher credit rating or official credit lines.

A third approach is to bring in non-sovereign official shareholders. BOAD, BDEAC, EADB, and TDB in Africa all have had African Development Bank as a shareholder for many years, and the European Investment Bank is also a shareholder of BOAD. These larger MDBs both bring AAA-rated share capital, which is extremely valuable for the MDB's bond rating, as well as access to low-cost credit lines. The role they play as shareholders in influencing MDB policy and administration is not entirely evident, but likely includes some pressure on loan standards and financial policy. BSTDB apparently sees the value of this approach and has prioritized finding a top-rated MDB "with a large presence on the global development stage" as a member, with the aim of "providing a boost to the Bank's credit and financial profiles" (BSTDB 2018, 23).

A final option, currently pursued at scale only by TDB in Africa, is to attract financial institutions as shareholders. As of 2020, TDB had 18 institutional investors as members (mainly regional insurance and pension funds). The benefit of such a strategy is to provide new capital to TDB from institutions with no policy agenda of their own. The downside is that these shareholders expect a return on their investment. That requires TDB to generate sufficient net income to pay a dividend, which puts pressure on TDB's ability to make development loans at attractive financial terms. This trade-off is one that other borrower-led MDBs have decided is not beneficial, at least thus far.[5] In spring 2020 TDB announced plans to launch a new share class for international impact investors, further ramping up its strategy of opening share capital (Humphrey 2021a).

Lending patterns

Borrower-led MDBs tend to have different lending patterns than the legacy MDBs (although with considerable variance), for two main reasons. On the one hand, the countries backing borrower-led MDBs may have different ideas on what constitutes "development" compared to the major shareholders of the legacy MDBs. On the other, the financial realities facing borrower-led MDBs—higher cost of funding and the need to maintain bond ratings—embeds strong incentives to lend to projects and borrowers that are at times closer to what a commercial bank might fund. While this does not necessarily make borrower-led MDBs less useful, it does mean that their development additionality is sometimes more difficult to clearly establish compared to the legacy MDBs.

A first key variance is whether an MDB lends more to governments and state-owned enterprises versus private sector companies. Why would an MDB prefer to provide loans to government borrowers or to the private sector? Developmental orientation is a key factor. EBRD, for example, was created to support the growth of a market economy in the former socialist countries, and as a result is much more focused on private sector lending compared to the other legacy MDBs. A similar breakdown is apparent in borrower-led MDBs (Figure 4.3). Those based in Latin America and Africa—regions with a more traditional "developmentalist"

---

[5] EADB also has a group of institutional investors that can receive a dividend, but the bank has not paid out dividends in recent years due to poor financial performance.

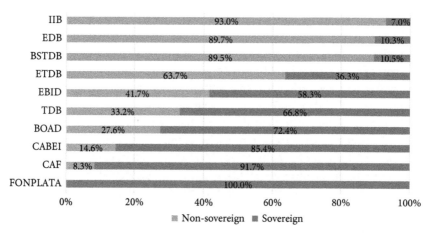

Figure 4.3 Sovereign vs. Non-Sovereign Share of Loan Portfolios (2020).
Source: 2020 MDB financial statements.
Note: "Sovereign" refers to loans guaranteed by the government, even if the loan is to a private or state-owned enterprise. Breakdown not available for BDEAC or EADB.

ethos—are more heavily weighted toward public sector lending (80–90 percent of lending in Latin America's CAF and CABEI, and 60–70 percent for TDB, BOAD, and EBID in Africa). By contrast, BSTDB, EDB, and IIB in Eastern Europe and western Asia lend around 90 percent to private sector borrowers.

Lending to governments has the added benefit of strengthening an MDB's loan portfolio quality, as sovereign borrowers are less risky than private sector borrowers. Governments are likely to repay loans to financial institutions of which they are themselves shareholders—the basis of preferred creditor treatment. Borrower-led MDBs, several of which have historically struggled with bad loans and have at times had non-performing loan levels up to 15–20 percent or more of their portfolio, have a strong incentive to lend more to governments as a way to strengthen their financial profile and bond rating. BSTDB's strategy emphasized its intention of increasing its share of public sector loans for the explicit purpose of "conferring a more favorable risk profile to the Bank's portfolio" (BSTDB 2018, 12).

However, the interest rates offered by borrower-led MDBs are often too high to be attractive to governments, many of whom can access cheaper loans from legacy MDBs or sometimes even bond markets directly. BSTDB attributed its low public sector lending to "the insufficient price competitiveness relative to AAA-rated MDBs who offer public sector lending at flat low rates" (BSTDB 2019, 46). CAF and CABEI in Latin America have had more success lending to governments in large part because of their high bond rating and hence low funding costs. FONPLATA lends entirely to governments, but it also lends only its (cost-free) shareholder equity, meaning it can offer very good financial terms, although this appears likely to change going forward.[6] Some MDBs in Africa make substantial public loans despite low bond ratings because of access to concessional credit lines from official sources like bilateral donor agencies and export agencies. The relative high cost of market-based funding by MDBs in Eastern Europe and Central Asia raise make their loan prices less competitive for government borrowers, which partly explains why they lend more to private borrowers.

The project sector is also shaped strongly by financial considerations. Projects oriented toward poverty reduction, social protection, primary education, and basic health—top priorities of the legacy MDBs—are almost entirely absent in the loan portfolios of borrower-led MDBs. Instead, the operational focus is on financial services, industry, commerce, and infrastructure. From a borrower country's point of view, higher-priced loans from borrower-led MDBs should not be used for social programs, but rather for projects that are financially bankable. As an Ethiopian Finance Ministry official put it: "The World Bank and AfDB lend in areas where we don't expect financial returns. For funding from other sources, we use it where we expect a financial return" (interview, October 14, 2016). For the MDBs themselves, the likelihood of being repaid is much higher for projects that generate financial returns. As a TDB staffer put it, "Projects have to be commercially viable for us to support ... Even a public sector project has to be attached to a cash flow that has to be sustainable. Otherwise we are not handing money out" (interview, May 15, 2017).

Several borrower-led MDBs engage in trade finance as opposed to more traditional project finance. TDB moved heavily into trade finance since the early 2000s as a key part of its growth strategy, with trade loans amounting to 58 percent of its portfolio in 2020. IIB's strategy is explicitly targeting growth in trade finance going forward (see IIB 2017). Trade finance makes sense for an MDB seeking to promote regional integration, and also makes sense financially. Trade finance is extremely safe (as the traded good itself serves as collateral), short term, and simple to prepare and process. On the other hand, the developmental value-added of trade financing is not always clear, especially if it is financing consumption goods imported from outside the region.

Bureaucracy, safeguards, and policy role

The challenges faced by borrower-led MDBs to access low-cost funding has a major impact on their ability to be a useful source of development finance to

---

[6] FONPLATA issued its first bond in 2019 and in the same year modified its statutes to permit non-sovereign lending. As a result of this new funding strategy, the interest rates it offers on its loans is likely to increase.

their members. A key way that they offset their price disadvantage is by being as "borrower-friendly" as possible in other aspects of their operations—including bureaucracy and decision-making, safeguard standards, and policy role. While these strategies have had considerable success in maintaining demand for lending, they also pose risks to an MDB's reputation and development impact.

Decision-making and bureaucracy

The speed of project approval and disbursement is a critical advantage for borrower-led MDBs. As discussed in Chapter 3, the legacy MDBs are extremely bureaucratic, taking up to two years or more to move a loan project through the approval process to first disbursement, and requiring complex paperwork and multiple project preparation missions. Alleviating that burden can go a long way to offsetting the price disadvantage of borrower-led MDB lending from the point of view of government officials eager to move ahead quickly with projects.

Borrower-led MDBs are well aware of this. As EDB's 2016 annual report states, "EDB is not in a position to offer competitive prices to customers as compared to the largest state-owned banks or national and international development institutions ... In these conditions, EDB concentrated on strengthening its competitive advantages that are unrelated to prices. This is, in the first place, the short time for project preparation and consideration" (EDB 2017b, 6). Similarly, IIB's 2018–2022 strategy outlines a number of internal efficiency reform measures "to reduce the time frame of the credit process, and also, if possible, to decrease the number of participants and documents used. If properly optimised, the credit process could give the Bank a real competitive advantage compared to other IFIs [international financial institutions], and possibly some commercial players" (IIB 2017, 24).

Evidence suggests that many borrower-led MDBs are succeeding in this effort. Government official interviewees in ten Latin American and Caribbean countries emphasized how much faster CAF and CABEI are in designing and approving loans compared to the World Bank and IDB. As one former Peruvian vice-minister of finance said, "The main reason we would use the CAF is that it disburses very quickly. The World Bank takes eighteen months, the IDB twelve months and the CAF three months. They [CAF] can even do it in a month and a half if you really need it" (interview, June 8, 2009, author's translation). A former director of public credit in Panama agreed with this assessment of CAF, and added that "CABEI is more like CAF, it is a lot faster [then the World Bank and IDB] in approving projects" (interview, November 14, 2013, author's translation).

The ability of borrower-led MDBs to prepare, approve, and disburse financing quickly is a direct result of the fact that unlike the legacy MDBs, they do not have non-borrower shareholders imposing rigid strictures to ensure that staff do not deviate from their views on development. Borrower-led MDBs can follow a much more streamlined set of procedures to approve and disburse loans. TDB's lead project finance official described the process:

We put together a concept paper, and then once that is approved, it goes to term sheets to negotiate with clients. If the client can move fast, then our due diligence can be done in two or three weeks, then we submit our proposal to the Operations and Technical committee, and then a week after that to the Credit Committee. If the loan is less than US$10 million, the Credit Committee can approve it by itself, and if it's more it goes to the board. But we don't usually have to wait long for board approval, since they can approve loans electronically without having to wait for a physical meeting.

(interview, May 16, 2017)

Other borrower-led MDBs for which information is available follow a similar process—first a concept review, then some type of operations committee to assess the technical and developmental merits, then a credit review to consider the financial and portfolio impacts of the project, followed by board approval. The shareholders of several borrower-led MDBs, including BSTDB, CAF, ETDB, and TDB, delegate project approval of certain types and below a defined financial threshold to the MDB president or credit committee. This type of authority granted by shareholders is revealing of the trust they have in management and the alignment of views between the two. By contrast, the legacy MDBs have only just begun delegating limited authority for project approval to management, and only in specific, highly restricted circumstances.

Board administration is also markedly different at borrower-led MDBs. Unlike the full-time executive boards of legacy MDBs, borrower-led MDB boards are almost entirely non-resident (CABEI being the only exception of the twelve in this chapter) and meet a few times a year or, if needed, take votes electronically without physically meeting at all. Board members are usually higher-level officials, often vice-ministers, ministers, or central bank governors, meaning they are empowered to take decisions without consulting with their governments. This accelerates decision-making and depoliticizes the activities of the board compared to the legacy MDBs.

Environmental and social standards

Another marked difference between the legacy and borrower-led MDBs is environmental and social safeguard policies. Borrower countries have long objected to the environmental and social safeguards of legacy MDBs, and borrower-led MDBs have unsurprisingly avoided imposing the same kind of requirements. Instead, they rely heavily on following the laws and regulations of the country in which a project is implemented. Of the twelve MDBs reviewed in this chapter, only six have any type of published policy on environmental and social impact.[7] In almost

---

[7] BSTDB (2016); CAF (2016); ETDB (2007); EDB (undated); IIB (2015); TDB (2020).

all cases the documents are brief and focus on the requirement of the MDB to comply with all local laws and regulations—very different from the extremely detailed, legalistic, and ex ante safeguard policy requirements of the legacy MDBs.

Despite this general deference to country standards and laws, many borrower-led MDBs are starting to adopt new policies to manage environmental and social impacts. This is driven in part by a desire to access low-cost concessional financing. Many sources of concessional financing—like the European Investment Bank, the Global Environment Facility, the Green Climate Fund, or Germany's GIZ aid agency—require borrower-led MDBs to have certain environmental and social standards before they can access low-cost credit lines or co-finance projects. Examples of the link between external agencies and a greater focus on environmental and social issues on the part of borrower-led MDBs are myriad. CABEI established an Office of Environmental and Social Sustainability in 2017 (with technical assistance from Germany's GIZ), and shortly after began accessing financing from the GCF (CABEI 2019b, 1, 15, and 108). BSTDB's strategy calls for policy changes to be able to receive accreditation from the GCF, as it "would enhance the business profile of BSTDB and improve access to climate financing on more favorable terms" (BSTDB 2018, 20).

While the initial impetus to reformulate approaches to environmental and social issues may come from external influences, that does not mean it is purely a cynical façade to access low-cost financing. It is not realistic to expect an MDB controlled by developing countries to impose rigid safeguards on their members. At the same time, the desire of these MDBs to access other sources of finance, to be perceived as top-class development institutions, and to avoid problematic projects all orient toward a gradual strengthening internal standards on what sorts of projects they take on and how they implement them. This process could move toward finding a balance between promoting international standards (pushed by the legacy MDBs) while still respecting the rights of countries to set their own priorities and development paths (favored by borrower-led MDBs).

Policy conditionality and technical assistance

A final major operational difference between borrower-led and legacy MDBs is their influence on the policies of recipient governments. Borrower-led MDBs do not engage in policy pressure on governments, in line with their overall approach of respecting the sovereignty of their members. Several borrower-led MDBs do offer financing that serves as de facto budget support, but none come with policy conditionality akin to the legacy MDBs.

CAF is the only one of the twelve MDBs considered in this chapter explicitly engaging in policy-based budget loans (since 2010), although CABEI intends to begin offering policy loans in the future (CABEI 2019, 10). In 2020, CAF policy lending amounted to US$2.3 billion in loan approvals, about 16 percent of total approvals that year. The policy content of the loans is not publicly available, but interviews with government officials in Latin America consistently emphasized that CAF does not impose policies on borrowers. As a high-level CAF official said in an interview, "We are much more respectful of internal politics of countries, to impose conditions would go against the principle of our shareholders" (interview, August 23, 2011, author's translation). A Dominican Republic Finance Ministry vice-minister agreed, saying "The CAF doesn't have these preconceived views, like what's the role of the state in specific industries or not, as is the case of the IDB and the World Bank" (interview, November 20, 2013, author's translation).

The flip side of not attempting to shape policies is that borrower-led MDBs have relatively little to offer in the way of knowledge and expertise to go along with their financing. This is a key strength of the legacy MDBs that is highly valued by many governments. The vast majority of government officials interviewed in fourteen countries in Africa and Latin America explicitly noted that the high quality of expertise and technical assistance offered by the World Bank in many cases offsets bureaucratic hassles. Borrower-led MDBs are, for the most part, not equipped to provide this sort of support to recipients. In cases where the borrower has clear ideas of project goals and design, this is not an obstacle, but when borrowers seek technical support they may prefer to work with a legacy MDB instead.

Several borrower-led MDBs intend to ramp up their knowledge and technical support services as a way of strengthening their competitive offer to recipients. But in-house expertise requires substantial investment in highly qualified staff. Borrower-led MDBs work tirelessly to bring down their administrative budget, and hiring top-notch sectoral experts would increase administrative costs and put pressure on the cost of their loans. It is no accident that the borrower-led MDBs advancing the most with knowledge and technical services are CAF and CABEI, which have high bond ratings and relatively low funding costs. For most others, building such capacity is not realistic in the near term.

CAF: Pathbreaker for Borrower-Led MDBs

CAF in Latin America has by far the most successful trajectory of all borrower-led MDBs and has served as a model for what an MDB controlled by developing countries can do.[8] It is no surprise that the BRICS nations closely examined CAF's history when designing the NDB. From an inward-looking and money-

---

[8] Portions of this section were first published in Humphrey 2016a and 2016b.

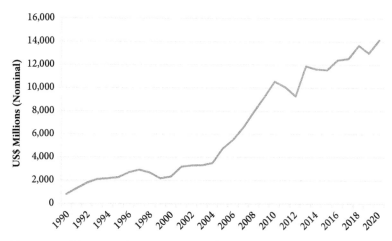

Figure 4.4 CAF Annual Loan Approvals (1990–2020).
Source: CAF annual reports, 1990–2020.

losing organization in the 1970s, CAF has transformed into a major source of development finance across the Americas. As with many smaller MDBs in Latin America and Africa, CAF was originally intended to promote regional economic integration (Fresard 1969). CAF's rapid growth starting in the 1990s (Figure 4.4) has shown other borrower-led MDBs what is possible based on a clear strategy and internal reform, and without the need to accept high-income shareholder countries.

CAF's first two decades did not look promising. Among the many problems when it opened for business in 1970, by far the most pressing was raising resources. The six founding countries had committed US$25 million in capital, but this would be paid in over the course of several years, making it essential that CAF quickly find other resources to on-lend. This proved to be no easy task. USAID provided a US$15 million soft loan in 1971, and Canada soon followed suit with another US$5 million, but what CAF originally saw as "initial" loans (CAF 1971, 34, author's translation) were never renewed. Further financial support expected from the World Bank and the IDB (ibid., 33) never materialized. Neither U.S. nor European capital markets showed any inclination to invest in CAF bonds, despite repeated visits to major investment banks (ibid., 34 and CAF 1974, 23).

Project lending was also problematic, with the bank's mandate of promoting regional integration running up against the more parochial interests of member governments. CAF sent out an initial mission in 1971 to put together a portfolio of potential projects. However, as that year's annual report noted, "The most common characteristics of these projects and initiatives was their limited integration content. The majority had strictly national characteristics" (CAF 1971, 21, author's translation). This problem was mentioned repeatedly in early annual reports. Lending declined further in the late 1970s as a result of the withdrawal of Chile (following a coup by a right-wing military dictatorship) as well as easy access by member governments to commercial loans during the petrodollar lending boom of the 1970s.

Changing direction in the 1980s

By the early 1980s CAF's finances were in a precarious state, with three years of net losses, negative reserve levels, and only US$15 million in loans committed in 1981. From this low point, CAF began to reform itself. In his 1981 inaugural speech, President José Corsino Cárdenas called for CAF to "adjust its institutional structure and launch new initiatives such that it can convert itself into ... a true financial agent for its shareholders and an organization that does more than just survive" (CAF 1981, 13, author's translation).

This meant, first and foremost, boosting CAF's attractiveness as a lender. The board approved a new Operations Policy in 1983, designed to "overcome the limitations of the existing operations policy, designed basically for industrial programming and free trade within the Andean Group" and turn to "other areas previously not addressed by the CAF" (CAF 1986, author's translation). In other words, regional integration—CAF's original *raison d'être*—was no longer the top priority. As well, loans increasingly went directly to governments or state-owned enterprises, rather than higher-risk private sector borrowers.

As a result, loan commitments climbed from US$40 million in 1982 to US$263 million in 1990. CAF also began selecting projects much more carefully, as indicated by the reduction in canceled projects from 43 percent of total value during 1971–1980 to 11 percent in 1982–1986 (CAF 1986). Net income rose from US$1.8 million in 1980 to US$35 million in 1990, and financial reserves grew from US$300,000 in 1980 to US$22 million in 1986 and US$200 million by 1993 (Figure 4.5).

The quantum leap in the CAF's performance came when former IDB staffer Luis Enrique García became president in 1991 and set about reorienting CAF's funding toward capital markets. He was clear about his goal right from the start, as he described in a later interview: "When I joined the CAF, particularly because of my experience with the IDB, I saw the future of the CAF as an institution relying essentially on CAF's ability to tap the international capital market. Because if it was only relying on the old capital or short-term lines of credit or even loans from the IDB, the institution really had no chance to grow" (Latin Finance 1998, 147).

Immediately after taking charge in 1991, García traveled to New York to obtain a rating from S&P and Moody's. This was an ambitious request, considering that not a single country in Latin America had investment grade and four of the five CAF government shareholders were among the most notorious debt trouble spots in the

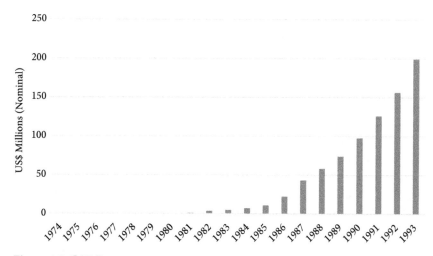

Figure 4.5 CAF Reserves.
Source: CAF annual reports, 1974–1993.

world during the 1980s. García hired a former World Bank vice president to help overhaul internal processes and revise operational and financial policies "with the aim of broadening its sources of financing" (CAF 1992, 57, author's translation). As a result, S&P and Moody's awarded CAF an investment grade rating in 1993 (CAF 1993). During the same year, CAF issued three bonds for a total of US$289 million in Europe and Japan, raising more freely usable resources in one year than it had in its entire previous two decades combined.

From an Andean MDB to Development Bank of Latin America

In parallel with the overhaul of internal policies and financial strategy, CAF began a concerted drive to expand membership. Mexico joined in 1990, Chile returned in 1992, Trinidad and Tobago joined in 1993, and Brazil—the biggest country in Latin America—joined in 1995. By 2020, CAF had nineteen member countries. Initially, the five founding members reserved "A" shares for themselves, while new members could only join as "B" or "C" class shareholders. This gave the founders more governance power, as CAF's Articles of Agreement (CAF 2015) stipulate that a unanimous vote of A shareholders is required to modify the Articles of Agreement (Art. 15) and A shares have a greater weight in Board of Governor votes (Art. 17). But in 2005, CAF opened up ownership of A shares to all member countries—a key shift in paradigm. By 2020, Argentina, Brazil, Panama, Trinidad and Tobago, and Uruguay were all A shareholders.

New members expanded the bank's capital base, increasing its financial capacity and greatly diversifying CAF's loan portfolio, which (as discussed in Chapter 2) is a key risk factor in the eyes of bond ratings agencies. In a less tangible but equally important sense, membership growth was a vote of confidence in CAF's relevance as a multilateral institution that strengthened its standing in bond markets and the international development community. Not coincidentally, since 2010 CAF began rebranding itself as the "Development Bank of Latin America."

CAF considered opening membership to non-borrower countries to improve its standing in capital markets. As García described it in an interview, inviting OECD countries was his "Plan B" if his initial reforms did not show results (Rubio 2015, 141–142). In the end, only Spain and Portugal—two shareholders with strong links to Latin America—became members in a minority position. CAF has since maintained a de facto policy of allowing a maximum shareholding of 10 percent to non-regional members (ibid., 142). As of end-2019, Spain and Portugal had 4.5 percent and 0.2 percent of total shareholding, respectively, and did not own the more powerful class "A" shares. García himself was clear about the trade-off of giving a major governance role to non-borrower countries: "Having triple-A countries as members would improve CAF's ratings but might mean a change in terms of CAF's objectives and policies" (Institutional Investor 1997).

CAF's expanding membership combined with a stellar repayment record—no government had ever not repaid its loans on time until Venezuela in 2017[9]—fueled steady improvements in its bond rating to AA– (S&P), AA– (Fitch), and Aa3 (Moody's) by 2018. This reduced CAF's cost of funding and hence the loan prices it charges to borrowers, which is a major factor in making CAF more attractive to borrowers. As one Panamanian Finance Ministry official put it, "CAF has strongly funded itself to achieve loan prices competitive with the World Bank and IDB. At first our portfolio with CAF was minimal, because of its price. But as they became more competitive, we were more interested in taking out loans" (interview, November 21, 2013, author's translation). Despite improvement, CAF still cannot match the loan pricing of the AAA-rated World Bank and IDB, and was downgraded to A+ by S&P in 2019 mainly due to late payments on loans made to Venezuela. The difficulties in strengthening its bond rating further, perhaps coupled with the retirement in 2017 of García (who championed the policy of not having non-borrower shareholders), could explain rumors in early 2021 that China may soon join CAF (Humphrey and Chen 2021).

CAF's governance arrangements give it other competitive advantages that borrower governments find attractive and help offset its higher loan costs. CAF's loan approval procedure is far faster than the legacy MDBs. Major loans routinely

---

[9] Starting in 2017, Venezuela became the first government to delay repayments to CAF, due to its ongoing crisis. Even though it had as of late 2021 not gone past 180 days overdue (which would trigger a "non-performing loan" status), CAF was forced to design a creative financial workaround to technically avoid a default (S&P 2020a).

move from conception to final approval within three months, or even faster if the country needs it. Loans below a certain level ($75 million for sovereign and $50 million for non-sovereign) can be approved directly by management without Board review. "We have definite advantages in terms of flexibility and reaction time compared to the other multilaterals," said one operations staffer. "This is from our operating design and type of administration. We are much less rigid than the other multilaterals, which have certain impositions from donating countries that we do not" (interview, November 25, 2009, author's translation).

This is exemplified in the dynamics of the BoD, which unlike the legacy MDBs does not sit in permanent session. As former CAF President Garcia pointed out in 2005, "I do not have a resident board here. CAF has a board that meets three to four times a year and they are all finance ministers or central bank governors. This means that all high-level decisions are taken very quickly. [Governments] have to delegate to management" (Barham 2005, 20). According to a top CAF finance officer, "Our administration is given more control over day-to-day operations; we don't have a sitting board. This eliminates or reduces almost to zero political interference in our operations" (interview, December 14, 2010, author's translation).

Borrowers find this reduced bureaucracy extremely attractive. A former minister in Trinidad and Tobago said this was a key reason why his country became a full A shareholder in CAF. "Within three months CAF was able to say, 'This is our frame. If you can meet that, we will go.' I spent a year with the IDB without knowing whether they were in or they were out" (interview, November 27, 2013). This flexibility also relates to modifying ongoing projects, as a Uruguayan official noted:

> CAF is very flexible and has a lot less internal bureaucracy. They didn't have to go back to their board to approve a supplement for our project. The World Bank came down for a week worth of missions, and as I'm ducking in and out of meetings, I sort everything out with CAF on the supplementary loan for US$5 million with a couple of telephone calls.
>
> (interview, November 11, 2013, author's translation)

Environmental and social safeguards is another area where CAF is more borrower-friendly than the legacy MDBs. Rather than impose externally-mandated standards on borrower countries for a project, as legacy MDBs do, CAF for most of its history focused on following national laws and regulations. "The reason is fundamentally from the composition of the board," said a CAF operations staffer (interview, August 23, 2011, author's translation).

> If for example we had Nordic and European countries on our board, environmental issues are very important to them, the bar is a lot higher ... At end of day,

since this is a Latin bank, for the board to put on conditionality that is stricter than local laws would be to shoot themselves in the foot, because they would be requiring expensive conditions that they have to pay themselves.

As CAF has begun to a rebrand itself as a modern, responsible MDB on a par with the legacy banks in recent years, it published a new set of safeguards in 2016 (CAF 2016). Although the policy is stronger than previously (Gallagher and Yuan 2017 and Conectas 2018), it still prioritizes national laws rather than imposing external safeguards, and takes a more flexible, case-by-case approach rather than the legalistic style of the legacy MDBs. As one Panamanian official noted, "For CAF, the issues of environment and relocation are quite important. But they adapt more to the internal processes of the country, the needs of the government, so we can go ahead with the project" (interview, November 14, 2013, author's translation).

A final operational advantage of CAF over the legacy MDBs is that it does not attempt to push borrower officials into certain kinds of project design, much less try to shape their policy frameworks. As President García stated bluntly in a 2008 interview, "the philosophy of CAF is not to impose things—we give members what they ask for" (cited in Rubio 2015, 139). For developing countries accustomed to the heavy-handed approach of the World Bank and to a lesser degree the regional MDBs, this can be a welcome relief. Numerous officials in ten countries across Latin America and the Caribbean repeatedly noted that CAF never tried to push them on their development agenda, in stark contrast to the World Bank and IDB.

The other side of the coin is that CAF offers little in the way of technical assistance or knowledge services. A Uruguayan sanitation official said, "CAF don't have such a big staff, so they can't offer as much in that way ... They will provide resources in the loan to contract consultants if needed. But their own teams are mainly just project finance specialists, whereas IDB and World Bank also have people who are specialists on impacts, design, etc." (interview, November 11, 2013, author's translation). CAF has in recent years begun to build up its research team, but it cannot yet compete on knowledge services with the legacy MDBs.

The combination of CAF's increasing access to bond markets and client-friendly approach has been remarkably successful. A former CAF operations staffer working at the World Bank stated,

CAF cannot compete in terms of price, because it doesn't have the rich donor countries behind it and it has a higher cost of borrowing to pass on. So instead it competes on speed and easy conditions. If a country needs a loan, the CAF can deliver it a lot faster, without a lot of safeguards and with much more convenient conditions. This is why the CAF is growing so rapidly.

(interview, June 1, 2009)

A Brazilian Finance Ministry official agreed, saying, "We don't have to push the CAF to be more flexible, they are already doing that. CAF is a master at this, they adapt so they can lend more and more" (interview, November 6, 2013, author's translation). As a result, CAF now lends $12–14 billion annually, more than the public and private sector operations of the World Bank in Latin America and the Caribbean.

Conclusions

The dozen MDBs discussed in this chapter may be much less well-known compared to the legacy MDBs, but they face exactly the same challenges inherent in the MDB model—accessing finance at reasonable terms, balancing quality control with speed and efficiency, and meeting the demands of borrowers while fulfilling their development mandates. Because of governance control by borrower country shareholders, these challenges play out in very different ways compared to the legacy MDBs. This is due to the divergent interests of these countries compared to the wealthy non-borrower nations that dominate the legacy MDBs and translates into a very different set of policies and operating characteristics.

Borrower-led MDBs are in a process of change and growth. Global investors are increasingly open to emerging market debt, and these MDBs have started to take advantage of that to broaden their access to finance. This trend—pioneered by CAF starting in the early 1990s and taken up since the 2000s by a growing number of borrower-led MDBs—has gone hand in hand with internal reforms to professionalize their activities, better manage risks, and focus more clearly on their comparative advantages as providers of development finance.

Until now, this group of MDBs has been at the margins of broader discussions of international development finance and cooperation to tackle global challenges. That appears to be changing, albeit slowly. One sign is the increasing efforts to channel climate finance from major global funds like the Green Climate Fund, Global Environmental Facility, and Adaptation Fund, among others, through borrower-led MDBs. The legacy MDBs have also started to consider MDBs more seriously as partners, as evidenced by a $835 million financing package (combining a direct loan and loan guarantees) to TDB by the World Bank, to help TDB expanded sustainable infrastructure lending in its countries of operation (World Bank 2020e).

A more concerted effort to incorporate borrower-led MDBs into international cooperation addressing climate change and other development challenges makes sense. Borrower-led MDBs have many flaws, not least of which is a tendency to focus on deal-making while losing sight of development goals. But they have important strengths such as intimate country knowledge and close relations with member governments, and their governance arrangements are in many ways better suited to a post–Bretton Woods world of developing countries taking charge of their own agenda.

5

New MDBs Step onto the Stage

Asian Infrastructure Investment Bank and New Development Bank

The most dramatic shift in the multilateral development landscape for decades occurred at the start of 2016, with the operational launch of the Asian Infrastructure Development Bank (AIIB) and the New Development Bank (NDB). By the end of 2020, five years after opening their doors, AIIB and NDB were both well on their way to establishing themselves as major new players in global development finance, with a substantial shareholder capital, a rapidly growing staff, and over US$20 billion in approved loans each (Table 5.1).

Founded by China and a group of mainly emerging market and developing countries (EMDCs), these two banks embody fundamental shifts underway in the world economy and geopolitics. These are not the modest-sized borrower-led MDBs discussed in the previous chapter, but rather well-capitalized banks with member countries representing a substantial share of the world population and economy. In financial scale, operational innovation, political relevance, and international standing, AIIB and NDB have the potential to rival the legacy MDBs almost right from the start. It is no surprise that their creation has been compared to a second Bretton Woods (Summers 2015).

While some observers perceive these new MDBs as a threat to the international order dominated by the G7 nations since the middle of the past century, in a broader perspective the creation of AIIB and NDB is a hopeful sign. In an era where a commitment to international cooperation by the U.S. and some other countries has at times appeared to be in retreat, rising nations are establishing new multilateral institutions to address global challenges. EMDCs could have channeled their efforts and resources via existing national financing agencies such as China Development Bank, Brazil's BNDES, or the Development Bank of Southern Africa. The fact that at least some constituencies within the governments of China and other EMDC see the value of multilateral institutions bodes well for the future of global cooperation.

AIIB and NDB are in broad terms following very similar institutional patterns to those laid down at Bretton Woods with the creation of the World Bank. Their founding nations see the core MDB model as useful to achieve their objectives, and

Financing the Future. Chris Humphrey, Oxford University Press. © Christopher Humphrey (2022).
DOI: 10.1093/oso/9780192871503.003.0006

Table 5.1 Overview AIIB and NDB

	Launch Year	Sovereign Members	Borrower Voting Power	Disbursed Portfolio (US$ million)	2020 Financing Approvals (US$ million)
Asian Infrastructure Investment Bank	2016	86	100%*	8,397	9,980
New Development Bank	2016	9**	100%	6,612	8,171

Source: Annual reports and financial statements.
Notes: * Formally all AIIB members—including wealthy countries—are eligible to borrow from the bank. ** NDB had five members until 2021, when it admitted two new member countries (Bangladesh and United Arab Emirates) and began the admission process for two more (Egypt and Uruguay).

have replicated many aspects of the organizational design, governance structures, and financial and operational policies used by other MDBs. By following this model, AIIB and NDB are facing the same tensions and trade-offs faced by the other MDBs discussed in this book. These are playing out in unique ways, however, due to the context in which they were founded and the constellation of countries making up their membership.

The role of China in both AIIB and NDB is particularly important, and points to how the evolving global geopolitical and economic context of the early twenty-first century is pushing at the edges of the MDB governance framework followed in this book. The emergence of China as a global power is a harbinger of the changing role of major middle-income and upper-middle-income nations like Korea, Brazil, India, South Africa, and Indonesia that blur the lines between "developed" and "developing" countries. What does this mean for MDB governance? As Wang (2019) notes, China has attributes of both: on the one hand in close allegiance with developing borrower countries and in opposition to the traditional G7 powers, but on the other hand the largest creditor nation in the world and a rapidly rising power with multiple agendas across the globe.

As this chapter will show, China is still very much a "borrower" nation in the framework of MDB governance, both technically (it has taken loans from both AIIB and NDB) as well as in its policy priorities. But because of its growing role as a global creditor and major power, China is beginning to develop new interests that may begin to diverge from other borrower countries and align more with non-borrowers. This is not happening quickly, due to the strongly felt views on development of China's administration that continue to largely align with other borrowers as well as its interest to continue positioning itself as a champion of developing countries against the western-led international order. As well, China's closed political system means that it does not face the kind of pressure group lobbying that plays an important role in shaping the policies of major non-borrower shareholders at the legacy MDBs.

This evolution of China's position in global governance is illustrated neatly in the divergent roles it has played in AIIB and NDB, and in their very different operational characteristics. China is using the AIIB to establish itself as a responsible leader in international development. It has made a concerted effort to bring in other non-borrower members (including five of the G7), and has agreed to many of the quality standards, transparency rules, and environmental safeguards of the legacy MDBs, although with some important differences. AIIB is, in short, similar to the legacy MDBs, but with China as the leader shareholder rather than the U.S. At NDB, on the other hand, China has equal voting power to the other four BRICS nations (Brazil, Russia, India, and South Africa), and has been willing to play a cooperative role to build a bank much more aligned with borrower country priorities. The result is an MDB that is similar to the borrower-led MDBs reviewed in Chapter 4, but with substantially more financial power and global scope right from the start. The trajectories of AIIB and NDB highlight the continued relevance of the borrower vs. non-borrower governance framework for analyzing and comparing MDBs, but also hint that in coming decades it may begin to erode as formerly developing countries begin to grow in economic power and their interests and priorities evolve.

This chapter explores how these governance dynamics and financial realities play out in the first five years of AIIB and NDB. The goal is to better understand how and why AIIB and NDB are similar and different from existing MDBs, and from each other. The chapter begins with a brief review of the background of and motivations for the creation of AIIB and NDB, before moving on to their governance, operations, environmental and social safeguards, and financial performance.[1]

Background and Motivations to Create AIIB and NDB

The idea of founding these new MDBs dates back to a 2009 proposal by a Chinese think tank for an Asian bank, and to the growing cooperation among the BRICS nations in the early 2000s (Callaghan and Hubbard 2016 and Chin 2014). The formal commitments to create both banks were announced in 2013—the AIIB by Chinese President Xi on a trip to Southeast Asia, and the NDB at the fifth BRICS summit in South Africa. NDB's Articles of Agreement were finalized in July 2014, it was legally created a year later, and began full operations at the start of 2016.[2] AIIB's Articles were finalized in June 2015 and the bank officially opened on January 1, 2016.

What motivated the founding countries to create these two new MDBs? An entire cottage industry has arisen in academic and policy circles attempting to

[1] Portions of this chapter are taken in modified form from Humphrey 2020a.
[2] See Noguiera 2021 for a fascinating account of NDB's creation and early operations by an insider

answer this question.[3] This chapter does not add to the conclusions of previous studies, beyond emphasizing two points.

First, it is worth taking seriously the reasons stated by founding members themselves. From the start of discussions to create both banks through their early years of operations, member country officials and senior management have emphasized that AIIB and NDB respond to three key problems with the legacy MDBs: governance, administration, and infrastructure investment.

- *Governance.* For years China and other EMDCs have pushed to reform the voting shares at the legacy MDBs and IMF, with minimal success (Summers 2015 and Morris 2016). The BRICS' share of global GDP grew from 16% in 1992 to 31% in 2020, but their collective voting share at the World Bank increased only from 11% to 13.3% over the same time span (Figure 5.1). Despite having almost exactly the same share of global GDP as the BRICS in 2020, the G7 countries control 40% of IBRD votes, three times the voting share of the BRICS. China in particular is underrepresented according the IBRD's own shareholding formula (World Bank 2020b, 4). Japan has more than twice the voting power of China (12.8% vs. 5.4%) at ADB, despite its economy being about one-fifth the size, while India has similar voting power to Canada at the World Bank (3% vs. 2.8%) even though its economy is about five times larger. As the BRICS stated in a 2012 summit declaration: "We therefore call for a more representative international financial architecture with an increase in the voice and representation of developing countries."

- *Administration.* The lengthy project processing times, bureaucratic requirements, and policy conditions of the legacy MDBs have long been extremely frustrating to EMDCs. AIIB and NDB have stated their intention to, as AIIB President Jin put it, "avoid institutional obesity" and "not be tied down with bureaucracy" (Gu 2018, 5–6). Similarly, NDB's Corporate Strategy states: "Organizational structures and procedures will be streamlined to minimize unnecessary bureaucracy and facilitate rapid project preparation and delivery" (NDB 2017a, 6), and that "NDB's mandate does not include prescribing policy, regulatory and institutional reforms to borrowing countries" (ibid., 11).

- *Infrastructure.* The stated operational goal of both new MDBs is to scale up infrastructure investment, which EMDCs see as undersupported by the legacy MDBs. An article by two NDB staffers notes that "The immense investment gap in infrastructure, especially in BRICS and other EMDCs, is another important reason that drove the creation of the NDB"

---

[3] See among many others Callaghan and Hubbard 2016, Chin 2014 and 2019, de Jonge 2017, Gabusi 2019, Hameiri and Jones 2018, He 2016, Ikenberry and Lim 2017, Li and Carey 2014, Liao 2015, Ming 2016, Wang 2019, Weiss 2017, Xiao 2016, Yang 2016 and Yeo 2018.

(Suchodolski and Demeulemeester 2018, 581). The theme is emphasized repeatedly in management interviews and strategy documents of both banks.

A further reason behind the creation of AIIB and NDB is an implicit recognition of the enduring viability and relevance of the MDB model. For all the discussion of how these new banks are revolutionizing global governance, it is striking how closely they follow the institutional design patterns first established at Bretton Woods. The structure of shareholder capital, linkage between shareholding and voting power, basic administrative and decision-making arrangements, and main financial and operational policies are very much in line with existing MDBs. Creating new MDBs makes a great deal of sense for EMDCs in purely pragmatic terms, as the up-front capitalization costs are relatively modest and MDBs mostly pay

Share of World GDP (PPP)

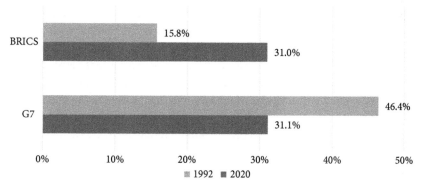

IBRD Voting Power

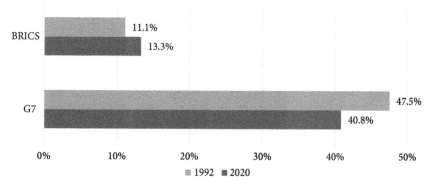

Figure 5.1 Share of Global GDP (PPP) and IBRD Voting Power (1992–2020).
Source: World Development Indicators for GDP; IBRD 1992 and 2020 financial statements for voting power.

for themselves going forward. And the potential benefits in terms of development promotion and geopolitical influence are substantial.

Despite the similar factors favoring the creation of both new MDBs, the underlying governance dynamics behind AIIB and NDB are different, and this has resulted in markedly divergent operational policies and characteristics.

AIIB is unquestionably China's creation, announced unilaterally as a Chinese initiative by President Xi in 2013. China is acting as a "hegemon" at AIIB, investing its own prestige and resources into a multilateral organization that reflects its rising global ambitions and interests. No one is surprised that China has reserved substantial governance power over AIIB and that it is playing a leading role in shaping its policies and organization. For other EMDCs or wealthier European nations, joining AIIB signals support for or at least acceptance of China's rising global power. China, in turn, has an interest in accommodating (to a degree, at least) the views of these nations on AIIB's design, as broad AIIB membership is an important diplomatic win for China and helps confer global legitimacy on AIIB.

NDB, by contrast, was created by a group of nations with aspirations for a global leadership role but not entirely certain of their status, common interests, or ability to work collectively. Russia has military might but a narrow economy and small and declining population; India a huge population but not yet sustaining economic take off; Brazil and South Africa regional powers with stop-and-start growth cycles and unstable politics. The BRICS agree on the need to build international institutions to counter G7 dominance and to increase the supply of infrastructure finance. But beyond that, relations among the BRICS and their role as a collective in the broader international system are far from settled. This contributes to a less clearly articulated vision for NDB, and the uncertainty with which other countries view it.

Membership and Governance

AIIB and NDB were created in part to afford greater decision-making power to EMDCs and their membership and governance structure reflects that, although in contrasting ways.

AIIB membership and governance

When President Xi first announced the creation of AIIB in 2013, it was expected to begin as a regional MDB led by China and composed of other Asian nations (He 2016, Xiao 2016, and Zhu 2019). However, a number of non-regional countries signed on as founding members in 2015, including wealthy nations such as U.K., France, Germany, Switzerland, and Sweden, for a variety of motivations (Gabusi 2019 and Callaghan and Hubbard 2016). By end-2020, AIIB had a total of eighty-six member countries and another seventeen prospective members. The majority of shareholders are Asian, but five of the G7 are now members, as are countries as disparate as Sudan, Rwanda, Argentina, Ecuador, and Serbia. AIIB is now the second-largest MDB in the world by membership behind the World Bank.

AIIB's membership represents both an impressive diplomatic victory for China as well as a challenge for the way the bank operates. China quickly recognized the advantages of bringing in high-income member countries, both for financial strength as well as AIIB's international credibility, but also realized that this would change the character of the bank. With most Asian members generally willing to follow China's lead, the thorniest discussions in AIIB's negotiations were between China and the European founding members. For the Europeans, environmental and social safeguards and other standards on project oversight and procurement were essential, and here China proved flexible. As well, China agreed to partially dial back the amount of operational authority it originally intended to give to the AIIB president compared to the Board of Directors. Europeans were unsuccessful in two key areas: China insisted that AIIB's Board of Directors would be a non-resident board (unlike the legacy MDBs) and would not reduce the amount of proposed initial shareholding capital from US$100 billion.

Beyond those issues, China was willing to accommodate the needs of the Europeans and other non-borrowers such as Australia, New Zealand, and subsequently Canada as a relatively small price to pay for the benefits they brought with them. AIIB has made this cooperation evident by hiring top officials from non-regional countries with experience at the legacy MDBs, particularly from the World Bank. This included the designer of AIIB's environmental and social safeguard policies and the architect of the Articles of Agreement (both U.S. nationals) and European officials for three of AIIB's first five vice presidents as well as the chief risk officer. The non-borrower shareholders, in turn, have been willing to move forward with policies that are more flexible and less legalistic than at the legacy MDBs.

China is the largest shareholder of AIIB, with 27.4 percent of AIIB voting power (including the votes of Hong Kong) at end-2020. Other traditional borrower members—including those outside of Asia—account for 45.7 percent of votes, while traditional non-borrower nations collectively control 26.9 percent of AIIB votes (Figure 5.2). The borrower vs. non-borrower distinction is a bit murky at AIIB since all members technically can borrow from the bank. Nonetheless, the split is likely to remain relevant as traditional non-borrower countries—western European nations, Canada, and Australia—are more inclined to push for policies on higher environmental and social standards, tighter project oversight, and a greater focus on poverty and social outcomes compared to traditional borrower countries.

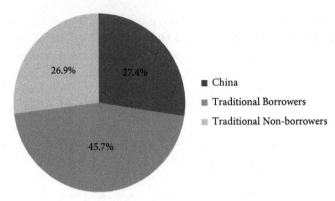

Figure 5.2 Voting Power at AIIB (December 2020).
Source: AIIB website, "Members and Prospective Members of the Bank,"
accessed January 10, 2021.
Note: "Traditional non-borrowers" and "Traditional borrowers" are
classified according to Part I and Part II countries for the World Bank's IDA
as of 2020.

AIIB's Articles of Agreement[4] stipulate that a 75 percent majority of voting
power is required for significant decisions such as modifying the capital structure,
Board of Directors, or the statutes (AIIB 2015, Article 28 [2]). Hence, China by
itself has veto power over these decisions at AIIB, very similar to the veto power
wielded by the U.S. at the Inter-American Development Bank (IDB). At the same
time, shareholders report that China has been circumspect on major policy discussions at AIIB, not using its voting power bluntly and making an effort to arrive at
compromise positions that satisfy all members. One G7 shareholder official said:
"We haven't seen any evidence so far of China throwing weight around, given
their voting power" (interview, August 2, 2019). An official from another European
member country agreed but noted that there was concern about China asserting
itself more going forward. "This is something we [the Europeans and Canada] are
all nervous about," the official said (interview, May 15, 2019).

AIIB President Jin indicated in a public talk at Boston University (October 18,
2019) that China may allow its voting power to be diluted below the 25 percent
veto threshold, although even if it did, it would take very little effort for China to
find allies to support it in a veto vote. In an implicit dig at the U.S., Jin stated in
an interview that "What matters is not the influence of a big shareholder. Rather,
the issue is what kind of influence the big shareholders or shareholders play, and
the way they exercise their power of influence" (Gu 2018, 6). Thus far, the Chinese government "has provided the AIIB the 'strategic space' it needs to foster its
multilateral character, and to sustain the growth of its multilateral culture, and by
extension, its international credibility," as Zhu (2019, 653) puts it.

---

[4] For a detailed account of the design of AIIB's Articles of Agreement by its lead author, see
Lichtenstein (2018).

Unlike the legacy MDBs, AIIB's Board of Directors (BoD) is non-resident and meets several times a year rather than sitting in permanent session—an issue on which China refused to compromise with European shareholders. While the non-resident BoD has led to concerns about oversight, some non-borrowers are willing to try something new in light of the politicization, bureaucracy, and expense of resident BoDs at the legacy MDBs. One G7 government official said of AIIB's non-resident BoD, "It has a lot of good features. The extra politics that come with a resident board is not always a good thing. So we are definitely happy to continue with this experiment" (interview, September 8, 2019). An article by two German Finance Ministry officials concluded that AIIB's non-resident BoD appeared well-designed to encourage "strategic thinking" (von Müller and Baumann 2019)—perhaps an indication of Germany's frustration with the resident BoDs of the legacy MDBs. Nonetheless, it is telling that Austria, Germany, and France base AIIB representatives at their respective embassies in Beijing, to more closely monitor AIIB operations in the absence of a full-time BoD (German Federal Ministry of Finance 2019).

AIIB's shareholders have delegated more authority on day-to-day operational matters from the BoD to its president compared to the legacy MDBs, including allowing AIIB's president to approve certain loans without formal board review. Several legacy MDBs have begun in recent years to streamline board approval, but none go as far as AIIB. The relevant regulations (AIIB 2019a) specify that the authority to approve all projects is by default delegated from the BoD to the president, and then lists specific criteria for projects where such delegation is not permitted. The main restrictions apply to first-time projects and loan sizes above a given threshold (US$200 million initially, though expected to increase). European shareholders lobbied for a provision allowing any single director to call a project in for BoD debate for any reason, as a backstop arrangement to ensure that the AIIB president cannot completely bypass them (German Federal Ministry of Finance 2019).

NDB membership and governance

As of end-2020, NDB had only the five BRICS nations as shareholders—seven years after finalizing its Articles of Agreement and over four years since the approval of the formal terms and conditions for new members (NDB 2017b). NDB's Articles state that all United Nations members are eligible to join the bank, and membership expansion is a stated goal in NDB's corporate strategy. "NDB must operate at scale, and that means bringing in new members beyond the founding five shareholder countries," with the aim of including a "mix of advanced, middle-income and lower-income countries" (NDB 2017a, 26). Interviews with former NDB staff as well as a book written by a former

NDB vice president (Noguiera 2021) suggest that internal disagreements among shareholders (particularly Russia) about which countries to accept as members as well as lack of interest by some potential target member countries are the main factors holding back membership expansion. In 2021, the first four new countries had joined NDB: Bangladesh and United Arab Emirates were admitted as full members by year-end, while Egypt and Uruguay had formally begun the admission process (NDB 2021). As a result, the BRICS nations are no longer completely in charge of NDB governance. Details of the shareholding granted to new members were not available at the time of publication.

Unusually among large MDBs, the five founding countries contributed exactly the same amount of capital and have equal voting power. This was an important political choice and contrasts with the AIIB, which has followed a shareholding model closer to the legacy MDBs wherein wealthier nations contribute more capital and have more voting power (Noguiera 2021). In so doing, NDB has foregone a larger capital base, as China could easily have contributed substantially more capital while others among the BRICS do not have the same economic strength. By prioritizing equality among the founders over a potentially higher capitalization, NDB made a powerful statement that its approach to governance is different from AIIB and the legacy MDBs.

The risk is that voting power equality could make it difficult to reach agreement on major decisions, in light of potential divergent interests among the BRICS. As He (2016, 8) notes, "The likelihood of reaching an impasse along the way to a final decision is greater under such a model." China, India, and Russia have complex relationships with one another on numerous economic and geopolitical issues—not least China's ambitious Belt and Road Initiative (BRI), which India has strongly opposed (see Ming 2016). Both South Africa and Brazil have faced economic downturns and political turmoil since NDB was created, weakening their international engagement and, in the case of Brazil, radically changing the policy stance of its administration. In such a context, NDB's governance arrangements could hinder establishing a clear strategic direction for the bank.

The BRICS have reserved considerable NDB governance power for themselves, even as membership expands. The Articles of Agreement stipulate that the BRICS will always collectively have at least 55 percent of voting power and no other member can have more than 7 percent (NDB 2014, Art. 8). The only other MDBs with a statute-mandated majority to founding members are the Black Sea Trade and Development Bank and the Central American Bank for Economic Integration. Major decisions at NDB's BoG, such as changes to the capital structure, amending the Articles of Agreement, modifying the composition and powers of the BoD, and admitting new members, all require special majorities that include the support of four of the five BRICS. The BoD—non-resident, as at AIIB—can have a maximum of ten chairs, five of which are permanently reserved for the BRICS (ibid., Art. 10). By statute, the NDB presidency rotates among the five BRICS nations (ibid., Art. 13a), while the four vice presidencies are reserved for each BRICS nation not in control of the presidency (ibid., Art. 13c). The president and vice presidents comprise the Credit and Investment Committee (CIC) that must approve all loan projects (ibid., Art. 13b ii and NDB 2016a, 9), meaning the BRICS will always have statutory control of NDB's loan pipeline.

The fact that NDB's governance arrangements are by statute dominated by the BRICS, even as membership expands, may contribute to wariness on the part of other prospective member countries. Large middle-income nations who would be potentially natural members—and would greatly contribute to NDBs international profile, capital base, and loan portfolio quality—might not like the prospect of remaining permanently subordinate to the BRICS. A relevant parallel can be seen at CAF, which was founded and controlled by five countries initially, but opened membership more broadly in the 1990s and the founding member countries relinquished any special governance powers. This coincided with the beginning of CAF's extraordinary growth in both membership and financial capacity over the subsequent decades. The BRICS may find—as CAF's founders did in the 1990s—that statutory dominance of governance can hinder NDB's growth prospects.

The role of China in AIIB and NDB governance

China played a major role in founding and shaping AIIB and NDB from the start, but the precise nature of that role is not entirely clear. The country was the driving force behind AIIB and continues to have a dominant share of AIIB's voting power. At NDB, China is more the *primus inter pares*: nominally on equal footing with the other four shareholders, but the one supplying the most political and financial credibility to the project. It is interesting and—at first blush—somewhat puzzling that AIIB and NDB have charted such divergent trajectories in terms of governance arrangements and operational characteristics, considering China's major role in both MDBs.

Wang (2019) and Serrano (2019) attribute this divergence to, respectively, ambiguity within China's own policy community and contrasting approaches to institutional formation between China and Brazil. While both of these explanations are plausible, it seems just as likely that China is simply experimenting or hedging its bets—helping launch two MDBs with very different approaches and seeing which proves most useful for which purposes. This is entirely in line with the pragmatic, experimental approach used by China in its own domestic development path since the 1980s (Ang 2016). It should come as no surprise that policymakers would take the same approach in the multilateral sphere. China policymakers will have looked closely at the trajectory of other MDBs as they considered the design of AIIB and NDB, and may well have concluded that both the legacy MDB model and the borrower-led model each have their own strengths and weaknesses, and might each be useful in different developmental contexts. Since the actual cost of capitalizing the MDBs is negligible, especially for a country with tremendous foreign currency reserves mostly invested in low-yield government bonds of G7 nations, founding two with divergent approaches has little downside.

As well, the geopolitical usefulness of the two MDBs may be as important to China as their operational characteristics. AIIB allows China to take the lead in negotiating directly with other major shareholders—notably the Europeans and Canada, but also other EMDCs—from a position of strength, as the hegemonic power behind AIIB. China can decide which policies it is willing to compromise on and which ones not, thus balancing its own vision for what it wants from AIIB with a clear-eyed calculation of the benefits of bringing in other countries as members. NDB, on the other hand, is more of an expression of solidarity among developing nations, a role China has long cultivated. The characteristics of the NDB itself may be less important to China than building and maintaining relations with the other BRICS. Particularly with India and Russia—two neighboring powers with which China has complex relations—NDB can be a useful, non-threatening platform for dialogue and engagement, which may be more important than any disputes about NDB's policies. Since China can already push its own vision for how to build an MDB with AIIB, it is less concerned about the direction of NDB, and more inclined to acquiesce to the views of the other four members. Other observers have noted that China has done so already in relation to equal voting power, agreeing to award India the first presidency, and opening branch offices in South Africa and Brazil in the first two years (He 2016 and Ming 2016).

The broad membership and legacy MDB-style approach of AIIB provides China important international legitimacy and standing, while NDB maintains China's role as a partner of other EMDCs and to other approaches to promote economic development (Humphrey and Chen, 2021). Thus, China can take advantage of both MDB models. This neatly matches the somewhat split personality of China's role, as described by Wang (2019): a huge creditor nation and ambitious global power that at the same time seeks to maintain its traditional solidarity with the Global South. Situated within this context, the divergent models of AIIB and NDB supported by China are less puzzling than they first appear.

Developmental Approach, Administration, and Operational Performance

This section discusses the overall approach taken by AIIB and NDB toward fulfilling their operational mandates, followed by an outline of key aspects of their administrative set-up and procedures. The remainder of the section reviews the operational performance of both MDBs in their first five years.

Development vs. growth

The focus of both AIIB and NDB is infrastructure finance, in line with the prioritization of China and other EMDCs of infrastructure to support economic growth, although both MDBs can lend for other purposes based on client needs (AIIB 2015, Art. 2 (i) and NDB 2017a, 21). This contrasts with the legacy MDBs, which have since the 1970s moved away from infrastructure projects as described in Chapter 3. Neither MDB has an explicit focus on poverty reduction per se, which is also fundamentally different from the legacy MDBs. Rather, the founders of both banks consider economic growth and job creation to be their primary goals. As AIIB President Jin put it in an interview, "We do not aim at direct intervention in poverty, but what we try to achieve in promoting broad-based economic and social development through investments in infrastructure and other productive sectors will make a huge difference in the overall economic situation of our members. Poverty will be reduced as a result" (Gu 2018, 2).

Neither bank has a "concessional" lending window like the World Bank's International Development Association (IDA) to offer zero interest loans or grants to the poorest countries. All government borrowers from both banks receive the same interest rate, regardless of their level of economic development, as at the legacy MDBs. AIIB does have a Project Preparation Special Fund seeded with contributions initially from China (US$60 million) and subsequently also by the U.K. (US$50 million) and Korea (US$18 million). The Fund provides grant resources for project preparation to countries that are classified as IDA borrowers by the World Bank. NDB has created a similar but smaller fund.

Administration

AIIB and NDB have both expressed a determination to avoid the bureaucracies and project processing times that EMDCs have long complained about at the legacy MDBs. This drive has translated into a focus on keeping overall staff numbers low and instituting a streamlined administrative apparatus. As of end-2020, NDB had only 185 professional staff while AIIB had 316, compared to 12,400 at the World Bank.

While limiting the growth of administrative bureaucracy is laudable goal, it comes with trade-offs. The first is staff capacity. The ability to offer in-house expertise and technical assistance to borrowers is shaped in part by how much an MDB invests in hiring specialized staff and dedicating resources to research, which boost administrative costs but are essential to build value-added beyond simply supplying financing. This is one of the strengths of the legacy MDBs: their ability to offer unparalleled expertise in a huge variety of development topics, which many borrowers value highly. The main reasons China has continued borrowing from the

World Bank, despite its huge foreign currency reserves, is precisely to benefit from this expertise.

The second potential trade-off is quality control. One reason why legacy MDBs have such frustratingly long project approval processes is the multiple levels of review that all projects must go through prior to approval. There can be little doubt that many of the review "gates" in the project cycle are overly complex or unnecessary, driven by excessive oversight zeal from non-borrower shareholders. At the same time, borrowers know that they will end up with a project that has been closely examined for design, development impact, financial terms, environmental and social sustainability, and more—all of which can avoid delays during implementation and which often result in high quality projects.

AIIB and NDB have both insisted that they will substantially accelerate process approval without sacrificing quality and oversight. The former is clearly being achieved thus far. Interviews with three borrower country officials (August 7, 16, and 30, 2019)—including one that has arranged projects from both banks—reveal that the process is notably quicker than at the legacy MDBs. Officials from both banks confirmed that their internal data showed the same, but public information is not available. Whether this speed is married with quality control equal to the legacy MDBs remains to be seen. AIIB's strategy of starting off by co-financing many projects with other MDBs has helped substantially, as it in effect "outsourced" much project preparation and oversight to co-financing partners. NDB has done almost no co-financing, but has instead taken on a large share of projects already designed by borrower governments, with limited input on the part of NDB staff. While this relieves NDB of considerable administrative burden, it poses risks and may be a factor in NDB's lower disbursement numbers (see below).

AIIB had as of end-2021 no offices apart from its Beijing headquarters, in line with President Jin's efforts to maintain a slim, non-bureaucratic administration. However, it seems likely that this will have to happen, to develop better country knowledge, build a project pipeline, keep tabs on project implementation, and address inevitable project delays and problems. As one European shareholder official put it, "We aren't pushing for AIIB to open loads of offices everywhere, but we do need eyes on the ground" (interview, August 2, 2019). NDB has moved more quickly to open country offices, with one opened in South Africa in August 2017 and further offices in Brazil and Russia by 2021.

Project approvals and disbursements

Both MDBs have gotten off the ground quickly, ramping up project approvals steadily over their first five years of operations (Figure 5.3). By end-2020, NDB had approved a total of US$25.5 billion vs. US$21.7 billion by AIIB. Despite the

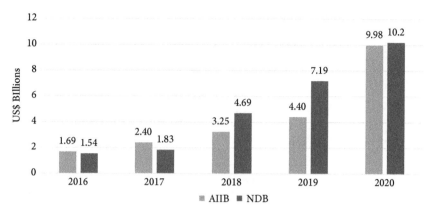

Figure 5.3 Annual Project Approvals (2016–2020).

Source: AIIB project databases; NDB 2016–19 loan data supplied directly to author by NDB; 2020 from NDB database.

Note: Does not include two cancelled NDB projects.

somewhat higher rhythm of approvals by NDB compared to AIIB thus far, the ratio of NDB disbursements is considerably lower. Only US$6.6 million had actually been disbursed by end-2020, or about 26 percent of total NDB approvals, compared to $8.4 billion by AIIB (40 percent of approvals).

A senior NDB management official suggested that the slower rhythm of disbursements is because NDB is developing almost all of its projects on its own, whereas AIIB is co-financing many projects designed and negotiated by other MDBs (interview, August 1, 2019). Another possible explanation is that NDB is approving projects to which borrowers are not fully committed or which are not fully vetted. For example, two NDB loan projects—a US$250 million loan to a state-owned bank in India and a US$69 million loan for a road in Russia—have been canceled, while a loan for a port project in South Africa stopped disbursing due to procurement problems (The Citizen 2019). Whether this is a sign of deeper problems with NDB project approval processes or not remains to be seen, but it is unquestionably an issue the bank will need to monitor closely as project disbursement is an important indicator of MDB efficiency.

Geographic distribution

Through end-2020, NDB had approved nearly 30 percent of its loans to India, and about 20 percent each to China and Brazil (Table 5.2), with less for Russia and South Africa. The strong lending to China—despite the country's obvious lack of need for financing and the absence of any technical assistance by NDB—suggests that it is helping build up the NDB's portfolio by taking out loans. That is, these

Table 5.2 Share of Top Five Country Recipients of
Financing Approvals, to end-2020

NDB		AIIB	
India	28.2%	India	22.7%
China	20.5%	Turkey	9.9%
Brazil	19.7%	Indonesia	9.7%
South Africa	17.3%	Bangladesh	8.5%
Russia	14.3%	Pakistan	5.8%

Source: AIIB and NDB project databases.
Note: AIIB has approved 8.3 percent of its financing to
pan-Asian infrastructure funds

loans indicate more that China is seeking to help NDB, rather than the other way
around. India's high borrowing is a function of the strong pipeline of shovel-ready
projects in line with the Modi administration's ambitious development agenda.
Brazil's lending had been extremely low through 2019 (only 10 percent of total
approvals)—possibly due to a lack of interest support for NDB by the right-wing
Bolsonaro administration—but jumped sharply in 2020 as a result of three large
budget support operations related to the Covid-19 crisis. The addition of four
new member countries in 2021—Bangladesh, Egypt, United Arab Emirates, and
Uruguay—will help NDB diversify its loan portfolio.[5]

AIIB's approved loan portfolio is much less concentrated compared to NDB.
Project approvals were distributed across twenty-seven countries as of end-2020,
with a further 8 percent of approvals to funds investing in multiple countries across
Asia. India has been the largest recipient of AIIB approvals thus far, although
AIIB management indicated that it will seek to improve portfolio balance moving forward. As noted above, the Indian government has a substantial pipeline
of finance-ready projects, which match up well with AIIB's limited project ini-
tiation capacity at start-up. China itself has received four loans from AIIB for a
total of $1.1 billion (5.3 percent of AIIB approvals). AIIB can lend to non-Asian
members under the rather broad requirement that the loans "foster economic
development, create wealth or improve infrastructure connectivity in Asia" (AIIB
2018a, 1). AIIB had by end-2020 made three non-Asian loans, two to Egypt for
US$319 million in total and a third to Ecuador for $50 million. The prospect of
AIIB loans likely played a role in several non-Asian countries joining the bank,
including European nations such as Italy (Asia Times 2019). Neither AIIB nor
NDB appear to be focusing their lending on China's Belt and Road Initiative thus
far (Box 5.1).

[5] The Ukraine crisis and subsequent financial sanctions on Russia in early 2022 may pose a serious
challenge to NDB's already concentrated loan portfolio (Humphrey 2022).

Box 5.1: Are AIIB and NDB Supporting Belt and Road?

Early lending patterns do not suggest that AIIB and NDB are vehicles to support China's BRI, at least thus far. China, India, and Brazil combine to total about 70 percent of NDB's loan approvals through 2020. China is of course the funder, not recipient, of BRI investments; India has vocally opposed BRI; and Brazil is not a BRI target country. For Russia and South Africa, only five projects could be considered relevant to BRI objectives,[*]This considers mainly connective infrastructure, particularly for transport. One can also take a broader view of BRI's objectives beyond transport infrastructure, following Macaes (2018). one of which (a container port in South Africa) has been suspended due to corruption allegations and a second (a road project in Russia) was canceled. Even including these, projects with a clear BRI link total only 3.8 percent of NDB's approval loans through end-2020.

The link between AIIB lending and BRI is more difficult to assess, as almost all AIIB borrowers are linked in some way to BRI. However, early loan approval patterns do not reveal an obvious trend toward BRI. India has to date received 23 percent of AIIB approvals, and it is not a BRI country. About 13 percent of AIIB total financing (fifteen out of a total of 106 projects) is clearly targeted to transport and communications infrastructure—mainly roads, but also ports and telecoms—that has an obvious potential link to BRI. Six of those projects are co-financed with EBRD, ADB, and World Bank, suggesting that considerations beyond BRI were involved in project selection.

The evidence is only preliminary, but it does suggest that China is not taking a short-term, direct approach to steering AIIB or NDB lending in favor of BRI. This could in part be part of longer-term strategy on the part of China to strengthen international perceptions of AIIB and NDB independence early in their organizational lives. The panorama could change as AIIB and NDB grow.

Project sectors

Through end-2019, project approvals by both banks focused entirely on infrastructure, with the exception of one judicial reform project by NDB to Russia (US$460 million in 2017). Energy and transport facilities were top priorities, accounting for over two-thirds of NDB's approvals through 2019 and 60 percent of AIIB's (Figure 5.4). AIIB's share of financing to transport and energy was in reality higher, as five approved projects were to general infrastructure funds that are likely to emphasize energy and transport. Each bank seems to be to a degree specializing, with NDB focusing more on transport while AIIB dedicated relatively more financing to energy, but this may be a function of early demand rather than a

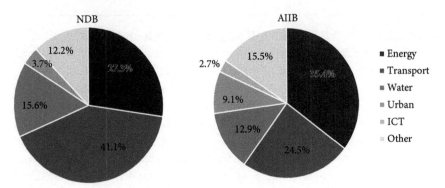

Figure 5.4 Sector of Approved Projects, 2016–2019.

Source: Compiled by author from NDB and AIIB project databases.

preconceived sectoral focus. Both MDBs have said they will support a wide range of infrastructure subsectors, depending on borrower demand and project feasibility. AIIB has published three sectoral strategies—energy, transport, and urban (AIIB 2018b, 2018c, and undated)—and the drafts of strategies for water and ICT in 2019. NDB has not yet released sectoral strategies, beyond the description in its corporate strategy (NDB 2017a, 20–21).

The situation changed sharply in 2020 as a result of the Covid-19 pandemic. Policy-based budget support lending like those controversially used by the legacy MDBs was not intended to form a significant part of AIIB or NDB's lending, if at all. But both banks adapted quickly to help their member countries face the crisis. NDB approved six emergency budget support operations for $1 billion each in 2020, and another two operations to Brazil for $2.2 billion total to national development banks to support the economy in the crisis. AIIB approved twenty-three projects with budget support components for a total of $6.5 billion across seventeen countries, the majority co-financed with the World Bank or ADB, and several containing policy conditions on the loans. Both banks may be tempted to continue these sorts of operations going forward, although it was not part of their original intentions, as they are attractive to borrowers and are an easy way to make large, fast-disbursing loans that are less complicated to prepare and disburse than infrastructure projects. Should AIIB and NDB continue with budget support loans beyond the Covid-19 crisis, the existence and content of policy conditionality will be highly revealing about how the views and policy stances of their major shareholders are evolving.

Public vs. private sector lending

AIIB and NDB can lend to public and private sector clients, but both have focused largely on public clients to date. This makes sense, as public sector lending poses less repayment risk to an MDB and is a good way to quickly build a financially solid loan portfolio. AIIB is moving more quickly toward private sector lending, while NDB is prioritizing working directly with governments. AIIB had approved 23.5 percent of its loans to private sector borrowers by end-2019, although this dropped to 15 percent by end-2020 due to heavy lending to governments in response to Covid-19. NDB, by contrast, had lent only 4 percent of projects to private sector borrowers by end-2020 (down from 4.6 percent at end-2019). As well, AIIB is quickly moving into innovative financial structures with private investors, like bond funds, a pan-Asian equity fund, and special-purpose vehicle to securitize loans of Asian commercial banks, while NDB has focused entirely on traditional long-term loans. AIIB's securitization arrangement, structured with a financial institution controlled by Singapore's sovereign wealth fund in November 2019, is particularly noteworthy in light of the resistance of some non-borrower shareholders to similar proposals at the legacy MDBs (Hay 2019).

This sectoral contrast fits with the different sets of shareholders behind the two banks. Despite its nominal communist ideology, the Chinese government has long favored intense engagement with private markets for its own development, and this aligns well with the increasing push among non-borrower countries— including many AIIB shareholders like the U.K., Germany, and Switzerland—to mobilize greater private sector participation in development finance. NDB's shareholders, on the other hand, have historically taken a more state-led approach to economic development. Although that is changing to a degree, it seems to have seeped into NDB's operational culture—in part via the many national development bank staff seconded by the founder countries to help design NDB's initial policies and form the core of its management (Serrano 2019).

Environmental and Social Sustainability and Safeguards

The question of how AIIB and NDB address environmental and social issues has hung over the two banks from the beginning. U.S. administration officials criticized the proposed AIIB shortly after it was announced, casting doubt that it would uphold environmental and social standards. "How would the Asian Infrastructure Investment Bank be structured so that it doesn't undercut the standards with a race to the bottom?" an unnamed senior U.S. administration official rhetorically asked (Perlez 2014). AIIB and NDB themselves have both made ambitious claims about the environmental and social sustainability of their operations. AIIB officials frequently repeat their "lean, green and clean" mantra, while NDB committed to having two-thirds of approvals in the first five years be for "sustainable infrastructure" (NDB 2017a, 7).

This laudable rhetoric is in line with what the international development community—especially major non-borrower countries—have come to expect from MDBs. At the same time, the operational realities of a strong commitment to environmental and social sustainability can conflict with the interests of some shareholders. EMDCs have for years complained about what they perceive to be overly rigid and intrusive rules on environmental and social issues imposed on the legacy MDBs by non-borrower shareholders. It would be surprising if two new MDBs created mainly by EMDCs follow the path of the legacy MDBs. This section examines how these tensions have played out in practice thus far with reference to i) how each MDB selects the kinds of projects it will finance and ii) policies to mitigate the environmental and social impacts of projects.

Defining and operationalizing sustainable infrastructure

Clear definitions, indicators, and targets are essential for an MDB to systematically support sustainability goals through its projects. Without these, MDB staff do not have the guidance or incentives to promote sustainable infrastructure projects with borrowers or any way to measure progress. Both AIIB and NDB have gotten off to a slow start in this area. AIIB has not yet defined what it means by being a "green" bank in a way that can be measured and verified, nor has it set any operational targets related to green or sustainable projects. Similarly, NDB had as of 2021 not followed up the commitment of two-thirds sustainable infrastructure approvals with definitions, policies, or strategies to bring this laudable commitment into reality. Nor has NDB made concrete commitments toward renewable energy, mass transit, efficiency, or emissions targets at the project or portfolio level.

Despite the lack of definitions and targets, the operational results of AIIB and NDB are reasonably strong compared to the legacy MDBs in the area of sustainability, according to categorization criteria laid out in Bhattacharya et al. (2019). In aggregate terms, 55 percent of AIIB's infrastructure investments to end-2019 classify as sustainable compared to 65 percent for NDB. These numbers include only projects that could be classified and exclude several general infrastructure projects that were not explicitly defined in project documents. Most sustainable infrastructure facilities were in urban mass transit, but both banks also dedicated substantial resources to renewable energy and water projects.

AIIB and NDB have stated that they will avoid funding coal-based projects, and if they do, only utilize technology that would reduce emissions from the borrower country's current level. As a senior NDB official put it, "If you have plan for renewable energy, we will finance that. But coal generation is still going on around the world. What we try to do is support the countries so that they can move marginally away from higher carbon energy sources" (interview, August 1, 2019). This contrasts with the legacy MDBs, which have—after much pressure from NGOs and non-borrower shareholders—largely ceased supporting coal projects. At AIIB, European shareholder officials stated that moving more toward renewable energy is a top priority for them in the coming years. "We'd like to see more green financing overall," said one European official. "We are pushing for that and we will continue to do so" (interview, September 8, 2019). AIIB does appear ready to commit to not funding any coal energy generation plants as part of its new energy strategy as of 2022 (Zhao, 2021). NDB has faced less pressure from its shareholders on this issue, and NGOs have found little leverage through BRICS government to influence NDB policy to the same degree as in G7 nations. As a result, it is more circumspect about sustainability or achieving the two-thirds target set in its strategy. The senior NDB official stated: "To be frank, that's a goal that we try to move toward, but in quantitative terms I cannot say we will achieve two-thirds" (interview, August 1, 2019).

The fact that AIIB and NDB's performance in sustainable infrastructure does not fully live up to their rhetoric is unsurprising. Their shareholders are on balance more focused on economic growth compared to the legacy MDBs, and less on sustainability issues. As a result, AIIB and especially NDB face less shareholder pressure to impose strict definitions and rules that might limit their operational flexibility. The legacy MDBs themselves still resist such restrictions, for example, opposing the call by climate advocates to set overall portfolio emissions targets (Igoe 2018), although they have moved much further due to years of pushing by non-borrower shareholders and the NGO community. Borrowers have their own priorities related to transportation infrastructure and energy generation, and AIIB and NDB have to strike a balance between that reality and shareholder interests if they wish to remain developmentally relevant. One way to find that balance would be to dedicate resources and time to build up expertise in designing sustainable infrastructure facilities, which would help stimulate demand among borrowers for sustainable projects. It remains to be seen if AIIB and NDB will follow that strategy.

Environmental and social protection policies

Starting in the 1980s, legacy MDBs instituted environmental and social safeguard policies to reduce the negative impacts of their projects (see Chapter 3). These policies require borrower countries to go beyond their own national legislation and regulations when implementing MDB projects, which many borrowers oppose. NDB and AIIB have taken different approaches to environmental and social protection issues compared to legacy MDBs and compared to one another. NDB prioritizes the use of a country's own legislation and regulations, and will (in theory) only intervene with additional requirements in cases where it considers the national framework to be inadequate. AIIB initially appeared to be moving in the same direction, but according to interviews with one Asian and four European shareholder officials were involved in negotiations (April 25, May 15, May 17, August 2, and September 8, 2019), these plans shifted when the U.K. and other European nations decided to join. The result is a set of AIIB safeguards similar in many ways to those of the legacy MDBs, although less prescriptive and with a degree of flexibility more in tune with the views of borrower countries. Both approaches are a direct result of the varying interests and governance power of their shareholders.

AIIB

AIIB Environmental and Social Framework (ESF) policy (AIIB 2019b) was issued in 2016.[6] The policy was designed largely by a former top World Bank safeguards specialist and borrows many aspects and language from the safeguard frameworks of the legacy MDBs. The ESF has three safeguard standards: environment, involuntary resettlement, and indigenous peoples. AIIB categorizes each project in one of four risk categories (ibid., 10) and specifies certain requirements for each category, including consultations, public disclosures, grievance mechanism, and decision-making steps, among others. It covers much of the same ground as the World Bank's new ESF (World Bank 2017e), but it is more in line with borrower desires for greater flexibility and speed, and fewer ex ante requirements. Areas of difference with the World Bank's ESF include:

- **AIIB permits projects to move ahead in certain circumstances even if full impacts are not clear** by using a "framework" approach (AIIB 2019b, 17–18, 39, and 43). The World Bank's ESF has similar provisions but is more categorical in ensuring that the bank approves all plans and actions before moving ahead. AIIB also permits a **"phased approach" in vaguely defined circumstances**, by which borrowers undertake required actions following project approval (ibid., 18–19). The World Bank's ESF has no similar provision.
- The **timeline for public information release** is similar to the World Bank ESF, with draft environmental and social documentation to be released prior to appraisal for sovereign-guaranteed projects and just after for non-sovereign projects (AIIB 2019c 7–8). However, AIIB management can defer disclosure for legal or commercial reasons at its own discretion (AIIB 2019b, 21), which is not permitted in the World Bank's ESF.
- AIIB's **policy on indigenous peoples** requires that in certain circumstances the client must undertake "free, prior and informed consultations" with the support of independent experts (ibid., 44–45). The World Bank's ESF, by contrast, requires that in similar circumstances the borrower must *obtain* "free, prior and informed *consent*" (World Bank 2017e, 79–80). Obtaining consent is a considerably higher hurdle than undertaking consultations.
- Projects undertaken via **financial intermediaries** (a significant portion of AIIB operations and expected to grow in the future) are categorized as "FI," which partially delegates responsibilities to the borrower (ibid., 10). This contrasts with the more rigorous approach of the World Bank's IFC to managing

---

[6] Public consultations were launched in 2020 to review the policy (AIIB 2021b)

environmental and social risks with financial intermediaries, which has been under implementation since 2014 (IFC 2015).

NGOs have been critical of the ESF in comparison to the legacy MDB safeguards, with one saying that it "lacks clear and mandatory implementation rules" (Hirsch et al. 2019, 37) and another noting that it gives "plenty of latitude to handle "mandatory" requirements in a rather flexible manner" (Horta 2019, 25). European shareholder officials appear comfortable with AIIB's policies, at least thus far. In part, this is driven by a recognition that these issues had become major political battlegrounds at the legacy MDBs. "There's a feeling that this is a chance to try a new approach, and we are open to staying flexible and seeing how well it goes," said the AIIB desk officer for one European country. "We could have spent quite a bit of time tweaking policies. Let's get it to as good as we can and get using it rather than spending ages battling at the board" (interview, August 2, 2019). An AIIB desk officer from another European country said, "We are reasonably comfortable [with the ESF], but we learn as we go along" (interview, September 8, 2019). One AIIB borrower country official felt that the ESF was strong and praised AIIB staffers as being proactive in addressing social concerns about project-related involuntary resettlement (interview, August 30, 2019).

NDB

NDB has taken a markedly different approach to managing environmental and social impacts. As NDB's corporate strategy states, "National sovereignty is of paramount importance to NDB in its interactions with member countries" (NDB 2017a, 11). In line with this, NDB prioritizes the use of national legislation and regulation to manage environmental and social risks, rather than imposing external safeguard policies. "The Bank's policies are directed toward the goal of using and strengthening country systems. Instead of starting from externally-designed set of standards, NDB will take a country's systems as the starting point, and see where weaknesses may need to be addressed to meet the Bank's requirements" (ibid., 16).

The NDB ESF (NDB 2016b) is in broad strokes similar to AIIB's in that it is comprised of a statement of policy followed by three standards related to environment, involuntary resettlement, and indigenous peoples. It utilizes the same project screening framework to assess each project into one of four categories with similar requirements for each. However, NDB's ESF is considerably more flexible and less prescriptive compared to AIIB, including much less detail and fewer mandated requirements for either the borrower or NDB itself. The result is more of a statement of principles rather than a set of prescribed actions to follow based on predefined criteria.

The ESF offers no details on how NDB will evaluate the adequacy of country systems or identify and address any potential gaps. The ESF states: "NDB conducts environmental and social due diligence review, as an integral element of its appraisal to ensure the consistency of use of country and corporate system with the core principles and key requirements of this Framework. This assists in NDB deciding whether to finance and, if so, the manner in which it requires the client to address environmental and social aspects" (ibid., 11). NDB management has stated that country system assessments have been undertaken for all five member countries as of end-2020, and that the results were satisfactory to NDB. However, it provided no information about those assessments, including what criteria where used, who undertook the reviews, or which aspects of the legal and regulatory framework were reviewed.

The NDB ESF mandates that all projects categorized A and B require clients to produce an environmental and social assessment, as well as (where relevant) resettlement and indigenous peoples' plans, and that these documents will be disclosed prior to project appraisal (ibid., 15, 22, and 24). This implies a total of at least forty-seven projects as of end-2020—thirty-two rated as B and fifteen rated as A. However, as of January 2020, not a single environmental or social-related project document had been posted on NDB's website (unlike AIIB, which has disclosed all ESF-mandated assessments as of end-2020). This is a worrying indication that either the assessments have not been completed or that NDB is not following its own information disclosure rules.

Thus far, it appears that NDB has elected to leave management of environmental and social risks largely in the hands of borrower governments—in line with its stated intention of giving borrower countries the freedom to decide their own approach to environmental and social issues. However, NDB's hands-off approach poses dangers that its projects could lead to serious social and environmental problems, which can in turn damage NDB's reputation and lead to project delays or cancellations. Based on the available evidence, NDB had as of 2021 done little more than offer lip service to managing the social and environmental impacts of its projects. The hiring of a dedicated safeguards specialist in 2019 is a positive sign, but it remains to be seen how this will impact actual operations.

Accessing External Finance

Unlike other MDBs set up mainly by borrower nations, AIIB and NDB began life with strong financial prospects. Both are amply capitalized and have strong bond ratings. This bodes well for their ability to quickly grow into development finance institutions with considerable financial capacity and potential impact on a global scale.

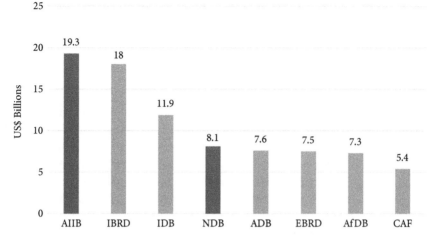

Figure 5.5 Paid-in Capital Stock, Selected MDBs.
Source: 2020 MDB financial statements.

Capital structure

Frustration with the low level of shareholder capitalization at the legacy MDBs was a contributing factor pushing China and the BRICS to create AIIB and NDB. The overall subscribed capital levels of both banks as of end-2020 was substantial—US$100 billion for AIIB and US$50 billion for NDB (Figure 5.5). Of that, 20 percent is actual paid-in cash capital, while the remainder is "callable" capital—a guarantee committed by shareholders in case an MDB faces financial difficulties. NDB's shareholders have contributed their capital ahead of schedule (NDB 2019, 59), while AIIB's shareholders have kept up to schedule for the most part, with a few cases of delayed payments thus far in small amounts (AIIB 2019d, 24). The larger total capital contribution of AIIB's shareholders gives it stronger prospects for portfolio growth in the coming years compared to NDB (Humphrey et al. 2015).

Resource mobilization

The ability of AIIB and NDB to raise resources from capital markets at good financial terms will shape their ability to operate as useful development finance institutions. The financial terms of AIIB and NDB loans are an essential component of their value proposition, particularly for larger middle-income countries with various borrowing options, and those financial terms will depend on the ability of the MDBs to fund themselves cheaply and reliably. In their early years, paid-in capital was sufficient to cover loan disbursements, giving the MDBs some space to enter capital markets when conditions were favorable. But as disbursements accelerate—particularly the fast-disbursing budget support loans both MDBs supplied in 2020 in response to Covid-19—issuing bonds at low interest rates has become increasingly important.

International markets

To issue debt in dollar and euro capital markets—the two deepest capital markets in the world—AIIB and NDB require ratings from at least one of the three largest bond rating agencies: Standard and Poor's (S&P), Moody's, and Fitch. While other ratings agencies do exist, the top three dominate the market and are deeply embedded in financial regulations of many countries and the internal rules of institutional bond investors (Abdelal and Blyth 2015, Griffith-Jones and Kraemer 2021). AIIB has a top AAA rating by all three agencies (Standard and Poor's 2019a, Fitch 2019a, and Moody's 2019b) and appears well positioned to join the legacy MDBs with excellent access to the major capital markets. NDB is rated one notch down at AA+ by S&P and Fitch and has not been rated by Moody's (Standard and Poor's 2019b, Fitch 2019b).

Although the difference between the ratings of the two MDBs is only one notch, AIIB's AAA rating gives it a number of advantages that NDB will not have in the near term, including:

- **Better financial terms:** Marginally lower funding costs will allow AIIB to either charge lower loan terms to borrowers than NDB or allow AIIB a wider loan margin and thus generate higher net income (which can be allocated to reserves or other purposes).
- **Countercyclical access:** AAA-rated issuers can raise debt even times of regional or global crises due to the "flight to quality" syndrome—highly useful for a development bank to assist borrower members facing financial difficulties.
- **Regulatory advantages:** AAA-rated MDBs currently are not required to reserve liquid assets to back up derivative positions, and Basel rules classify AAA-rated MDB bonds as zero risk-weighted assets on the books of bond buyers (Basel Committee 2019).
- **Engagement with private investors:** MDBs are increasingly working with private sector actors, especially institutional investors and commercial banks, and these are more inclined to work with AAA-rated MDBs.

The difference in AIIB and NDB ratings comes down to the former's perceived advantage in the main components of an MDB's bond rating. Looking at the methodology of S&P—the largest of the agencies—an MDB's bond rating is comprised of a *financial profile*—capital adequacy, portfolio quality, and liquidity—and *enterprise profile*—a more subjective set of indicators related to policy role, governance, and administration (Standard and Poor's 2020b, 42–69). Together these combine to arrive at the "standalone" rating, which can be adjusted upward if S&P believes that an MDB would receive *shareholder support*, to arrive at the final rating.

The **financial profile** of AIIB and NDB are both given the top classification of "extremely strong" by S&P. With several billion in paid-in capital and only a very small portfolio of outstanding loans, capital adequacy is not a binding constraint. This will change in coming years, and NDB will come under more pressure than AIIB due to its lower capitalization. As well, NDB's loan portfolio is highly concentrated, with about half of approvals thus far to only two countries. Portfolio concentration is heavily penalized by S&P's methodology, which gives added impetus for NDB to expand membership and diversify its loan portfolio.

For the **enterprise profile**, AIIB is classified as "very strong" by S&P, while NDB is marked one notch down as "strong." S&P notes that NDB faces "difficulties in finding viable bankable projects in Russia, Brazil, and South Africa," which negatively impacts its policy relevance. S&P's description of AIIB and NDB's administration is similar, but it notes AIIB's "high standards" and points out that AIIB has no nationality restrictions to employment, unlike NDB, which restricts staff to citizens of member nations only. Based on the mechanics of S&P's methodology, NDB cannot reach a AAA standalone rating with only a "strong" enterprise profile.

S&P calculates **shareholder support** based on its view of the likelihood that shareholders will pay their callable capital should it be needed. S&P's methodology calculates this essentially[7] by adding callable capital provided by shareholder countries rated AAA and AA+ back into its capital adequacy calculation. A total of 15 percent of AIIB's callable capital is provided by member countries rated AAA or AA+, which could increase its rating up to three notches. As AIIB has a standalone AAA rating, this extra support is not necessary, but it may prove useful as its lending grows in future years. NDB has only one country shareholder rated A+ (China) and two of the five shareholders with ratings below investment grade (Brazil and South Africa). As a result, NDB's callable capital plays no useful role in supporting its bond rating from S&P. The methodologies of Fitch and Moody's are somewhat more generous than S&P in accounting for callable capital below AA+, but still result in minimal ratings uplift for NDB.

This obscure technical aspect of rating agency methodology is a major reason why AIIB benefited so much from the inclusion of major non-borrower nations as shareholders. It also explains why some within NDB lobbied to bring in non-borrower shareholders, despite the opposition of Russia (Noguiera 2021). One European official described being approached by NDB staff to discuss potential membership in 2016: "We had the impression that they were mainly interested in

[7] The actual methodology is somewhat more complicated. See Standard and Poor's 2020b for details.

getting our AAA rating. We weren't convinced they really wanted us on board" (interview, April 28, 2017).

Both MDBs have issued U.S. dollar bonds, but AIIB's higher rating has allowed it to raise more resources at better terms thus far. Through end-2020, AIIB had issued two "benchmark" dollar bonds totaling US$5.5 billion at five-year maturities, and another US$3 billion at three years. In January 2021 AIIB issued another five-year placement for US$3 billion at an extremely low interest rate of 0.5 percent fixed— just 14 basis points above comparable U.S. Treasury bonds (AIIB 2021a) and on a par with the rates of legacy MDB bonds. After initially only issuing bonds in China, NDB began issuing dollar-denominated debt in 2020 and had by year-end issued a total of US$3.55 billion in three bonds at maturities ranging from two to five years. It paid 0.625 percent for the five-year bond issued on September 22, 2020, which was 35 basis points above five-year U.S. Treasuries issued the same day—a very low rate, but more expensive than AIIB's funding terms.

Local currency markets

While the U.S. dollar and euro capital markets are by far the deepest and most liquid in the world, other capital markets are also potential sources for MDB borrowing, notably in China as well as Japan and several middle-income economies. These will be highly relevant for NDB, as it has stated its intention to provide local currency financing to borrowers and because it received a AAA rating by ratings agencies in Japan and China. AIIB has indicated that it will focus mainly on leveraging its AAA rating in international markets in the medium term, and only raise resources in other markets as opportunities arise.

NDB issued its inaugural bond on China's capital market in 2016, for 3 billion renminbi (US$450 million equivalent) and followed that with a second bond issue for another 3 billion renminbi in February 2019. With yields of 3.0–3.3 percent, the bonds were priced tight to China government's own bonds, which yielded about 3.1 percent for a five-year bond at end-2018 (Asian Bonds Online 2019). Both bond issues were three times oversubscribed, which bodes well for NDB continuing raising resources regularly in what is already the world's third-largest bond market (BIS 2019). In 2020, NDB issued two more renminbi bonds worth about US$1 billion, also at rates very close to Chinese government debt. The resources raised in renminbi are most useful for on-lending to projects within China itself, but they can also be swapped into other currencies (at a cost) for lending in other countries.

NDB has indicated that it intends to issue debt in other BRICS capital markets. Although these markets are considerably smaller than China's, they offer opportunities to raise resources for on-lending within the same country. NDB has officially registered a bond program with regulators in South Africa (April 2019) and Russia (November 2019). However, despite repeated comments by NDB officials that bond issues were imminent in India and South Africa (Goh

2018 and Xinhua 2019a), they had not occurred as of January 2021. The hold-up, according to a top NDB financial official, is obtaining regulatory permits in the other four BRICS nations (Xinhua 2019b)—not a positive sign of their support to NDB.

AIIB has thus far only issued one bond in China's capital market, a three-year bond for 3 billion renminbi in June 2020, priced at 2.4 percent. These terms are similar to an NDB three-year bond issued two months earlier the same market, suggesting that Chinese investors see the two MDBs as comparable and are willing to offer similar terms to both. AIIB has given no indication of issuing bonds in other capital markets, although it has established formal funding programs to access the Australian and New Zealand capital markets.

Conclusions

The creation of two new major multilateral finance institutions represents a momentous shift in international development finance and global governance more broadly. The fact that China and a group of other EMDCs have dedicated time and resources to lead the creation of AIIB and NDB suggests that they see cooperation within a multilateral framework as a useful approach to international engagement. Whatever else it may mean, the founding of AIIB and NDB is a vote of confidence by EMDCs in the continued relevance of the MDB model first created during World War II to the global context of the early twenty-first century.

In some ways, AIIB and NDB represent new versions of, respectively, the legacy and borrower-led MDB characteristics described in previous chapters. AIIB has broad membership of borrower and non-borrower countries, operational standards broadly in line with the legacy MDBs, a AAA bond rating, and full inclusion in the high-level debates on international development. NDB has no non-borrower members, is more vocally opposed to the Washington-centric approach to development, and has highly streamlined, borrower-friendly standards and procedures. But the analogy is not precise, because of the particular constellation of members and the unique geopolitical moment in which the two new banks were created.

The power of China has attracted dozens of other nations—including five of the G7 countries—to join AIIB, for both practical reasons related to development goals as well as more symbolic signaling that they accept China's growing international role. China is more amenable to compromise with other countries within AIIB's governance and less inclined to openly use its power for its own interests as the U.S. has been at the legacy MDBs. Other non-borrower AIIB shareholders have been more open to trying new approaches that go part way toward the views of borrower countries than they have at the legacy MDBs. AIIB shareholders have struck a balance, taking on many of the best characteristics of the legacy MDBs while dialing back on some of their more extreme bureaucratic and developmental impositions by non-borrowers.

Whether this happy medium continues is far from certain, and much will hinge on how China comports itself within AIIB governance in the coming years. The lack of domestic civil society pressure makes it very unlikely that China will push safeguards and other standards on AIIB as the U.S. has at the legacy MDBs. However, China could start using its voting power to more aggressively push its own views on development through AIIB projects, steer lending in line with its own geopolitical goals, and shape AIIB financial policies in a way that suit its interests as a major shareholder. Should this occur, it would suggest that a new class of "non-borrower" might be needed to analyze MDBs in the future—one that aligns with traditional non-borrower approaches in some areas, but not in others.

While the BRICS nations behind NDB are broadly aligned with the views of developing borrower countries, they are a disparate group, with rivalries and conflicting interests. Their main commonalities are a discontent with the existing international order and a desire to position themselves as global leaders—a status which only China is on a path to achieving in the near term. This uneasy and partial alliance is manifested in NDB's governance arrangements, with each nation having exactly equal voting power (despite vastly different economic strength) and collective control of the bank regardless of which other countries may join going forward. They have yet to articulate a clear and convincing vision for the NDB's future, which leaves potential member countries, financial markets, and the international development community uncertain about its prospects.

As a result, NDB had as of end-2021 just attracted its first four new member countries beyond the BRICS (Bangladesh, Egypt, United Arab Emirates, and Uruguay), and had not taken an active role in the broader development community as has AIIB. NDB has an opportunity to build a new type of bank that combines respect for national sovereignty, reduced bureaucracy, and greater flexibility of existing borrower-led MDBs with financial capacity and a global development vision. Its ability to achieve those ambitions will depend on whether its shareholders are able to open membership to a broader range of countries, accelerate the professionalization of the administration, and take a higher-profile role in the international development community.

The initial honeymoon phase of AIIB and NDB's founding is drawing to a close. The evidence of their founding and early years of operation suggests that they are both on a trajectory to become major MDBs with global influence, although each in their own way. The links between the different governance patterns of the two banks, and how these interact with the financial realities inherent in the MDB model, map well onto the patterns seen in other MDBs created in earlier years. But the unique moment in which they were founded—as the Bretton Woods order and the geopolitical power relations underpinning it start breaking down, and as new nations led by China gain wealth and step out onto the global stage—mean that AIIB and NDB do not perfectly fit into categories of legacy or borrower-led MDB. China and other rising EMDCs still have most of the same interests as other borrowers within the framework of an MDB's governance, but are beginning to evolve new views based on their shifting economic and geopolitical positions.

This suggests that the governance variable linked to borrower and non-borrower MDB shareholders remains highly relevant to understanding the policies and characteristics of different MDBs, but may require modification in coming decades. This variable was built around a global reality in which countries were either borrowers or non-borrowers, with almost no movement between the two categories. These categories may blur or break down as the twenty-first century proceeds. It seems unlikely that countries like China, the other BRICS, or Korea will quickly take on policy positions of the G7 or other current non-borrowers, at least not in the near term. But it does seem likely that their views and interests may begin to slowly diverge from lower-income countries on certain issues related to MDB operations. Whether this requires an entirely new framework to understand MDB governance, or possibly the creation of a new category of country ("former borrower shareholder"?) remains to be seen.

Looking Forward

The Future of MDBs in a Post–Bretton Woods World

The preceding three chapters reviewed the experiences of the World Bank and four major regional multilateral development banks, a dozen borrower-led MDBs, and the recently-created Asian Infrastructure Investment Bank (AIIB) and New Development Bank (NDB). The characteristics and trajectories of these MDBs are diverse, but one message comes through clearly: MDBs have proven to be extraordinarily useful to the international community since the World Bank was first founded almost eight decades ago in the forests of rural New Hampshire.

The MDB model is well adapted to help address the sorts of problems that have moved to the forefront in our increasingly globalized world. The Covid-19 crisis and other pandemics, reconstruction following violent conflict, extreme weather patterns resulting from climate change, rising global inequality, and ever greater cross-border migration flows are all examples of global challenges that are intensifying and which countries cannot tackle on their own. It is no surprise that member countries continue to support the legacy MDBs despite a continual barrage of criticism, that smaller MDBs are growing rapidly, and that major emerging nations like China are creating new ones.

MDBs provide a well-tested platform by which countries can voluntarily coordinate with one another to provide low-cost investment financing and technical assistance for specific development aims. Groups of nations can agree on a defined set of goals—even though they may disagree in other areas—contribute a relatively small amount of share capital out of their budgets, and then leverage external resources toward achieving those goals. MDBs are above all practical: they go beyond political summits, international agreements, and communiqués to make real investments that have concrete, visible results. And compared to bilateral aid agencies, they do so in a more efficient, cost-effective way that is trusted more by developing country recipients, as shown by the interviews conducted for this book as well as numerous studies (for example, Gulrajani 2016, Brookings Institution and Center for Global Development 2018 and Prizzon et al. 2022). MDBs have many flaws that urgently need to be addressed to improve their effectiveness, but the core of the organizational and financial model is sound. They are

Financing the Future. Chris Humphrey, Oxford University Press. © Christopher Humphrey (2022). DOI: 10.1093/oso/9780192871503.003.0007

one of the most useful and effective platforms for international cooperation ever invented—an extremely valuable tool in a world ever more beset by global problems yet at the same time one in which multilateralism is increasingly under threat by fragmented power and a retreat to national interest.

A Vision for the MDBs in the Twenty-First Century

When the delegates at Bretton Woods finished their deliberations, they had invented the basic structure of the world's first multilateral development bank. They might not have realized it at the time, but this new kind of international organization would be replicated many times over in subsequent decades. But the Bretton Woods delegates were less clear on exactly how this shiny new tool would be used. Was it to rebuild Europe after World War II? Promote industrialization in lower-income countries? Fight the spread of communism? Reduce poverty? Nobody had a definitive answer. As a result of this uncertainty—or flexibility, to look at it more positively—MDB operations have evolved considerably over the past decades, from the emphasis on heavy infrastructure in the 1950s and 1960s, to poverty reduction in the 1970s, to the neoliberal policy reforms of the 1980s, and institution-building and social safety nets in the 1990s and early 2000s.

The question of "what for?" still hangs over the MDBs. Driven by factors as diverse as shifting geopolitical realities, globalized economic production and financial markets, migration, the Covid-19 pandemic, and the increasingly obvious existential threat posed by a changing climate, MDBs are at an inflection point. A stream of think tank reports and high-level panels have come up with all manner of suggestions for how to reorient or even reinvent the MDBs, many with compelling arguments and useful ideas (notably G20 2018 and Birdsall and Morris 2016). Meanwhile, China and a group of other emerging market and developing countries (EMDCs)—joined by some OECD countries—have founded two new MDBs to pursue new approaches unencumbered by sclerotic governance hampering the World Bank and major regional MDBs. Other groups of EMDC governments are focusing on strengthening and expanding borrower-led MDBs to pursue their own development priorities.

The reality is that no one can tell an MDB what its priorities should be and how it should operate apart from its member country owners. Advocating some kind of top-down coordination among MDBs, conceiving of them as a single "system" that can be steered by a few powerful shareholders, has been tried repeatedly over the years and has always failed. MDBs are independent cooperative institutions, each based on a separate international treaty among a particular group of sovereign nations. G20 countries may be the dominant shareholders in several of the legacy MDBs, but that does not mean that the G20 countries can simply manipulate them as they see fit.

A much more promising approach is to articulate a compelling vision for how MDB strengths can be most usefully deployed to help address the myriad challenges facing our world in the coming decades. Such a vision will help convince shareholder governments to support MDBs with additional share capital and by resisting the urge to tie them down with mandates based on parochial domestic political concerns. It will orient building platforms for cooperation among the MDBs, bottom-up approaches that serve specific, practical purposes and which like-minded MDBs can join to improve coordination, efficiency, and impact. A shared vision will bring into focus the most promising directions for MDB reform—agreeing on the ends to help define the means.

A consensus of sorts is already beginning to coalesce around this vision, and it is centered on sustainability—economic sustainability, social sustainability, and environmental sustainability. This term is used so often in development discourse that it has become almost hackneyed, but that does not make it any less relevant for our times. One can easily criticize the grab-bag, utopian nature of the Sustainable Development Goals (SDGs), but these seventeen targets to be achieved by 2030 represent a global compact that is broadly accepted and helps orient action. Coupled with the SDGs, the urgent need to face the climate crisis—and the international discussion around that, embodied in the United Nations Framework Convention on Climate Change and the annual Conference of the Parties negotiations—are leading to clear, concrete ideas about the investments needed in the coming decades to keep our planet's climate on a livable trajectory. The huge upswing in terrifyingly destructive weather events, population migrations, unsustainable and poorly planned urban growth, ecosystem destruction, social unrest, and volatile economic crises all hammer home the need to make high-quality, long-term investments that generate public goods to make our world a better place. This is exactly what MDBs were designed to do, and nearly a century after the first MDB was created, no other type of institution is better placed to lead this push, as numerous commentators have noted (for example UN 2021 and Bhattacharya and Stern 2021).

MDBs should prioritize public investment

It is often argued that MDBs represent just a tiny fraction of total financial flows to the developing world. That is clearly true. But to conclude as a result that the core MDB model of providing long-term financing mainly to government borrowers for projects that generate public goods is obsolete, and that MDBs should be converted instead into levers for greater private sector investment, is to misunderstand how development occurs and the role MDBs can play. The vast majority of global financial flows have for decades been dominated by the private sector, and that will inevitably continue. MDBs—especially private sector-oriented MDBs like IFC and IDB Invest—can play a very useful role in facilitating those flows, especially in lower-income countries. But public sector investments oriented toward public goods that do not generate short-term profit, and hence are not attractive to private investors, are essential for long-term economic growth and development in EMDCs. Here the involvement of MDBs is vital.

Take the example of physical infrastructure. EMDCs desperately need to build out their energy and water supply, transportation networks, and communications technology to underpin economic growth and create jobs, opportunities, and better living conditions for their growing populations. Not only that, but they need to invest in newer, sustainable technologies that will not lock our planet into higher levels of carbon emissions for decades to come. This cannot be done by private investment on its own. Much infrastructure investment even in OECD countries is done by governments, despite their much more developed financial markets and greater investment security. Think about the tremendous economic impact of the U.S. highway system investment in the 1950s (Kahn and Levinson 2011) and the huge post-Covid Infrastructure Investment and Jobs program approved by the U.S. government in 2021. An estimated 83 percent of all physical infrastructure investment in EMDCs is undertaken by the public sector (World Bank 2017g). Considering the risk aversion of private investors as well as the scale and complexity of investments needed, that is not likely to change anytime soon. With their practical expertise built over decades, high quality standards, relationship with governments, and financial strength, MDBs are well placed to help EMDCs plan and implement infrastructure investments. The need for MDB support is even clearer with social investments like primary education, maternal health services, and social safety nets in EMDCs, which generate no financial profits and will never attract private investors.

For some stakeholders, the idea of prioritizing public sector investments in MDB operations is unsettling. Public investment is seen in some quarters as a last resort, as exemplified in the "cascade" approach articulated by the World Bank (2017c). Private investment by definition seeks private returns and is not interested in the public good. There's nothing wrong with that, and in many cases the workings of the market will lead to socially beneficial outcomes. Any cursory study of history makes it abundantly clear that government has a critical role to play, not only in setting the rules for the private sector but also in undertaking key investments to improve opportunities for all and allow markets to function more efficiently and generate more gains for society as a whole.

In many cases, this can and should be done in conjunction with the private sector, and MDBs can help bring public and private actors together. For example, many infrastructure investments generate public goods but also some private returns—like energy generation and transmission, water supply, and some types of transport systems like toll roads. MDBs can help EMDC governments design long-term plans, and make key initial investments to open the way for private investors.

They can help design standardized contracts that allow infrastructure developers to more easily issue bonds on local capital markets, advise on a regulatory framework conducive to long-term investment planning, or offer guarantees to cover political risk. In light of the tremendous volume of investments needed, it is essential to bring in the private sector. But it is also essential to maintain and indeed strengthen the role of MDBs as a provider of technical assistance to governments and in making direct catalytic public sector investments.

MDBs should continue operating in middle-income countries

Not only should MDBs continue making long-term loans to public sector borrowers, but they should continue to do so in middle-income countries (MICs). Some non-borrower shareholder governments in the legacy MDBs argue that MICs don't need help from MDBs, that they can access markets on their own and should be weaned off MDB support. This pervasive rhetoric is behind the push to reduce lending to MICs during the 2018 World Bank capital increase discussions, the proposals to charge MICs higher fees for MDB loans, and the difficulty of obtaining new capital for MDBs working largely in MICs.

There can be no doubt that more needs to be done to help the lowest-income countries, and both MDBs and donor countries need to step up their efforts. But that does not mean MDBs should wind down lending and technical support to MICs. That would misunderstand why MDBs were created in the first place. The World Bank's first borrowers were major European countries who (like MICs today) had access to private capital. The World Bank's founders recognized that it was in the interests of all of members to make specific kinds of investments, and to do them at scale and quickly. MDBs were not created as a cash machine of last resort for countries that can't borrow anywhere else, but to promote public policies that benefit all members, non-borrower and borrower countries alike. Continued MDB operations in MICs makes sense for at least three reasons.

First, if poverty reduction is the goal, then MICs must be involved. Over 60 percent of the world's poor live in MICs, many in regions of entrenched extreme poverty like northeast Brazil, southern Mexico, or parts of rural India. A World Bank report estimated that 80 percent of the 150 million people falling back into extreme poverty as a result of the Covid-19 crisis were in MICs (World Bank 2020f). MICs are also poles of economic growth, generating opportunities and investment for LICs in their regions—for example Kenya, Nigeria, and South Africa in their respective parts of Africa. They are the hubs of growth and trade that can pull up an entire region.

Second, MICs are where sustainability issues are most urgent. These countries are urbanizing and industrializing at a rapid rate and are right now building infrastructure facilities that will remain in place for the next fifty years or more. The types of infrastructure and the ways different facilities work together in a broader system will go a long way to defining the climactic and social trajectory of our planet over the coming decades. MICs don't need just rural roads and water wells, but highly complex investments like multimodal transport facilities to support exports and public transport networks and waste water systems for cities with millions of people. MDBs are well placed to help design and implement the kind of infrastructure facilities needed, providing advice to refine legal and regulatory frameworks, making catalytic investments, and showing the way for private investors to follow.

Third, continued engagement with MICs benefits the ability of MDBs to support LICs. Much of the vaunted expertise of MDB staff comes from the practical knowledge and experience gained from decades of designing and implementing projects in MICs around the world. MDB staff can transfer the lessons and experiences of the MICs to LICs further behind in their development trajectory. Without engaging directly with MICs, the hands-on, applied knowledge of MDB staff will deteriorate. MIC lending is important for MDB financial strength as well, as it generates substantial net income, which builds MDB reserves and supports research budgets (not to mention transfers to support concessional lending to LICs). MIC loans strengthen MDB balance sheets in the eyes of bond markets, underpinning their superlative funding costs. An MDB that lends only to LICs would be very difficult to sustain, as LICs take smaller loans (more expensive to prepare relative to loan size), face more challenges in implementation (more frequent delays and cancellations), and face higher repayment risks (using up more lending space per dollar value of loan).

Take the case of the European Investment Bank (EIB). The EIB lends for projects intended to achieve specific public policy goals like environmental sustainability, job creation, and social equity, and it does so in some of the highest-income countries in the world. The wealth of the recipient country is less relevant than a project's impact and whether or not it would be funded by private investors without EIB support. Other MDBs should take the same approach. Setting up arbitrary per capita income cut-off points for MDB lending misses the point of why MDBs were created in the first place: to achieve collective public policy goals.

An Agenda for MDB Reform

Despite the inherent strengths of the model, MDBs have weaknesses that limit their ability to fulfill their public policy mandates. These weaknesses have multiple sources, a number of which have not been touched on in any detail in this book, including self-interested MDB staff, path-dependent organizational culture, flawed applications of academic development ideas to real-world situations, insufficient transparency and accountability mechanisms, and the inherent challenges of working in countries with variable democratic accountability, institutional capacity, and control of corruption. Underneath it all, this book argues that the key to the ability of MDBs to better serve the public interest lies in their governance and finances. These two factors, more than any others, should be the first point of departure for any agenda to reform and improve MDBs, individually and collectively.

Grappling with the mechanics of how MDBs function is essential for any reform agenda to have a chance of success. All too often, well-intentioned proposals are detached from the reality of what MDBs actually do and where their resources come from. For example, the idea of the World Bank as a "knowledge bank" rather than a lender gained considerable backing in the early 2000s. However, knowledge transfer cannot be detached from lending, for two reasons. First, the World Bank's knowledge services are paid for by the revenue from lending—without loans, either donors would have to pay for research and technical assistance out of their own budgets or the bank would have to start charging for consultancy services, neither of which are realistic options. Second, much of the knowledge and expertise of the World Bank and other MDBs come directly from the experience of MDB staff implementing loan operations. That's why this knowledge is so valuable—it comes not from a textbook, but from decades of practical experience working hand in hand with government officials implementing projects on the ground. Any reform plan must keep in mind the practical lessons of how MDBs function.

While reforms are urgently needed to help MDBs face the challenges of coming decades, that does not mean that MDBs need to be reinvented. This book has argued that the model of channeling resources from capital markets and other sources to development projects via low-cost, long-term loans is fundamentally sound. MDBs need to become more nimble and innovative, take more risks, cut back on their bureaucracy, engage more creatively with private finance, and be closer to their member countries. The core MDB model should be maintained and strengthened. The baby should be given a thorough scrubbing, but not thrown out with the bathwater.

Getting the governance right

The interests and decision-making power of different member countries within an MDB's governance is the core factor shaping much of its organizational structure, policies, and operational characteristics. MDBs are owned and controlled by governments, and the ways in which those governments negotiate and arrive at decisions is at the root of how each MDB functions. This may sound obvious, but it is remarkable how often MDB shareholders, think tanks, and academics either overlook or willfully ignore this fact when advocating MDB reform. It may be tempting (and politically expedient) to focus on problems with MDB staff, an MDB's organizational structure, or specific policies. But the point of departure for any serious effort to improve development effectiveness must be MDB governance.

A classic example of trying to solve a governance problem with a technical solution was the ill-fated organizational reform launched by President Jim Kim at the World Bank in 2014. The complex and controversial restructuring—masterminded by well-paid management consulting firms—involved a wholesale reorganization of senior staff into "global practices" in an effort to improve information flow, internal cooperation, and service delivery (World Bank 2019c). But the fundamental problems facing the World Bank related to its "creeping irrelevance" to many borrower countries are due to policies and an operational style that do not suit their needs (Harding 2014). These, in turn, derive directly from the interests and power of a group of non-borrowing shareholders, as detailed in Chapter 3. The organizational reform was a distraction from these core issues and in some cases even worsened them, as pointed out by an internal evaluation (World Bank 2019c). Unsurprisingly, much of the reorganization was subsequently scrapped (Edwards 2019), while the problems facing the World Bank remain largely unchanged.

This is not to suggest that technical solutions are never possible. New financial instruments can better meet the fiscal needs of borrower governments, for example by offering a greater range of pricing and repayment options for different types of projects. Bureaucratic incentives can be fine-tuned to encourage MDB staff to focus more on development outcomes rather than making large loans. Information can flow more efficiently within MDBs to evaluate and manage project risks or to encourage learning from past successes or failures. But underlying governance issues must first be addressed before the technical solution can be truly effective.

Governance dynamics also have deeper impacts on the long-term relevance and viability of an MDB, beyond day-to-day operations and policies. If a group of member countries feels that they are shut out of MDB governance, not truly part of the cooperative, then they will be far less likely to support that MDB, as noted by Woods (1999, 5). That has practical consequences. Disenchanted member countries may opt for other sources of external finance if they become available, even if their cost is higher and development impact lower, and become less interested in policy advice or technical assistance from an MDB that they don't see as a true partner. They may feel less inclined to always repay an MDB on time, weakening the preferred creditor status that is so important to its financial strength. And they may not wish to invest fiscal resources if an MDB needs a capital injection to increase its operational capacity in the face of a crisis or to tackle new development challenges.

Is there a specific model of MDB governance that all should aspire to, such as, for example, complete equality of voting power among members? The answer is obviously no. Different country groupings can divide governance power within an MDB any way that suits their needs and according to whichever criteria they choose—including economic size, geopolitical power, ability to contribute to MDB capital, or equality among members, among others. Nor is it inherently better for an MDB to be more controlled by borrower country members compared to non-borrowers—each approach has trade-offs that might be more appropriate for different purposes. The proof of the pudding is in the eating: how the details of a particular MDB's governance arrangements impact its ability to operate effectively and be perceived as legitimate in the eyes of all of its members.

Legacy MDBs

The key unifying trait of the legacy MDBs discussed in Chapter 3 is that they are controlled by wealthy non-borrower member countries. This brings with it numerous advantages. The most obvious is financial—non-borrower member countries help MDBs obtain a top bond rating, reducing the cost of loans to borrowers, and can contribute more capital to give an MDB greater operational capacity. Non-borrower country shareholders also bring new perspectives on development from their own experiences, a push for quality standards, transparency and accountability, and a focus on higher-level development goals beyond simply supplying finance. However, non-borrowers have also imposed a set of operational policies and characteristics that restrict the attractiveness of the legacy MDBs in the eyes of developing countries and which chip away at their legitimacy and relevance. The problem at the legacy MDBs is twofold: the lopsided dominance of non-borrowers despite major geopolitical shifts and the way that some powerful non-borrowers act within MDB governance.

The shape of the world economy has changed drastically in the past three decades, with the share accounted for by the U.S. and G7 nations falling and that of other nations rising. This change has not been reflected to a meaningful degree in the voting shares of the legacy MDBs, a fact that has caused resentment in major emerging nations. To take the most dramatic example, China's economy in 2020 was larger than all six G7 countries apart from the U.S. combined, even though these six nations controlled 25 percent of IBRD voting power among them, compared to China's 4.7 percent. This dominance of non-borrower countries was embedded into the legacy MDBs at their founding and has been perpetuated through seemingly technical shareholding formulas and voting rules that are in fact deeply political.

Non-borrower dominance is problematic enough for the legacy MDBs, but worse is how some non-borrower shareholders—especially the U.S.—have exercised their voting power. Too many non-borrower governments prioritize domestic considerations, such as lobbying from NGO and business communities or their own foreign policy interests, over the development effectiveness of the MDBs. All too often MDBs are viewed by non-borrowers as the source of a potential domestic political problem—as "risks to be managed rather than as productive assets," as one observer put it (Morris 2016, 11). The U.S. has been by far the worst culprit, as noted by Morris (ibid., 18): "Historically, the reaction of other MDB shareholders to U.S. positions has barely registered as a consideration in U.S. decision-making, which has been overwhelmingly focused on the reactions of congressional actors and independent groups that lobby Congress." As AIIB President Jin Liqun said laconically, answering a question about China but clearly referencing the U.S., "What matters is not the influence of a big shareholder. Rather, the issue is what kind of influence the big shareholder or shareholders play, and the way they exercise their power of influence" (Gu 2018, 6).

Is it realistic to significantly change the governance of the legacy MDBs? It may not be. Too many non-borrower government ministries and domestic lobbying groups have grown accustomed to imposing their vision and interests on MDB policies. With a lock on decision-making power, non-borrowers can continue to resist change as long as they collectively wish. This would be a mistake. For all their flaws, the legacy MDBs are tremendously powerful assets to help pursue global public policy goals that benefit all countries, borrower and non-borrower alike. Allowing them to become encumbered with policies that suit the interests of a subset of powerful shareholders, and in some cases respond to parochial domestic concerns rather than development effectiveness, means they will have less ability to set the development agenda and maintain relevance as partners to many developing countries. On a deeper level, if the legacy MDBs are perceived to be run by and serve the interests of the major shareholder countries, it will weaken their legitimacy in the eyes of other countries and undermine their efforts to serve as trustworthy, apolitical honest brokers.

Meaningful governance reform at the legacy MDBs would require:

- A more rapid adjustment of shareholding to better reflect changing global economic realities. Giving borrowers more voice and a greater stake in decision-making is essential for the long-term health of the legacy MDBs.
- Institute merit-based selections for legacy MDB leadership, rather than the "backroom" agreements that have dominated to date.
- Reorganize Board of Director chairs to give greater representation on a rotating basis to smaller countries and allow chairs at all MDBs to "split" their votes to ensure all members have their views fully represented even if they don't sit at the table.

- Continue reducing the role of the Board of Directors in approving loan operations and give more authority to MDB presidents and senior management, coupled with a clear accountability framework to hold management responsible. The excessive role of the Board in day-to-day operations is a sign of the mistrustful, almost adversarial relationship major non-borrowers have with MDB staff. The EIB functions perfectly well without a sitting Board, as does the new AIIB. It is time to move the legacy MDBs in the same direction.
- Resist the urge to use replenishment rounds for the concessional lending windows of the African Development Bank and the World Bank as levers to force through policy reforms at the main lending windows. Replenishment round policy discussions should only relate to concessional lending to low-income countries, while policy discussions for non-concessional lending should occur at regular board meetings or during capital increase negotiations.
- Strike a better balance between placating domestic interests and saddling MDBs with excessive rules and mandates. Non-borrowers should be more proactive and vocal in defending MDBs to domestic constituents as highly effective and very low-cost cooperatives to pursue goals that benefit their own citizens, and not take the politically expedient (and disingenuous) route of portraying them as benevolent giveaway money from rich countries to the global poor.
- Rethink the imposition of MDB-led rules that supersede national laws on issues like environment, indigenous peoples, relocating project-affected peoples, and procurement. MDBs must have high standards, but they should not impose them on the political systems of recipient countries—that is a direct infringement of sovereignty and explicitly prohibited by MDB statutes (see for example World Bank 2012a, Art. IV Section 10). The legacy MDBs should find a new way to maintain standards, follow national laws and regulations scrupulously, and decline to provide financing if the national framework of a given project does not meet MDB standards (Humphrey 2016c). That would convert MDB standards into an incentive for a country to change its approach—affecting all projects in a country, not just those with an MDB— rather than serving to "safeguard" the reputation of MDBs to the NGO community and non-borrower shareholders, as is currently the case.

Borrower-led MDBs

Borrower-led MDBs comprise roughly twenty MDBs distributed across the globe (twelve of which were considered in Chapter 4), with considerable variation in terms of membership, financial scale, and objectives. One unifying feature is that by having membership exclusively or mainly composed of the same country governments eligible to borrow from the MDBs, their governance is much less conflictive than at the legacy MDBs. Borrower country shareholders are more likely to have relatively aligned views and interests on key questions of MDB policy and operations. This, in turn, permits a streamlined set of governance and administrative procedures, more responsibility to MDB management, and less need for the thicket of bureaucratic procedures that bedevil the legacy MDBs.

The danger is that borrower-led MDBs become little more than cash machines for borrower governments, with uncertain developmental value-added or quality control. There's nothing wrong if a group of countries want to create a cooperative bank to access lower-cost financing. But it is a limited mandate, and not what these MDBs could do. Led by EMDCs, borrower-led MDBs have potential to shift development practices, focusing more on the "country ownership" approach embedded in the Paris, Accra, and Busan agreements on effective development finance. Borrower-led MDBs can do this through their own direct operations as well as in partnership with larger MDBs and bilateral aid agencies. The decision to focus more on developmental additionality must come from the country shareholders themselves, and in line with their own definition of "development."

Within the diversity of governance arrangements that characterize borrower-led MDBs, the model of relatively equitable, balanced power among a diverse group of shareholders seems to have worked the best. Both CAF in Latin America and Trade and Development Bank in Africa have twenty-odd shareholder countries with none in a dominant position. This governance set-up has encouraged shareholders to allow these MDBs to develop a strong institutional identity and financial track record, and also encouraged other countries to join. As a result, both CAF and Trade and Development Bank have grown rapidly and are now important development finance players in their respective regions. Other MDBs like FONPLATA in Latin America, West African Development Bank, and the Black Sea Trade and Development Bank also have relatively balanced governance and show strong prospects for future growth.

Several other borrower-led MDBs have governance arrangements that appear less balanced. In some cases, such as Islamic Development Bank (Saudi Arabia), Eurasian Development Bank and International Investment Bank (Russia), and Ecowas Bank for Investment and Development (Nigeria), one country is the dominant shareholder, which naturally leads to suspicions that the MDB is more an instrument of one country's own interests rather than the aims of all shareholders. For example, the International Investment Bank has made strenuous efforts to reposition itself as not a Russia-dominated bank, in part by moving its headquarters from Moscow to Budapest. However, as a public letter from management posted on the IIB website makes clear, these suspicions are not easily assuaged due to the reality of Russia's voting power.[1] Other MDBs like the Central

---

[1] The statement attempts to refute accusations that the IIB is "Russia's International Investment Bank," that it is a tool to help Russia circumvent economic sanctions, and that it is a "Trojan horse of the Russian secret service" (IIB 2020). At the time of writing, several Eastern European countries announced their departure as IIB members due to Russia's invasion of Ukraine and their continued perception that IIB is essentially a Russian tool (Humphrey 2022).

American Bank for Economic Integration, East African Development Bank, and ECO Trade and Development Bank have reserved special governance authority for a subset of member countries, often the founders. Splitting shareholding into two unequal groups creates negative governance dynamics, with potential new members less inclined to join as "second class" shareholders and minority shareholders less interested in supporting the MDB by using its services or contributing capital. This is a lesson CAF learned during the early years of its growth phase—the benefits of MDB governance control are far outweighed by the potential upside of opening up membership on relatively equal terms to all, and thus engendering a stronger cooperative dynamic among members.

AIIB and NDB

The two new MDBs founded by China and other emerging nations only began full operations in 2016, which makes judgments on the efficacy of their governance arrangements premature. Early patterns of decision-making and comparisons with existing MDBs do allow some tentative conclusions. The main one is that while both MDBs were created in part because of perceived flaws in the governance of the legacy MDBs, they have in many ways replicated existing MDB governance models, with a twist reflecting new geopolitical realities.

AIIB appears very similar to the model of the legacy MDBs, but with China in the dominant position instead of the U.S. As with the U.S. between 1945 and 1989, other nations recognize the rising power of China and have ceded it the leading role in shaping AIIB. A desire to signal acceptance of China's growing international role in part explains the rapid membership growth of AIIB to eighty-six countries as of end-2020. At the same time, China has been a more flexible "hegemon" compared to the U.S., willing to strike compromises with other shareholders on issues like safeguards and project oversight. China has also been willing to allow AIIB to develop its own institutional identity and has not pushed AIIB to lend heavily for Belt and Road projects, for example (at least initially). This compromise-oriented approach would seem to be a perfect governance model, but it depends entirely on the benevolence of China. Should the calculations of the Chinese administration change, due to new leaders or new circumstances, China has the power to be every bit as domineering in AIIB's management as the U.S. is at the legacy MDBs.

By contrast, NDB has followed the model of many borrower-led MDBs, with governance divided equally among the five BRICS shareholders in its first five years. While this approach among the BRICS is in many ways admirable, it contrasts with virtual monopoly over NDB decision-making that the five BRICS granted themselves as new countries join. This has led to the internal NDB administration becoming overly politicized and made membership in NDB less attractive to potential new members. The dominance of the BRICS has played a role in the fact that other major middle-income countries that would be a natural fit for NDB membership have kept their distance thus far. The joining of four new countries in 2021—Bangladesh, Egypt, United Arab Emirates, and Uruguay—is a positive sign, but pales in comparison with the AIIB. While BRICS dominance may have made sense to get the NDB up and running in line with the vision of its founders, it is critical for the BRICS to revamp NDB governance arrangements, open up membership on more equitable terms for new members, and reduce their heavy-handed control over the bank.

Bolster MDB lending capacity with share capital and financial innovation

Channeling private resources for development via MDB bond issues is an efficient and sustainable model for generating substantial volumes of development finance. How these resources are used is a worthy topic of debate, but the basic financial machinery has worked extremely well. The tensions between market forces and development goals limits what an MDB can do, but the limitations are offset by the much greater financial capacity MDBs have at their disposal. It also imposes a degree of discipline by forcing MDBs to keep an eye on their financial bottom line and to remain sensitive to the needs of borrowers—areas where budget-funded aid agencies often fall short.

Nonetheless, the model does have problems. Chief among them is that the shareholder capital of MDBs does not align with what member countries are pushing them to do—particularly at the legacy MDBs. Member countries are quick to ask MDBs to play major roles tackling huge global challenges, but they are reluctant to contribute even the relatively modest amounts of capital MDBs need to realistically undertake these missions. The recent capital increases at the World Bank (agreed in 2018) and African Development Bank (agreed in 2019) were sufficient only to keep lending on its current trajectory (or not even that, in the case of the African Development Bank), rather than increasing lending capacity in line with global development needs (Humphrey and Prizzon 2020).

Shareholders should contribute more capital to the MDBs—it's as simple as that. This is especially the case for MDBs oriented toward public sector lending, which are most capital-constrained and have the most potential to help achieve development and climate goals in EMDCs. The amount of share capital needed to double or even triple annual MDB lending (Bhattacharya and Stern 2021) is a fraction of what most wealthy countries spend every year in their bilateral aid programs. Rather than budgeting that money to bilateral agencies every year, MDB shareholder capital is leveraged up to five times in lending, year after year going forward. Steering resources to MDB capital is far more financially efficient than bilateral aid, and more developmentally effective and valued by recipients as well. If we want MDBs to lead the way in helping face the challenges of the coming decades, they need the resources to do the job.

Despite the compelling arguments in favor of capitalizing the MDBs, political support among shareholders is hard to come by. Many wealthy countries accuse MDBs of being wasteful and plead dwindling political support for overseas aid. Many developing countries say they don't have fiscal capacity to contribute capital. Trying to square the circle of restricted capital and ever more public policy mandates, MDBs are groping for new solutions: pushing capital adequacy limits and mobilizing new sources of finance. Both of these approaches have their merits, but also pose risks.

Doing more with the same: MDB capital adequacy

If shareholders are stingy with contributing more capital to MDBs, one solution is to lend more with the same capital. For international organizations that for much of their history have obsessively sought to build a reputation for financial probity, that is a deeply unnerving prospect. And it is made even more unnerving because no one is quite sure how to decide whether an MDB's capital is "adequate" or not. The topic of capital adequacy is complex and cannot easily be solved, but three proposals would move discussions in the right direction:

- **Reform internal MDB capital adequacy metrics**. For decades MDBs have managed their finances very conservatively, in part to avoid even the slimmest chance that the MDBs might need to be bailed out with callable capital. This possibility is vanishingly remote—the legacy MDBs are extraordinarily safe in financial terms, as they are essentially always repaid by their borrowers. Internal MDB capital adequacy models can be recalibrated to better account for their superlative repayment record (especially by government borrowers), thus expanding lending space. The models could also incorporate a portion of highly-rated MDB callable capital, which all three major rating agencies give credit for in their MDB evaluations, but the MDBs themselves ignore entirely (Humphrey 2020b). Shareholders need to push MDBs to modify capital adequacy policies to make better use of the scarce capital provided by their taxpayers. If done prudently, in combination with a capital increase, and in coordination across several MDBs, this would be very unlikely to lead to any negative impact on MDB funding ability. An independent review of MDB capital adequacy may help provide clarity to shareholders in evaluating MDB capital needs (G20 2021), although the work was not yet completed by the time this book went to press.[2]
- **Encourage reform and convergence in ratings agency methodologies**. Ratings agencies have taken on an increasingly prominent role in MDB operational decision-making. Because MDBs are a confusing mix of financial institution and aid agency, and because they are unregulated, ratings agencies

---

[2] The author is a panel member in the review. This book does not include any information from the panel's data gathering, deliberations, or conclusions.

have no clear guidelines on how to evaluate them. Each of the three main rating agencies have very different methodologies that pull MDBs in different directions, which impacts their lending capacity. The work of the G20 external capital adequacy review (G20 2021) could help encourage rating agencies to rationalize their methodologies in a way that reduces uncertainty among MDB finance staff and allows more efficient use of capital. Clear signaling from major shareholders is critical to how MDBs are perceived by market participants.

- **AAA rating are a means, not an end**. The legacy MDBs manage their finances to maintain a AAA bond rating, which brings many advantages. The superlative repayment record of especially sovereign-focused MDBs suggests that this top rating is fully warranted. However, in some cases, maintaining a AAA rating has meant that MDBs need to restrict lending. For example, the Inter-American Development Bank and especially the African Development Bank were forced to dial back lending during the Covid-19 crisis due to capital constraints leading to pressure on their bond rating (Humphrey and Prizzon 2020). If African Development Bank had a AA or AA+ bond rating, loan pricing would be slightly higher but still well below commercial rates and the bank's lending could expand substantially. This is even more the case for private sector-focused MDBs like IFC, IDB Invest (which is already sub-AAA), and EBRD—the trade-off between slightly higher pricing and a much greater ability to take on riskier projects could be a net gain for development. This book is not recommending that MDBs should be downgraded—in many cases, there is no reason why they should not remain AAA (especially MDBs lending mainly to sovereigns). But the trade off between bond rating, financial terms and lending capacity should be considered empirically and dispassionately, rather than taken as an article of almost religious faith as is currently the case.

- **Get more creative with MDB capital**. For decades, the legacy MDBs have been locked into a low-equilibrium dynamic. Major non-borrower shareholders have been very reluctant to increase MDB capital, and are not willing to let other countries like China to contribute more capital as this would rebalance shareholding and dilute their voting power. Getting more creative to allow different kinds of share classes—including non-voting shares or even shares for investors—could open up new channels for major institutional investors or sovereign wealth funds to capitalize the MDBs without major shifts in governance power. Borrower-led MDBs like TDB and CAF have already shown that different share classes can work.

- **Eliminate MDB statutory limits**. Most MDBs have rules in their founding statutes that define how much they can lend based on their capital. While these rules may have made sense in the 1940s, when the World Bank was founded, they are now obsolete and entirely ignored by bond market actors.

The statutory limits give a false sense of security but bear little relation to financial reality and serve mainly to confuse shareholders about an MDB's financial position. Eliminating them would reduce this confusion and help reposition discussions about MDB capital needs on firmer terrain.

Financial innovation, but with clarity about limitations and trade-offs

Shareholders have pushed the MDBs ever more insistently to mobilize private sector investment, beyond their traditional technique of borrowing from bond markets. This can mean, for example, an MDB offering a guarantee on a bond issued by a middle-income government to improve its financial terms, or an MDB lending jointly with a commercial bank for a new port facility, or even an MDB selling loans off its balance sheet to a commercial bank to clear space for more lending. The concept is for MDBs to use their balance sheet strength to target key investments or risk mitigation needed to mobilize much larger shares of private resources—the so-called "billions to trillions" agenda (World Bank 2017f). A signal of the importance of this drive is that MDBs now jointly produce a report detailing their mobilization each year (IFC 2019). While the legacy MDBs have been at the forefront of the mobilization agenda, a number of borrower-led MDBs are active as well.

The drive to use scarce MDB resources to catalyze other investments is a positive step. In an era of huge development needs and limited shareholder capital, there's no reason why the traditional MDB approach cannot be improved. For example, rather than keeping an infrastructure loan on its books for twenty or thirty years, an MDB could make shorter loans during the risky construction phase of a project, and private investors can move in when the facility is built and generating revenue. The MDB can then turn around and make other loans, "recycling" its capital more quickly. An MDB can offer a political risk guarantee to target the specific risk holding back private investment in a politically unstable country or take an equity stake in a risky but high-potential private firm in a low-income country that can be later sold off to private investors when the company has an established track record. Or an MDB can blend its low-cost loans with higher-cost commercial financing to provide borrowers a much larger loan package at below market rates but slightly above traditional MDB loans. In short, MDBs can become more flexible and creative in employing their lending and advisory services to design tailored solutions for individual projects with high potential development impact.

This agenda of financial innovation is just beginning at most MDBs, held back by institutional inertia, shareholder caution, and the need to reorient the skill set of MDB staff. Shareholders should push ahead, but it is important not to lose sight of the limitations and risks of this new approach. While part of the motivation is to make more efficient use of scarce MDB resources, it is also driven in part by an ideological inclination among some non-borrower countries favoring private investment, and also as a substitute for the fact that MDBs are undercapitalized.

A number of considerations should lead to caution about the MDB private sector mobilization drive:

- **Private investors are only interested in a subset of the investments need for the SDGs.** Investors will support a project if it has some chance of generating a profit, like electric power, transport facilities, or private schools. It is worth bringing in as much private investment as possible in the appropriate projects, and MDBs can help with that. But the great majority of investments needed to meet the SDGs generate no financial profit and are of no interest to private investors. They must be undertaken by the public sector. While it is possible to mobilize private investors into public sector MDB project lending, it is complicated and often requires a donor subsidy that is not easy to come by.
- **In their eagerness to mobilize, MDBs might give away too much subsidy to investors.** Investors know very well that MDBs are being asked to mobilize and use that in their favor to seek more subsidy. MDBs were not created to be deal-makers for investors and moving too far in that direction could undermine their credibility as development organizations, and also may be less financially efficient compared to traditional lending. It should come as no surprise that major private investors like BlackRock's Larry Fink favor MDBs shifting their business model to de-risk private sector investment (Schatzker 2021)—that means more profit and less risk for investors. Catalytic mobilization is one thing, but helping private investors reap easy profits with minimal risk is something else altogether.
- **MDBs need to build staff expertise.** Public sector development economists have formed the core of MDB staff (at least at the legacy MDBs), but this training is not so suitable for mobilizing private investors. Private sector experience and financial expertise will become more important. MDBs need to be cautious that this does not go too far and that the expertise of development specialists is not lost. The staff of some MDBs focused mainly or entirely on the private sector already act at times more like deal-making investment bankers rather than development specialists. It is essential that public sector-focused MDBs don't go too far in that direction and lose their sense of development mission.
- **Mobilization can weaken the official relationship of MDBs and borrowers.** MDBs operate in the public interest. If borrowers start to feel that their loans are being sold off to private investors or that an MDB is structuring deals to attract investors rather than to achieve development goals, the MDB may come to be perceived not as an international organization with official standing and a public purpose, but as just another external financier. That would undermine one of the foundation blocks of the MDB model, including the preferred creditor status that supports their financial strength.

Mobilizing private investment and adapting MDB activities to new economic real-ities makes sense in light of the massive investment needs facing the world today. Stakeholders must be clear on the trade-offs involved and move ahead cautiously and with eyes open. It may in many cases be more financially and developmentally efficient to simply capitalize the MDBs and have them issue more bonds on global capital markets, as they have for decades, rather than engaging in complex new mobilization techniques.

Nor should MDB policy and convening roles be overlooked in mobilizing pri-vate investors for development. MDBs can provide pragmatic advice and technical assistance, informed by experiences from countries across the world, on how developing country governments can establish better conditions to attract pri-vate investment. This goes well beyond the famous (and controversial) World Bank Doing Business Indicators, which focus on cutting bureaucratic red tape and increasing investor security. Many developing countries have pools of resources from local pension funds or insurance companies that are invested mostly in low-risk assets in OECD countries. Modernized regulatory frameworks, stan-dardized public infrastructure contracts, and engagement with domestic bond market players can all reorient those savings to domestic public investment needs, as the cases of Malaysia (Yong 2017), Nigeria (GuarantCo 2016), and Colombia (World Bank 2015b) have shown. With the huge upswing in impact investment, the opportunities will only continue to grow.

A Tool to Finance Our Future

MDBs have come a long way since the World Bank was founded in 1944. Because of tectonic shifts in the global economy and geopolitics, they are in the process of adjusting to the realities of a new era. The Global Financial Crisis of 2008, the Covid-19 pandemic that began in 2020, and the long-running global climate crisis have shown with devastating clarity that public policy is essential to channel cap-italism toward more productive and less destructive paths, and that facing current and future crises requires cooperation among countries. MDBs are ready-made platforms for international cooperation, able to direct finance and knowledge toward public policy goals. One can argue about what goals an MDB has and about how to best improve the effectiveness of specific policies or operations. But the tool forged at Bretton Woods remains as useful as ever and can help us finance a better future.

Annex: Overview of MDBs (2020)

	Launch Year	Sovereign Members	Borrower Voting Power	Disbursed Portfolio (US$ million)	2020 Financing Approvals (US$ million)
Africa					
African Development Bank	1964	81	55.3%	32,004	5,314
Trade and Development Bank	1985	24	82.5%	5,363	3,657
West African Development Bank	1976	15	93.4%	4,363	485
Ecowas Bank for Investment and Development	1979	15	100%	771	361
East Africa Development Bank	1967	6	87%	381	184
Central African States Development Bank	1975	10	51%	680	466
Middle East					
Islamic Development Bank	1975	57	100%	22,198	10,900
Islamic Corporation for the Development of the Private Sector	1999	55	100%	2,554	307
Arab Bank for Economic Development in Africa	1976	18	0%	4,269	410
Americas					
Inter-American Development Bank	1959	48	50.02%	104.8	13,948
Development Bank of Latin America (CAF)	1970	19	100%	28,321	14,147
Central American Bank for Economic Integration	1960	15	64.1%	7,948	3,459
IDB Invest	1985	47	52.3%	4,177	6,782
Caribbean Development Bank	1970	28	55.2%	1,407	294
Financial Fund for the Development of La Plata Basin (FONPLATA)	1974	5	100%	1,237	537
North American Development Bank	1994	2	100%	1,017	248
Eastern Europe/Central Asia					
Eurasian Development Bank	2006	6	100%	2,730	1,336

Black Sea Trade and Development Bank (BSTDB)	1999	11	100%	1,973	933
International Investment Bank	1970	9	100%	888	186
ECO Trade and Development Bank	2005	6	100%	515	Not available
Europe					
European Investment Bank	1958	28	100%	555,218	115,440
European Bank for Reconstruction and Development	1991	69	13.8%	40,519	13,304
Nordic Investment Bank	1975	8	100%	25,528	6,815
Council of Europe Development Bank	1956	42	100%	21,054	7,260
Asia					
Asian Development Bank	1966	68	39.3%	132,054	28,232
Pacific Islands Regional Development Bank	1989	4	100%	12	2
Asian Infrastructure Investment Bank	2016	96	100%*	8,397	9,980
Global					
International Bank for Reconstruction and Development	1944	189	40.0%	204,231	27,976
International Development Association	1960	174	45.0%	160,961	30,365
International Finance Corporation	1956	184	35.1%	44,309	11,135
New Development Bank	2016	5	100%	6,612	8,171

Source: Annual reports and financial statements.

Notes: Non-concessional lending windows only for all MDBs. World Bank Group (IBRD, IDA, and IFC) use fiscal year July–June, all others use calendar year. Disbursed portfolio and annual approvals include project loans, trade financing, guarantees, and equity investments. In some cases MDBs report approvals (approved by MDB board), in others they report commitments (signed contract with borrower).

* Formally all AIIB members—including wealthy countries—are eligible to borrow from the bank.

References

Abdelal, Rawi and Mark Blyth. 2015. "Just who put you in charge? We did." In *Ranking the World: Grading States as a Tool of Global Governance*, edited by Alexander Cooley and Jack Snyder, 39–59. Cambridge: Cambridge University Press.

ADB. 1967. Annual Report. Manila: ADB.

ADB. 2009. Safeguard Policy Statement. Manila: ADB.

ADB. 2015a. "Enhancing ADB's Financial Capacity by Up to 50% for Reducing Poverty in Asia and the Pacific: Combining ADB's ADF OCR Resources." Press release, March 31, 2015. Manila: ADB.

ADB. 2015b. Enhancing Operational Efficiency of the Asian Development Bank. Policy paper, November 2015. Manila: ADB.

ADB. 2016a. "ADB, Sweden Unveil Innovative Risk Transfer Arrangement for Expanded Lending." News release October 3, 2016.

ADB. 2016b. Consultations with Stakeholders from the United States and Canada on "Road to 2030": ADB's New Strategy Note-to-File. October 17, 2016. https://www.adb. org/sites/default/files/page/181506/Note-to-file_Consultations-with-US-and-Canada-Stakeholders.pdf

ADB. 2016c. Consultations with Stakeholders from Europe on "Road to 2030": ADB's New Strategy Note-to-File. September 26, 2016. https://www.adb.org/sites/default/files/ page/181506/Note-to-file_Consultations-with-European%20Stakeholders-on-New-Strategy.pdf.

ADB. 2016d. Consultations with Stakeholders from India on "Road to 2030": ADB's New Strategy Note-to-File. August 31, 2016. https://www.adb.org/sites/default/files/page/ 181506/Note-to-file_India-Mission-on-New-Strategy.pdf.

ADB. 2016e. Consultations with PRC Stakeholders on Road to 2030: ADB's New Strategy Note-to-File. June 16, 2016. https://www.adb.org/sites/default/files/page/181506/Note-to-file_PRC-Mission-on-New-Strategy.pdf.

ADB. 2016f. Road to 2030: ADB's New Strategy Southeast Asia Consultations. March 24, 2016. https://www.adb.org/sites/default/files/page/181506/Note-to-File_ Southeast%20Asia%20Consultations_22-24%20Mar%202016_Hanoi.pdf.

ADB. 2019. "ADB Introduces New Loan Pricing for Higher Income Countries." News release, November 19, 2019. Manila: ADB.

ADB. 2020. Development Effectiveness Review (2019). Manila: ADB.

ADB. 2021. "ADB Sells Record $5 Billion 5-Year Global Benchmark Bond." News release, April 8, 2021. Manila: ADB.

AfDB. 2012. The Preferred Partner? A Client Assessment of the African Development Bank. Abidjan: AfDB.

AfDB. 2013. African Development Bank Operations Manual. Revised March 2013. Abidjan: AfDB.

AfDB. 2014. African Development Bank Group's Integrated Safeguard System: Policy Statement and Operational Safeguards. Abidjan: AfDB.

AfDB. 2020. Annual Development Effectiveness Review (2019). Abidjan: AfDB.

AfDB. 2021. "African Development Bank Launches $2.5 Billion 0.875% Global Benchmark Due 23 March 2026." Press release, March 18, 2021. Abidjan: AfDB.

AIIB. 2015. Asian Infrastructure Investment Bank Articles of Agreement. Beijing: AIIB.

AIIB. 2018a. Strategy on Financing Operations in Non-Regional Members. February 24, 2018. Beijing: AIIB.

AIIB. 2018b. Energy Sector Strategy: Sustainable Energy for Asia. April 11, 2018. Beijing: AIIB.

AIIB. 2018c. Sustainable Cities Strategy: Financing Solutions for Developing Sustainable Cities in Asia. December 2018. Beijing: AIIB.

AIIB. 2019a. Regulation on the Accountability Framework. Beijing: AIIB.

AIIB. 2019b. Asian Infrastructure Investment Bank. 2019c. Environmental and Social Framework. February 2019. Beijing: AIIB.

AIIB. 2019c. Asian Infrastructure Investment Bank. Directive on Public Information. November 2019. Beijing: AIIB.

AIIB. 2019d. Financial Statement. Beijing: AIIB.

AIIB. 2021a. Investor Presentation. May 2021. Beijing: AIIB.

AIIB. 2021b. Review of the Environmental and Social Framework. Outcome of the Phase 1 and Phase 2 Consultation Process. February 21, 2021. Beijing: AIIB.

AIIB. Undated. Transport Sector Strategy: Sustainable and Integrated Transport for Trade and Economic Growth in Asia. Beijing: AIIB.

Andersen, Thomas, Henrik Hansen, and Thomas Markussen. 2006. "US Politics and World Bank-IDA Lending." *Journal of Development Studies* 42 (5): 772–794.

Ang, Yuen Yuen. 2016. *How China Escaped the Poverty Trap.* Ithaca: Cornell University Press.

Ascher, William. 1990. "The World Bank and US control." In *The United States and Multilateral Institutions: Patterns of Changing Instrumentality and Influence*, edited by Margaret Karns and Karen Mingst, 115–139. Boston: Unwin Hyman.

Asia Times. 2019. "Italian BRI Decision Echoes UK Move on AIIB." *Asia Times*, March 15, 2019.

Asian Bonds Online. 2019. Database. http:asianbondsonline.adb.org.

Attridge, Samantha and Matthew Gouett. 2021. "Development finance institutions: the need for bold action to invest better." Overseas Development Institute Research Report, April 2021. London: ODI.

Avalle, Oscar. 2005. "The Multilateral Development Banks in Latin America and the Caribbean Region." *Vermont Journal of Environmental Law* 6 (2): 193–212.

Babb, Sarah. 2009. *Behind the Development Banks: Washington Politics, World Poverty, and the Wealth of Nations.* Chicago: University of Chicago Press.

Barham, John. 2005. "Outstanding Trajectory." *Latin Finance* 165, 20, March 18, 2005.

Barnett, Michael and Liv Coleman. 2005. "Designing Police: Interpol and the Study of Change in International Organizations." *International Studies Quarterly* 49 (4): 593–619.

Barnett, Michael and Martha Finnemore, M. 2004. *Rules for the World: International Organizations in Global Politics.* Ithaca: Cornell University Press.

Basel Committee. 2019. Calculation of RWA for Credit Risk. CRE20. Standardized Approach: Individual Exposures." January 1, 2019. Basel: BIS.

Bazbauers, Adrian and Susan Engel. 2021. *The Global Architecture of Multilateral Development Banks: A System of Debt or Development?* New York: Routledge.

Ben-Artzi, Ruth. 2016. *Regional Development Banks in Comparison: Banking Strategies Versus Development Goals.* New York: Cambridge University Press.

Bermeo, Sarah B. 2017. "Aid Allocation and Targeted Development in an Increasingly Connected World." *International Organization* 71 (4): 735–766.

Bhattacharya, Amar and Nicholas Stern. 2021. "Beyond the $100 billion: Financing a sustainable and resilient future." Policy Note November 2021, Grantham Research Institute on Climate Change and the Environment. London: London School of Economics.

Bhattacharya, Amar, Kevin Gallagher, Miguel Muñoz Cabré, Minji Jeong, and Xinyue Ma. 2019. "Aligning G20 Infrastructure Investment with Climate Goals and the 2030 Agenda." Foundations 20 Platform, a report to the G20. Brookings Institution and Boston University, June 2019.

Birdsall, Nancy and Scott Morris. 2016. *Multilateral Development Banking for this Century's Development Challenges: Five Recommendations to Shareholders of the Old and New Multilateral Development Banks*. Washington D.C.: Center for Global Development.

Birdsall, Nancy, ed. 2006. *Rescuing the World Bank. A CGD Working Group Report and Selected Essays*. Washington D.C.: Center for Global Development.

BIS. 2019. "Summary of Debt Securities Outstanding." June 17, 2019. Downloaded from BIS database "Debt Securities Statistics." http:www.bis.org/statistics/secstats.htm.

Bitterman, Henry. 1971. "Negotiating the Articles of Agreement for the IBRD." *The International Lawyer* 5 (1): 59–88.

Brookings Institution and Center for Global Development. 2018. Quality of Official Development Assistance Assessment database. https://www.cgdev.org/topics/quoda. Washington D.C.: Center for Global Development.

Broz, J. Lawrence and Michael Hawes. 2006. "U.S. domestic politics and International Monetary Fund policy." In *Delegation and Agency in International Organizations*, edited by Darren Hawkins, David Lake, Daniel Nielson, and Michael Tierney, 77–106. New York: Cambridge University Press.

BSTDB. 2016. Environmental and Social Policy. Thessaloniki: BSTDB.

BSTDB. 2018. Medium-Term Strategy and Business Plan 2019–2022. Thessaloniki: BSTDB.

BSTDB. 2019. Annual Report 2018. Thessaloniki: BSTDB.

CABEI. 2019. Memoria Anual de Labores 2018. Tegucigalpa: CABEI.

CABEI. 2020. Estrategia Institucional CABEI 2020–2024. Tegucigalpa: CABEI.

CAF. 1971. Reporte Anual. Caracas: CAF.

CAF. 1974. Reporte Anual. Caracas: CAF.

CAF. 1992. Reporte Anual. Caracas: CAF.

CAF. 1993. Reporte Anual. Caracas: CAF.

CAF. 1981. Discurso del Ing. José Corsina Cárdenas en el acto de toma de posesión de la Presidencia Ejecutiva de la Corporación Andina de Fomento, December 10, 1981. Supplied via PDF by CAF Centro de Información y Documentación. Caracas: CAF.

CAF. 1986. Discurso del Presidente Ejecutivo de la Corporación Andina de Fomento Ing. José Corsina Cárdenas con Motivo de la Finalización de su Periodo, December 9, 1986. Supplied via PDF by CAF Centro de Información y Documentación. Caracas: CAF.

CAF. 2015. Agreement Establishing CAF. Caracas: CAF.

CAF. 2016. Salvaguardas Ambientales y Sociales. Caracas: CAF.

CAF. Various years. Annual Report/Reporte Anual. Caracas: CAF.

CAF. Various years. Financial Statement/Estados Financieros. Caracas: CAF.

Callaghan, Mike and Paul Hubbard. 2016. "The Asian Infrastructure Investment Bank: Multilateralism on the Silk Road." *China Economic Journal* 9 (2): 116–139.

Canuto, Otaviano. 2020. "Latin America and the Multilateral World," video, Center for Macroeconomics and Development. December 4, 2020. Https://www.cmacrodev.com/2-videos-latin-america-and-the-multilateral-world-macroeconomic-policies-in-times-of-covid-19-in-emerging-markets-early-lessons/.

Caro, Robert. 1974. *The Power Broker: Robert Moses and the Fall of New York*. New York: Knopf.

Carr, Edward H. 2016. *The Twenty Years' Crisis: 1919–1939*. London: Palgrave Macmillan.

Chin, Gregory. 2014. "The BRICS-Led Development Bank: Purpose and Politics Beyond the G20." *Global Policy* 5 (3): 366–373.

Chin, Gregory. 2019. "The Asian Infrastructure Investment Bank—New Multilateralism: Early Development, Innovation, and Future Agendas." *Global Policy* 10 (4): 569–581.

Chwieroth, Jeffrey. 2008. "Organizational Change 'from within': Exploring the World Bank's Early Lending Practices." *Review of International Political Economy* 15 (4): 481–505.

CIEL. 2008. The Use of Country Systems in World Bank Lending: A Summary of Lessons from the Pilot Projects and Recommendations for a Better Approach. Washington D.C.: Center for International and Environmental Law.

Clifton, Judith, Daniel Diaz-Fuentes, and Ana Lara Gomez. 2018. "The European Investment Bank: Development, Integration, Investment?" *Journal of Common Market Studies* 56 (4): 733–750.

Comte, Jean and Jon Hay (2021). "Europe's review of EIB and EBRD veers toward status quo." *Global Capital*, April 22, 2021.

Conectas. 2018. "Country Systems and Environmental and Social Safeguards in Development Finance Institutions: Assessment of the Brazilian System and Ways Forward for the New Development Bank." May 2018. São Paulo: Conectas.

Conway, Ed. 2014. *The Summit: Bretton Woods, 1944*. New York: Pegasus.

Copelovitch, Mark. 2010. "Master or Servant? Agency Slack and the Politics of IMF Lending." *International Studies Quarterly* 54 (1): 49–77.

CSIS. 2013. "Our Shared Opportunity: A Vision for Global Prosperity." A Report of the CSIS Executive Council on Development. Washington D.C.: Center for Strategic and International Studies.

Culpeper, Roy. 1997. *Titans or Behemoths: The Multilateral Development Banks*. Boulder: Lynne Rienner.

de Jonge, Alice. 2017. "Perspectives on the Emerging Role of the Asian Infrastructure Investment Bank." *International Affairs* 93 (5): 1061–1084.

Delikanli, Ihsan Ugur, Todor Dimitrov, and Roena Agolli. 2018. *Multilateral Development Banks: Governance and Finance*. Palgrave Macmillan.

Dell, Sidney. 1972. *Inter-American Development Bank: Study in Development Financing*. New York: Praeger.

Dreher, Axel, Jan-Egbert Sturm, and James Vreeland. 2009. "Development Aid and International Politics: Does Membership on the UN Security Council Influence World Bank Decisions?" *Journal of Development Economics* 88 (1): 1–18.

Dreher, Axel, Valentin Lang and Katharina Richert. 2019. "The Political Economy of International Finance Corporation Lending." *Journal of Development Economics* 140: 242–254.

EBID. 2016. 2016–2020 Strategic Plan. Lomé: EBID.

EBRD. 2014. Environmental and Social Policy. May 2014. London: EBRD.

EBRD. 2021. "EBRD issues US$ 2.00bn 5-year Fixed Rate Note." Press release January 21, 2021. London: EBRD.

EDB. 2017a. Eurasian Development Bank Strategy (2018–2022). Almaty: EDB.

EDB. 2017b. 2016 Annual Report. Almaty: EDB.

EDB. *Undated. Environmental and Social Responsibility Policy*. Almaty: EDB.

Edwards, Sophie. 2019. "World Bank reforms found ineffective, bank shuffles senior staff." *Devex*, April 10, 2019.

EIB. 2015. "The Governance of the European Investment Bank". Luxembourg: EIB.

English, E. P. and H. Mule. 1996. *The African Development Bank*. Boulder: Lynne Rienner.

ETDB. 2007. Environmental Policy. Istanbul: ETDB.

ETDB. 2018a. Annual Report 2017. Istanbul: ETDB.

ETDB. 2018b. Business Plan (2018–2022). Istanbul: ETDB.

Fitch. 2019a. "Fitch Affirms AIIB at 'AAA'; Stable Outlook." July 9, 2019. London: Fitch Ratings.

Fitch. 2019b. "Fitch Affirms NDB at 'AA+'; Stable Outlook." July 31, 2019. Paris: Fitch Ratings.

Fitch. 2020. Supranationals Rating Criteria. April 30, 2020. New York: Fitch.

Fresard Roberto. 1969. *Corporación Andina de Fomento: antecedentes para su organización.* Washington D.C.: Corporación de Fomento de la Producción.

Frey, Bruno and Friedrich Schneider. 1986. "Competing Models of International Lending Activity." *Journal of Development Economics* 20: 225–245.

Frey, Bruno. 1997. "The public choice of international organizations." In *Perspectives on Public Choice*, edited by Dennis Mueller, 106–123. Cambridge: Cambridge University Press.

G20. 2018. *Making the Global Financial System Work for All.* Report of the G20 Eminent Persons Group on Global Financial Governance. October 2018.

G20.2021. Annex I: An Independent Review of Multilateral Development Banks' Capital Adequacy Frameworks Terms of Reference. Third Finance Ministers and Central Bank Governors Meeting, Venice, July 10, 2021.

Gabusi, Giuseppe. 2019. "Global Standards in the Asian Infrastructure Investment Bank: The Contribution of the European Members." *Global Policy* 10 (4): 631–638.

Gallagher, Kevin, Amos Irwin and Katherine Koleski. 2012. "The new banks in town: Chinese finance in Latin America." March 2012. Washington D.C.: Inter-American Dialogue.

Gallagher, K. and F. Yuan. 2017. "Standardizing Sustainable Development: A Comparison of Development Banks in the Americas." *Journal of Environment & Development* 26 (3): 243-271.

German Federal Ministry of Finance. 2019. "Asian Infrastructure Investment Bank achieves major milestones in its first three years." April 3, 2019. Berlin: BMF.

Gianaris, William. 1990. "Weighted Voting in the International Monetary Fund and the World Bank." *Fordham International Law Journal* 14 (4): 910–945.

Goh, Brenda. 2018. "BRICS Development Bank to Issue 780 million in yuan-denominated bonds." Reuters, May 28, 2018.

Gordy, Michael and Eva Lütkebohmert. 2013. "Granularity Adjustment for Regulatory Capital Assessment." *International Journal of Central Banking* 9 (3): 33–71.

Gould, Erica. 2006. *Money Talks: The International Monetary Fund, Conditionality and Supplementary Financiers.* Palo Alto: Stanford University Press.

Grande, Edgar. 1996. "The State and Interest Groups in a Framework of Multi-Level Decision-Making: The Case of the European Union." *Journal of European Public Policy* 3 (3): 318–338.

Greenhill, Romily, Annalisa Prizzon, and Andrew Rogerson. 2013. "The age of choice: Developing countries in a new aid landscape." ODI working paper 364, January 2013. London: Overseas Development Institute.

Griffith-Jones, Stephany and Jose Antonio Ocampo (editors). 2018. *The Future of National Development Banks.* Oxford: Oxford University Press.

Griffith-Jones, Stephany and Judith Tyson. 2018. "The European Investment Bank: Lessons for Developing Countries." UNU WIDER Working Paper 2013/019. Helsinki: UNU-WIDER.

Griffith-Jones, Stephany and Moritz Kraemer. 2021. "Credit rating agencies and developing economies." UN DESA Working Paper 175, December 2021. New York: UN DESA.

Griffith-Jones, Stephany, David Griffith-Jones, and Dagmar Hertova. 2008. "Enhancing the Role of Regional Development Banks." G-24 Discussion Papers, No. 50, July 2008. New York: UNCTAD.

Gruber, Lloyd. 2000. *Ruling the World: Power Politics and the Rise of Supranational Institutions.* Princeton: Princeton University Press

Gu, Qingyang. 2018. "Lean, Clean and Green: A New Model of Multilateral Development Bank for Building Infrastructure in Asia and Beyond—An interview with AIIB President Jin Liqun." *Journal of Infrastructure, Policy and Development* 2 (1): 1–10.

GuarantCo. 2016. "InfraCredit Nigeria." December 2016. https://guarantco.com/our-portfolio/infracredit/.

Gulrajani, Nilima. 2016. "Bilateral versus multilateral aid channels: strategic choices for donors." Research report April 2016. London: Overseas Development Institute.

Gutner, Tamar. 2002. *Banking on the Environment: Multilateral Development Banks and Their Performance in Central and Eastern Europe.* Cambridge: MIT Press.

Gutner, Tamar. 2005. "Explaining the Gaps Between Mandate and Performance: Agency Theory and World Bank Environmental Reform." *Global Environmental Politics* 5 (2): 10–37.

Hajjar, Bandar. 2020. "The children's continent: keeping up with Africa's growth." World Economic Forum Youth Perspectives, January 13, 2020. Geneva: WEF.

Hameiri, Shahar and Lee Jones. 2018. "China Challenges Global Governance? Chinese International Development Finance and the AIIB." *International Affairs* 94 (3): 573–593.

Harding, Robin. 2014. "World Bank: Man on a Mission." *Financial Times*, April 7, 2014.

Hawkins, Darren, David Lake, Daniel Nielson, and Michael Tierney (editors). 2006. *Delegation and Agency in International Organizations.* New York: Cambridge University Press.

Hawkins, Darren, David Lake, Daniel Nielson, and Michael Tierney. 2006. "Delegation under anarchy: States, international organizations, and principal-agent theory." In *Delegation and Agency in International Organizations*, edited by Darren Hawkins, David Lake, Daniel Nielson, and Michael Tierney, 3–38. New York: Cambridge University Press.

Hay, Jon. 2018a. "Supranationals to copy African Development Bank's securitization breakthrough." *Global Capital*, October 12, 2018.

Hay, Jon. 2018b. "AfDB finds London's insurers a deep pool for risk transfer." *Global Capital*, October 22, 2018.

Hay, Jon. 2019. "US will try to stop MDBs securitizing." *Global Capital*, January 10, 2019.

He, Alex. 2016. "China in the International Financial System: A Study of the NDB and the AIIB." CIGI Papers 106, June 2016. Waterloo: Center for International Governance and Innovation.

Helleiner, Eric. 2014. *Forgotten Foundations of Bretton Woods: International Development and the Making of the Postwar Order.* Ithaca: Cornell University

Hirsch, Thomas, Sophie Bartosch, Yao Anqi, Guo Hongyu, Yulia Menshova, Ajita Tiwari Padhi, and Md Shamsuddoha. 2019. "Aligning the Asian Infrastructure Investment Bank (AIIB) with the Paris Agreement and the SDGs: Challenges and Opportunities. A Civil Society Perspective from Bangladesh, China, India, Russia & Germany." April 2019. Bonn: Germanwatch.

Horta, Korinna. 2019. "The Asian Infrastructure Investment Bank (AIIB): A Multilateral Bank Where China Sets the Rules." Publication Series on Democracy Vol. 52. Berlin: Boell Stiftung.

Humphrey, Chris and Annalisa Prizzon. 2020. "Scaling up multilateral bank finance for the Covid-19 recovery." ODI Insight, November 2020. London: ODI.

Humphrey, Chris and Katharina Michaelowa. 2013. "Shopping for Development: Multilateral Lending, Shareholder Composition and Borrower Preferences." *World Development* 44: 142–155.

Humphrey, Chris and Katharina Michaelowa. 2019. "China in Africa: Competition for Traditional Development Finance Institutions?" *World Development* 120: 15–28.

Humphrey, Chris and Shakira Mustapha. 2020. "Lend or suspend? Maximising the impact of multilateral bank financing in the Covid-19 crisis." ODI Working Paper July 2020. London: ODI.

Humphrey, Chris and Yunnan Chen. 2021. "China's rise meets Bretton Woods: The diverse strategies of a new global power at multilateral banks." ODI Working Paper, August 2021. London: ODI.

Humphrey, Chris, Stephany Griffith-Jones, Jiajun Xu, Richard Carey, and Annalisa Prizzon. 2015. "Multilateral development banks in the 21st century: Three perspectives on China and the Asian Infrastructure Investment Bank." ODI Working and Discussion Paper, December 2015. London: ODI.

Humphrey, Chris. 2014. "The Politics of Loan Pricing in Multilateral Development Banks." *Review of International Political Economy* 21 (3): 611–639.

Humphrey, Chris. 2015a. "National Development Banks and Infrastructure Provision: A Comparative Study of Brazil, China, and South Africa." Working paper prepared for the Inter-Governmental Group of 24 and Global Green Growth Institute. Washington D.C.: G24.

Humphrey, Chris. 2015b. "The Impact of Credit Rating Agencies on Multilateral Development Banks." Policy paper for the Inter-Governmental Group of 24, October 2015. Washington D.C.: G24.

Humphrey, Chris. 2016a. "The Invisible Hand: Financial Pressures and Organizational Convergence in Multilateral Development Banks." *Journal of Development Studies* 52 (1): 92–112.

Humphrey, Chris. 2016b. "Shareholder interests and loan 'hassle factors' at multilateral development banks." In *Global Economic Governance and the Development Practices of the Multilateral Development Banks*, edited by Susan Park and Jonathan Strand, 143–166. New York: Routledge.

Humphrey, Chris. 2016c. "Time for a new approach to environmental and social protection at multilateral development banks." ODI Briefing Paper, April 2016. London: ODI.

Humphrey, Chris. 2017a. "He Who Pays the Piper Calls the Tune: Credit Rating Agencies and Multilateral Development Banks." *Review of International Organization* 12: 281–306.

Humphrey, Chris. 2017b. "Six proposals to strengthen the finances of multilateral development banks." ODI Working Paper, April 2017. London: ODI.

Humphrey, Chris. 2018a. "The Role of Credit Rating Agencies in Shaping Multilateral Finance: Recent Developments and Policy Options." Policy paper for the Inter-Governmental Group of 24, April 2018. Washington D.C.: G24.

Humphrey, Chris. 2018b. "Channeling private investment to infrastructure: What can multilateral development banks realistically do?" ODI Working Paper, April 2018. London: ODI.

Humphrey, Chris. 2019. "'Minilateral' Development Banks: What the Rise of Africa's Trade and Development Bank (TDB) Says About Multilateral Governance." *Development and Change* 50 (1): 164–190.

Humphrey, Chris. 2020a. "From Drawing Board to Reality: The First Four Years of Operations at the Asian Infrastructure Investment Bank and New Development Bank." April 2020 by the Inter-Governmental Group of 24 and Boston University Global Development Policy Center. Washington D.C.: G24.

Humphrey, Chris. 2020b. "All hands on deck: How to scale up multilateral financing to face the Covid-19 crisis." ODI Briefing Paper, April 2020. London: ODI.

Humphrey, Chris. 2021a. "New shareholders for multilateral development banks: A viable approach to increase development finance?" ODI briefing paper, April 2021. London: ODI.

Humphrey, Chris. 2021b. "The case for an external review of multilateral development bank capital adequacy." ODI, March 2021. London: ODI.

Humphrey, Chris. 2022. "What will the Ukraine conflict mean for multilateral development finance?" ODI Briefing Paper, March 2022. London: ODI.

Hussain, Ali Abid, Selim Jeddi, Kannan Lakmeeharan, and Hasan Muzaffar. 2019. "Unlocking private-sector financing in emerging-markets infrastructure." October 10, 2019, McKinsey and Company.

IDB. 1960. Annual Report. Washington D.C.: IDB.

IDB. 1965. "Resúmen del informe sobre aportación de recursos adicionales por países no miembros del BID." Washington D.C.: IDB.

IDB. 2005. Inter-American Development Bank Sustainability Review 2005. Washington D.C.: IDB.

IDB. 2011. Independent Advisory Group on Sustainability Final Report. January 2011. Washington D.C.: IDB.

IDB. 2013. "Mid-term Evaluation of IDB-9 Commitments: Financial and Risk Management." OVE Background Paper, March 2013. Washington D.C.: IDB.

IDB. 2016a. "Technical Note: Design and Use of Policy-based Loans at the IDB." Washington D.C.: IDB.

IDB. 2016b. Annual Report: Summary of Activities and Analysis of Policy-Based Lending. OVE 2016.

IDB. 2017. Financial Statement, Management's Discussion and Analysis. Washington D.C.: IDB.

IDB. 2018. Financial Statement. Washington D.C.: IDB.

IDB. 2019. Quarterly Business Review. Washington D.C.: IDB.

IDB. 2020. "IDB Executes Exposure Exchange Agreement with Asian Development Bank." News release, December 15, 2020. Washington D.C.: IDB.

IDB. 2021. "IDB issues a new 5-year fixed-rate global News benchmark transaction." Release, April 13, 2021. Washington D.C.: IDB.

IFAD. 2020. "IFAD becomes first UN fund to receive a credit rating, providing a boost to the world's poorest people." Press release, October 2, 2020. Rome: IFAD.

IFC. 2012. Performance Standards on Environmental and Social Sustainability. January 1, 2012. Washington D.C.: IFC.

IFC. 2015. "Update on IFC's Management of E&S Risks in its FI Business." October 2015. Washington D.C.: IFC.

IFC. 2019. Mobilization of Private Finance by Multilateral Development Banks and Development Finance Institutions. August 2019. Washington D.C.: IFC.

IFC. 2020. "Managed Co-Lending Portfolio Program (MCPP)." https://www.ifc.org/wps/wcm/connect/corp_ext_content/ifc_external_corporate_site/solutions/products+and+services/syndications/mcpp.

Igoe, Michael. 2018. "Why the World Bank decided against an emissions target." Devex, December 12, 2018.

IIB. 2015. Policy on Environmental and Social Sustainability of International Investment Bank. Budapest: IIB.

IIB. 2017. Strategy 2018–2022: Growing for Greater Development Impact. Budapest: IIB.

IIB. 2020. "Statement of the IIB Management Board." https://iib.int/en/about/statement-of-the-iib-management-board.

Ikenberry, John and Darren Lim. 2017. "China's emerging institutional statecraft: The Asian Infrastructure Investment Bank and the prospects for counter-hegemony." Project on International Order and Strategy. April 2017. Washington D.C.: Brookings Institution.

IMF. 2014. "Quota Formula: Data Update and Further Considerations." IMF Policy Paper, August 2014.

IMF. 2022. "A New Trust to Help Countries Build Resilience and Sustainability." IMF Blog, January 20, 2022.

Imre, Ahmet. 2006. "Financial Cooperation within the Black Sea Region: The Experience of the Black Sea Trade and Development Bank." *Southeast European and Black Sea Studies* 6 (2): 243–255.

Institute for Development Studies. 2000. *Foresight and Policy Study of the Multilateral Development Banks.* Sussex: University of Sussex IDS.

Iqbal, Munawar. 2007. "International Islamic financial institutions" in *Handbook of Islamic Banking*, edited by M. Kabir Hassan and Mervyn K. Lewis, 361–383. Northampton, MA: Edward Elgar.

Kahn, Matthew and David Levinson. 2011. "Fix It First, Expand It Second, Reward It Third: A New Strategy for America's Highways." The Hamilton Project Discussion Paper February 2011. Washington D.C.: Brookings Institution.

Kajimoto, Tetsushi. 2017. "ADB chief seeks to cooperate, not compete, with China-led OBOR, AIIB." Reuters, May 4, 2017.

Kappagoda, Nihal. 1995. *The Asian Development Bank.* Boulder: Lynne Rienner.

Kapur, Devesh, John P. Lewis, and Richard Webb. 1997. *The World Bank: Its First Half-Century, Vol. 1.* Washington D.C.: The Brookings Institution.

Kapur, Devesh. 2002. "The Common Pool Dilemma of Global Public Goods: Lessons from the World Bank's Net Income and Reserves." *World Development* 30 (2): 337–354.

Kellerman, Miles. 2019. "The Proliferation of Multilateral Development Banks." *Review of International Organizations* 14 (1): 107–145.

Keohane, Robert. 1984. *After Hegemony: Cooperation and Discord in the World Political Economy.* Princeton: Princeton University Press.

Kilby, Christopher. 2006. "Donor Influence in Multilateral Development Banks: The Case of the Asian Development Bank." *Review of International Organizations* 1 (2): 173–195.

Kilby, Christopher. 2011. "Informal Influence in the Asian Development Bank." *Review of International Organizations* 6 (3–4): 223–257.

Koremenos, Barbara, Charles Lipson and Duncan Snidal. 2001. "The Rational Design of International Institutions." *International Organization* 55 (4): 761–799.

Krasner, Stephen. 1981. "Power Structures and Regional Development Banks." *International Organization* 35 (2): 303–328.

Lake, David. 2007. "Delegating Divisible Sovereignty: Sweeping a Conceptual Minefield." *Review of International Organizations* 2: 219–237.

Landers, Clemence. 2021. "IDA-20: Donors Must Go Big, and IDA Must Too." Center for Global Development Notes, April 1, 2021. Washington D.C.: CGD.

Latin Finance. 1998. "In Their Own Words." *Latin Finance* (no author cited). July 1, 1998, 147.

Li, X. and Richard Carey. 2014. "The BRICS and the International Development System: Challenge and Convergence?" IDS Evidence Report 58, March 2014. Brighton: University of Sussex.

Liao, Rebecca. 2015. "Out of the Bretton Woods: How the AIIB is Different." *Foreign Affairs*, July 27, 2015.

Lichtenstein, Natalie. 2018. *A Comparative Guide to the Asian Infrastructure Investment Bank*. Oxford: Oxford University Press.

Lyne, Mona, Daniel Nielson and Michael Tierney. (2006). "Who delegates? Alternative models of principals in development aid." In *Delegation and Agency in International Organizations*, edited by Darren Hawkins, David Lake, Daniel Nielson, and Michael Tierney, 41–76. New York: Cambridge University Press.

Lyne, Mona, Daniel Nielson, and Michael Tierney. 2009. "Controlling Coalitions: Social Lending at the Multilateral Development Banks." *Review of International Organizations* 4 (4): 407–433.

Macaes, Bruno. 2018. *Belt and Road: A Chinese World Order*. London: Hurst & Co.

Mallaby, Sebastian. 2004. *The World's Banker A Story of Failed States, Financial Crises, and the Wealth and Poverty of Nations*. New York: Penguin.

Marshall, Katherine. 2008. *The World Bank: From Reconstruction to Development to Equity*. London: Routledge.

Mason, Edward and Robert Asher. 1973. *The World Bank Since Bretton Woods*. Washington D.C.: The Brookings Institution.

McHugh, Christopher. 2021. "Mobilizing Private Funding of Development Finance." *Journal of Development Studies* 57 (12): 1979–2001.

Mearsheimer, John. 1995. "The False Promise of International Institutions." *International Security* 19 (3): 5–49.

Meenai, Saeed Ahmed. 1989. *The Islamic Development Bank: A Case Study of Islamic Co-Operation*. New York: Routledge.

Meltzer, Allan. 2000. The Report of the International Financial Institution Advisory Commission.

Mertens, Daniel and Matthias Thiemann. 2019. "Building a Hidden Investment State? The European Investment Bank, National Development Banks and European Economic Governance." *Journal of European Public Policy* 26 (1): 23–43.

Milner, Helen. 2006. "Why multilateralism? Foreign aid and domestic principal-agent problems." In *Delegation and Agency in International Organizations*, edited by Darren Hawkins, David Lake, Daniel Nielson, and Michael Tierney, 107–139. New York: Cambridge University Press.

Ming, Liu. 2016. "BRICS Development: A Long Way to a Powerful Economic Club and New International Organization." *The Pacific Review* 29 (3): 443–453.

Mingst, Karen. 1990. *Politics and the African Development Bank*. Lexington: University of Kentucky Press.

Mistry, Percy. 1995. *Multilateral Development Banks: An Assessment of their Financial Structures, Policies and Practices*. The Hague: FONAD.

Mohammed, Aziz Ali. 2004. "Who Pays for the World Bank?" G-24 Research Papers. Washington D.C.: G24.

Moody's. 2019a. "Multilateral Development Banks and Other Supranational Entities." June 25, 2019. New York: Moody's.

Moody's. 2019b. "Rating Action: Moody's affirms AIIB's Aaa rating; outlook stable." March 28, 2019. New York: Moody's.

Morris, Scott. 2016. "Responding to AIIB: U.S. Leadership at the Multilateral Development Banks in a New Era." September 2015. Washington D.C.: Council on Foreign Relations.

Morris, Scott. 2019. "Parting Words: Stephen Groff on His Tenure at the Asian Development Bank." Center for Global Development, February 15, 2019. Washington D.C.: CGD.

Mosley, Paul, Jane Harrigan, and John Toye. 1995. *Aid and Power: The World Bank and Policy-Based Lending*. London: Routledge.

Munir, Waqas and Kevin Gallagher. 2020. "Scaling Up for Sustainable Development: Benefits and Costs of Expanding and Optimizing Balance Sheet in the Multilateral Development Banks." *Journal of International Development* 32 (2): 222–243.

NDB. 2014. Agreement on the New Development Bank. July 2014. Fortaleza: NDB.

NDB. 2016–2020. Annual Financial Statement. Shanghai: NDB.

NDB. 2016–2020. Annual Report. Shanghai: NDB.

NDB. 2016a. Policy on Processing of Loans with Sovereign Guarantee. January 2016. Shanghai: NDB.

NDB. 2016b. New Development Bank Environmental and Social Framework. March 2016. Shanghai: NDB.

NDB. 2017a. NDB's General Strategy: 2017–2021. Shanghai: NDB.

NDB. 2017b. Terms, Conditions and Procedures for the Admission of New Members. April 2017. Shanghai: NDB.

NDB. 2021. "NDB admits Egypt as new member." Press release, December 29, 2021. Shanghai: NDB.

Neumayer, Eric. 2003. "The Determinants of Aid Allocation by Regional Multilateral Development Banks and United Nations Agencies." *International Studies Quarterly* 1 (47): 101–122.

New Climate Economy. 2016. *The Sustainable Infrastructure Imperative: Financing for Better Growth and Development*. Washington D.C.: NCE.

NGO Statement. 2014. Civil Society Statement on World Bank Safeguards. http://nebula.wsimg.com/93718c692cf0e2e9451e4572e32ef5c9?AccessKeyId=BBECBE2DB5DCCE90DECA&disposition=0&alloworigin=1.

NIB. 2011. Nordic Investment Bank: Constituent Documents. Helsinki.

Nielson, Daniel, Michael Tierney, and Catherine Weaver. 2006. "Bridging the Rationalist-Constructivist Divide: Re-engineering the Culture of the World Bank." *Journal of International Relations and Development* 9 (2): 107–139.

Noguiera, Paulo. 2021. *The BRICS and the Financing Mechanisms They Created: Progress and Shortcomings*. New York: Anthem Press.

Ocampo, Jose Antonio and Victor Ortega. 2020. "The Global Development Banks' Architecture." Research paper, November 2020, Agence Francaise de Developpement. Paris: AFD.

OECD. 2005. Paris Declaration on Aid Effectiveness. OECD Publishing. http://dx.doi.org/10.1787/9789264098084-en.

OECD. 2011. Busan Partnership for Effective Development. OECD Publishing. http://doi.org/10.1787/54de7baa-en.

Park, Susan and Jonathan Strand. 2016. *Global Economic Governance and the Development Practices of the Multilateral Development Banks*. New York: Routledge.

Payer, Cheryl. 1982. *The World Bank: A Critical Analysis*. New York: The Monthly Review Press.

Perlez, Jane. 2014. "U.S. opposing China's answer to World Bank." *New York Times*, October 9, 2014.

Pfeffer, Jeffrey and Gerald Salanick. 1978. *The External Control of Organizations: A Resource Dependence Perspective*. New York: Harper and Row.

Prada, Fernando. 2012. "World Bank, Inter-American Development Bank, and Subregional Development Banks in Latin America: Dynamics of a System of Multilateral Development Banks." ADBI Working Paper No. 380. Manila: ADB.

Prizzon, Annalisa, Romily Greenhill, and Shakira Mustapha. 2016. "An age of choice for development finance: evidence from country case studies." Research Report April 2016. London: ODI.

Prizzon, Annalisa, Michael Josten and Hayk Gyuzalyan. 2022. "Country perspectives on multilateral development banks: A survey analysis." ODI Report April 2022. London: ODI.

Rappeport, Alan. 2019. "U.S. objects to World Bank's lending plans for China." *New York Times*, December 5, 2019.

Ray, Rebecca. 2019. "Who Controls Multilateral Development Finance?" GEGI Working Paper 026, March 2019. Boston: Boston University.

Reinsberg, Bernhard, Katharina Michaelowa, and Vera Eichenauer. 2015. "The rise of multi-bi aid and the proliferation of trust funds." In *Handbook on the Economics of Foreign Aid*, edited by B. Mak Arvin and Byron Lew, 527–554. Cheltenham: Edward Elgar.

Ren, Xiao. 2016. "China as an Institution-Builder: The Case of the AIIB." *The Pacific Review* 29 (3): 435–442.

Richardson, Jeremy. 2000. "Government, Interest Groups and Policy Change." *Political Studies* 48 (5): 1006–1025.

Rosero, Kristen Hudak and Luis Rosero. 2018. "Multilateral Development Banks as Conduits for South-South Cooperation." *Journal of Global South Studies* 35 (1): 29–55.

Rubio Vega, Veronica. 2015. "From lending in the Andes to thriving in Latin America: CAF's continuity, growth and long-term financing in the region." Thesis for Doctor of Philosophy in Global Governance, Wilfrid Laurier University.

Sagasti, Francisco and Fernando Prada. 2006. "Regional development banks: A comparative perspective." In *Regional Financial Cooperation*, edited by José Ocampo, 68–106. Washington D.C.: Brookings Institution.

Schatzker, Erik. 2021. "BlackRock's Fink Urges World Bank, IMF Overhaul for Green Era." *Bloomberg*, July 11, 2021.

Securities and Exchange Commission. 2022. "Staff Report on Nationally Recognized Statistical Rating Organizations." Washington D.C.: SEC.

Serrano, Omar. 2019. "The New Architects: Brazil, China, and Innovation in Multilateral Development Lending." *Public Administration and Development* 39 (4–5): 203–214.

Settimo, Riccardo. 2017. "Towards a More Efficient Use of Multilateral Development Banks' Capital." Occasional Paper Series 393, September 2017. Rome: Bank of Italy.

Shields, Stuart. 2016. "The European Bank for Reconstruction and Development as organic intellectual of neoliberal common sense in post-communist transition." In *Global Economic Governance and the Development Practices of the Multilateral Development Banks*, edited by Susan Park and Jonathan Strand, 191–210. New York: Routledge.

Shihata, Ibrahim. 2000. *The World Bank in a Changing World, Vol. 3.* New York: Springer.

Standard and Poor's. 2016. "How Much Can Multilateral Institutions up the Ante?" April 12, 2016. New York: S&P.

Standard and Poor's. 2019a. "Asian Infrastructure Investment Bank 'AAA/A-1+' Ratings Affirmed on Criteria Revision; Outlook Remains Stable." February 15, 2019. New York: S&P.

Standard and Poor's. 2019b. "New Development Bank 'AA+' Ratings Affirmed on Criteria Revision; Outlook Stable." February 27, 2019. New York: S&P.

Standard and Poor's. 2020a. "Corporacion Andina de Fomento Outlook Revised to Stable from Negative; 'A+/A-1' Ratings Affirmed." June 16, 2020. New York: S&P.

Standard and Poor's. 2020b. Supranationals Special Edition. New York: S&P.

Stiglitz, Joseph. 2002. *Globalization and its Discontents*. New York: W.W. Norton.

Stone, Randall. 2011. *Controlling Institutions: International Organizations and the Global Economy*. New York: Cambridge University Press.

Strand, Jonathan. 1999. "State Power in a Multilateral Context: Voting Strength in the Asian Development Bank." *International Interactions* 25 (3): 265–286.

Strand, Jonathan. 2001. "Institutional Design and Power Relations in the African Development Bank." *Journal of Asian and African Studies* 36 (2): 203–223.

Strand, Jonathan. 2003. "Measuring Voting Power in an International Institution: The United States and the Inter-American Development Bank." *Economics of Governance* 4 (1): 19–36.

Suchodolski, Sergio and Julien Demeulemeester. 2018. "The BRICS Coming of Age and the New Development Bank." *Global Policy* October 1, 2018.

Summers, Lawrence. 2015. "A global wake-up call for the U.S.?" *Washington Post*, April 5, 2015.

Swedlund, Haley. 2017. "Is China Eroding the Bargaining Power of Traditional Donors in Africa?" *International Affairs* 93 (2): 389–408.

TDB. 2018. "TDB breaks new ground with benchmark-sized Eurobond issue." Press release, June 21, 2018. Nairobi: TDB.

TDB. 2020. Environmental and Social Management System Summary. January 2020. Nairobi: TDB.

Thacker, Strom. 1999. "The High Politics of IMF Lending." *World Politics* 52 (1): 38–75.

The Citizen. 2019. "Transnet, CMI Emtateni terminate controversial R4.2bn Durban port expansion contract." May 21, 2019.

Tussie, Diana. 1995. *The Inter-American Development Bank*. Boulder: Lynne Rienner.

U.S. House of Representatives. 2018. Statement of Under Secretary David Malpass Before the U.S. House Financial Services Subcommittee on Monetary Policy and Trade. December 12, 2018.

U.S. Treasury. 2008. U.S. Position on Evaluation of the Initial Phase of the Pilot Program for Use of Country Systems for Environmental and Social Safeguards: Lessons Learned and Management Proposal for an Incremental Scale-Up of the Program, January 31, 2008.

U.S. Treasury. 2013. U.S. Position on the African Development Bank Group's Integrated Safeguards System (ISS), December 2013.

U.S. Treasury. 2014. United States Comments on the European Bank for Reconstruction and Development (EBRD) Environmental and Social Policy (ESP) Revision Draft for Consultation March 7, 2014.

U.S. Treasury. 2016. U.S. Position on the Review and Update of the World Bank's Safeguard Policies August 4, 2016.

U.S. Treasury. 2017. United States Comments on the Guidance Notes for the World Bank Environmental and Social Framework (ESF), Draft for Public Comment, November 1, 2017, December 2017.

U.S. Treasury. 2019. Report to Congress from the Chairman of the National Advisory Council on International Monetary and Financial Policies. April 2019.

UN. 2021. *Financing for Sustainable Development Report*. Inter-agency Task Force on Financing for Development New York: UN.

UN. 2008. Accra Agenda for Action. Third High-Level Forum on Aid Effectiveness, September 2–4, 2008. UN: Accra.

USAID. 2020. Fiscal Year 2020 Development and Humanitarian Assistance Budget. https://www.usaid.gov/sites/default/files/documents/1868/FinalFY20FactSheet.pdf.

Vaubel, Roland. 1986. "A Public Choice Approach to International Organization." *Public Choice* 51 (1): 39–57.

Vestergaard, Jakob. Undated. Voice Reform in the World Bank. For the Danish Institute of International Studies. https://um.dk/en/-/media/websites/umen/danida/partnerships/research/2010/voice-reform-in-the-world-bank-2010.ashx.

Von Bernstorff, Jochen and Philipp Dann. 2013. Reforming the World Bank's Safeguards. A Comparative Legal Analysis. GIZ-Publikation, 2013. Eschborn: GIZ.

Von Müller, Camilo and Elke Baumann. 2019. "On the AIIB's Non-resident Board: Strategic Trade-offs, Roles and Responsibilities." *Global Policy* 10 (4): 587–592.

Vreeland, James and Axel Dreher. 2014. *The Political Economy of the United Nations Security Council. Money and Influence.* Cambridge: Cambridge University Press.

Wade, Robert. 1996. "Japan, the World Bank and the Art of Paradigm Maintenance: The East Asian Miracle in Political Perspective." *New Left Review* 217: 3–36.

Wade, Robert. 1997. "Greening the Bank: The struggle over the environment, 1970–1995." In *The World Bank: Its First Half-Century, Vol. II*, edited by Devesh Kapur, John Lewis, and Richard Webb, 611–734. Washington D.C.: The Brookings Institution.

Wang, Hongying. 2019. "The New Development Bank and the Asian Infrastructure Investment Bank: China's Ambiguous Approach to Global Financial Governance." *Development and Change* 50 (1): 221–244.

Weaver, Catherine and Ralf Leiteritz. 2005. "'Our Poverty Is a World Full of Dreams:' Reforming the World Bank." *Global Governance* 11 (3): 369–388.

Weaver, Catherine. 2008. *Hypocrisy Trap: The World Bank and the Poverty of Reform.* Princeton: Princeton University Press.

Weiss. Martin. 2017. "Asian Infrastructure Investment Bank." Congressional Research Service report, March 2017. Washington D.C.: CRS.

Whitol, Robert. 2014. "Whither Multilateral Development Finance?" ADBI Working Paper 491. Manila: ADB.

Woods, Ngaire. 1999. "Good Governance in International Organizations." *Global Governance* 5: 39–61.

Woods, Ngaire. 2003. "The United States and the international financial institutions: Power and influence within the World Bank and IMF." In *US Hegemony and International Organizations: The United States and Multilateral Institutions*, edited by Rosemary Foot, S. Neil MacFarlane, and Michael Mastanduno, 92–114. Oxford: Oxford University Press.

Woods, Ngaire. 2006. *The Globalizers: The IMF, the World Bank, and Their Borrowers.* Ithaca: Cornell University.

World Bank 2021b. "A Changing Landscape: Trends in Official Financial Flows and the Aid Architecture." November 2021. Washington D.C.: World Bank.

World Bank. 1946. Annual Report. Washington D.C.: World Bank.

World Bank. 1961. Transcript of oral history interview with J. Burke Knapp held on July 1961. World Bank Archives. Washington D.C.: World Bank.

World Bank. 1991. Bolivia. Structural Adjustment Program Project: President's Report. August 12, 1991. Washington D.C.: World Bank.

World Bank. 1992. Peru. Structural Adjustment Program Project: President's Report. December 21, 1992. Washington D.C.: World Bank.

World Bank. 2000. Statement by Mr. Jin Liqun Vice Minister of Finance People's Republic of China, 61st Development Committee Meeting, April 17, 2000. Washington D.C.: World Bank.

World Bank. 2001. "Cost of Doing Business: Fiduciary and Safeguard Policies and Compliance." July 16, 2001. Washington D.C.: World Bank.

World Bank. 2004. Statement by Joseph Deiss, President of the Swiss Confederation, 70th Development Committee Meeting, October 2, 2004. Washington D.C.: World Bank.

World Bank. 2005a. Statement by H.E. Roberto Lavagna, Minister of Finance and Production Argentina 71st Development Committee Meeting statement on April 17, 2005, DC/S/2005-0028. Washington D.C.: World Bank.

World Bank. 2005b. Statement by Heidemarie Wieczorek-Zeul, Federal Minister for Economic Cooperation and Development Germany, 71st Development Committee Meeting, April 17, 2005. Washington D.C.: World Bank.

World Bank. 2006a. Statement by Luis Carranza Ugarte Minister of Economy and Finance Peru, 74th Development Committee Meeting September 18, 2006, DC/S/2006-0049. Washington D.C.: World Bank.

World Bank. 2006b. Statement by Eero Heinaluoma, Minister of Finance Finland 74th Development Committee Meeting, Sept. 18, 2006, DC/S/2006-0040. Washington D.C.: World Bank.

World Bank. 2006c. Statement by John Snow, U.S. Secretary of the Treasury, 73rd Development Committee Meeting April 23, 2006, DC/S/2006-0011. Washington D.C.: World Bank.

World Bank. 2007. Statement by James M. Flaherty Minister of Finance Canada, 75th Development Committee Meeting April 15, 2007, DC/S/2007-0016(E). Washington D.C.: World Bank.

World Bank. 2010. "Safeguards and Sustainability Policies in a Changing World." Independent Evaluation Group. Washington D.C.: World Bank.

World Bank. 2012a. International Bank for Reconstruction and Development Articles of Agreement. As amended June 27, 2012. Washington D.C.: World Bank.

World Bank. 2012b. World Bank's Safeguard Policies Proposed Review and Update Approach Paper, October 10, 2012. Washington D.C.: World Bank.

World Bank. 2014. FY2015 Budget, October 8, 2014. Washington D.C.: World Bank.

World Bank. 2015a. Brief of statement made by Mr. Subhash Chandra Garg, Executive Director for Bangladesh, Bhutan, India and Sri Lanka, at the Committee on Development Effectiveness on June 24, and July 1, 2015 on ESF Consultations for Safeguards. Washington D.C.: World Bank.

World Bank. 2015b. "Colombia Deep Dive: Building Local Currency Bond Markets to Finance Infrastructure." September 22, 2015. Washington D.C.: World Bank.

World Bank. 2016. "New US$1.485 Billion Package to Support Iraq's Drive to Counter Cost of War, Low Oil Prices." Press release, December 20, 2016. Washington D.C.: World Bank.

World Bank. 2017a. "Progress Report to Governors on Shareholding." World Bank/IMF Development Committee report September 19, 2017. Washington D.C.: World Bank.

World Bank. 2017b. "Additions to IDA Resources: Eighteenth Replenishment. Towards 2030: Investing in Growth, Resilience and Opportunity." January 12, 2017. Washington D.C.: World Bank.

World Bank. 2017c. "Forward Look: A Vision for the World Bank Group in 2030." Washington D.C.: World Bank.

World Bank. 2017d. Corporate Scorecard. Washington D.C.: World Bank.

World Bank. 2017e. World Bank Environmental and Social Framework. Washington D.C.: World Bank.

World Bank. 2017f. "Maximizing Finance for Development: Leveraging the Private Sector for Growth and Sustainable Development." World Bank/IMF Development Committee report September 19, 2017. Washington D.C.: World Bank.

World Bank. 2017g. "Who sponsors infrastructure projects? Disentangling public and private contributions." Public-Private Infrastructure Advisory Facility report. Washington D.C.: World Bank.

World Bank. 2018a. "2017 Survey of National Development Banks." Global Report, May 2018. Washington D.C.: World Bank.

World Bank. 2018b. "A Report to the Governors on Shareholding at the Spring Meetings, 2018." Development Committee Report 2018-0003/P, April 20, 2018. Washington D.C.: World Bank.

World Bank. 2018c. "Sustainable Financing for Sustainable Development" April 21, 2018. Washington D.C.: World Bank.

World Bank. 2018d. Client Surveys FY2018, FY2017, FY 2015. Supplied directly to author by World Bank Public Opinion Research Group in 2019. Washington D.C.: World Bank.

World Bank. 2018e. Corporate Scorecard

World Bank. 2019a. Statement by Maksim Oreshkin Minister of Economic Development Russia, 100th Development Committee Meeting, October 19, 2019. Washington D.C.: World Bank.

World Bank. 2019b. "IDA19: An Overview. Ten Years to 2030: Growth, People, Resilience." June 4, 2019. Washington D.C.: World Bank.

World Bank. 2019c. "Knowledge Flow and Collaboration Under the World Bank's New Organizational Model: An Independent Evaluation." April 8, 2019, Independent Evaluation Group. Washington D.C.: World Bank.

World Bank. 2020a. "Board of Directors." https://www.worldbank.org/en/about/leadership/directors.

World Bank. 2020b. 2020 Shareholding Review: Report to Governors at the Annual Meetings. Development Committee Report DC2020-0009, October 16, 2020. Washington D.C.: World Bank.

World Bank. 2020c. Project Cycle. https://www.worldbank.org/en/projects-operations/products-and-services/brief/projectcycle.

World Bank. 2020d. Procurement Contracts Award Summary, 2000–2019. https://www.worldbank.org/en/projects-operations/products-and-services/brief/summary-and-detailed-borrower-procurement-reports.

World Bank. 2020e. "World Bank Provides $425 Million to Support the Provision of Infrastructure Financing in Eastern and Southern Africa." Press release, June 30, 2020. Washington D.C.: World Bank.

World Bank. 2020f. Poverty and Shared Prosperity 2020: A Reversal of Fortunes. Washington D.C.: World Bank.

World Bank. 2021a. "World Bank USD 2.5 Billion 5-Year Bond Mobilizes Finance for Sustainable Development." Press release May 18, 2021. Washington D.C.: World Bank.

Xinhua. 2019a. "BRICS New Development Bank to issue bonds in South Africa, commercial paper in U.S. dollar." March 6, 2019.

Xinhua. 2019b. "BRICS New Development Bank Places Bond in China." February 26, 2019.

Xu, Jiajun, Kedi Wang, and Xinshun Ru. 2020. "Funding Sources of National Development Banks." NSE Development Financing Research Report 3. Beijing: Peking University.

Yang, Hai. 2016. "The Asian Infrastructure Investment Bank and Status-Seeking: China's Foray into Global Economic Governance." *Chinese Political Science Review* 1: 754–778.

Yeo, Yukyung. 2018. "China's Policy of 'Going Out' 2.0: Ideas, Interests, and the Rise of the Asian Infrastructure Investment Bank (AIIB)." *The Korean Journal of International Studies* 16 (3): 367–387.

Yong, Hee Kong. 2017. "Infrastructure Financing in Malaysia." *Nomura Journal of Asian Capital Markets* 1 (2): 26–30.

Zappile. Tina. 2016. "Sub-regional development banks: Development as usual?" In *Global Economic Governance and the Development Practices of the Multilateral Development Banks*, edited by Susan Park and Jonathan Strand, 187–211. New York: Routledge.

Zedillo, Ernesto (editor). 2009. "Repowering the World Bank for the 21st Century," Report by the High-Level Commission on Modernization of World Bank Group Governance. New Haven: Yale.

Zhao, Huanxin. 2021. "AIIB may officially end coal financing in 2022." China Daily, August 6, 2021.

Zhu, Jiejin. 2019. "Is the AIIB a China-controlled Bank? China's Evolving Multilateralism in Three Dimensions (3D)." *Global Policy* 10 (4): 653–659.

Index

Figures, Tables, and Boxes are marked *f*, *t*, and *b* and are listed on page *viii*